D1590846

TERTULLIAN

Tertullian (*c.* AD 160–225) was one of the first theologians of the
Western Church and ranks among the most prominent of the early
Latin fathers. His literary output is wide ranging, and provides an
invaluable insight into the Christian Church in the crucial period
when the Roman Empire was in decline.

This book is the first accessible introduction in English to Tertullian's
works, providing translations of *Aduersus Iudaeos* (Against the Jews),
Scorpiace (Antidote for the Scorpion's Sting) and *De Virginibus Velandis*
(On the Veiling of Virgins). These crucial works, together with
Geoffrey D. Dunn's comprehensive commentary, illuminate the early
church's reaction to paganism, Judaism, Scripture and its development of a distinctive Christian ethic.

Geoffrey D. Dunn is an Australian Research Council Senior Research
Associate in the Centre for Early Christian Studies at the Australian
Catholic University. He is also a presbyter of the Catholic Diocese of
Cairns.

THE EARLY CHURCH FATHERS
Edited by Carol Harrison
University of Durham

The Greek Latin Fathers of the Church are central to the creation of Christian doctrine, yet often unapproachable because of the sheer volume of their writings and the relative paucity of accessible translations. This series makes available translations of key selected texts by the major Fathers to all students of the early church.

CYRIL OF JERUSALEM
Edward Yarnold, SJ

EARLY CHRISTIAN LATIN POETS
Carolinne White

CYRIL OF ALEXANDRIA
Norman Russell

MAXIMUS THE CONFESSOR
Andrew Louth

IRENAEUS OF LYONS
Robert M. Grant

AMBROSE
Boniface Ramsey, OP

ORIGEN
Joseph W. Trigg

GREGORY OF NYSSA
Anthony Meredith, SJ

JOHN CHRYSOSTOM
Wendy Mayer and Pauline Allen

JEROME
Stefan Rebenich

TERTULLIAN

Geoffrey D. Dunn

LONDON AND NEW YORK

First published 2004
by Routledge
11 New Fetter Lane, London EC4P 4EE

Simultaneously published in the USA and Canada
by Routledge
29 West 35th Street, New York, NY 10001

Routledge is an imprint of the Taylor & Francis Group

©2004 Geoffrey D. Dunn

Typeset in Garamond by Prepress Projects Ltd, Perth, Scotland
Printed and bound in Great Britain by TJ International, Padstow, Cornwall

British Library Cataloguing in Publication Data
A catalogue record for this book is available from the British Library

Library of Congress Cataloging in Publication Data

Dunn, Geoffrey D., 1962–
Tertullian/Geoffrey D. Dunn.
p. cm. – (Early church fathers)
Includes bibliographical references (p.   ) and index.
1. Tertullian, ca. 160–ca. 230. 2. Theology – Early works to 1800.
I. Tertullian, ca. 160–ca. 230. *Aduersus Iudaeos*. English. II. Tertullian,
ca. 160–ca. 230. *Scorpiace*. English. III. Tertullian, ca. 160–ca. 230.
De virginibus velandis. English. IV. Title. V. Series.
BR65.T7D86 2004
230'.13'092–dc22

2003026276

ISBN 0–415–28230–6 (hbk)
0–415–28231–4 (pbk)

CONTENTS

v

CONTENTS

PREFACE

I came to Tertullian indirectly. My initial area of research interest some fifteen years ago was fourth-century Christianity at the time of Constantine. The scholarship of Professor Timothy Barnes impressed me and when I looked for what else he had written, I was introduced to Christianity in North Africa in the Severan age. The debt I owe to Professor Barnes' biography is obvious in the pages of this volume.

It is only when one undertakes the laborious task of translating that one realizes the truth of the oft-found comments by predecessors about the difficulty of Tertullian's Latin. The problem is not so much with his grammar as with the density of his thinking and the obscurity of his style. I wish to thank friends and colleagues who have helped me in these labours. In particular, I would like to thank Professor Pauline Allen, who suggested this volume to me and offered encouragement along the way, Dr Bronwen Neil, who generously read through every word of my translation and made countless suggestions to save me from inaccuracy and inelegancy, and John Cawte, who offered his painstaking linguistic expertise with one of the texts. My debt to them is enormous. I am sure that it is only my foolhardiness that is responsible for me not taking every one of their suggestions on board. I am also grateful to the professional encouragement and suggestions from Richard Stoneman of Routledge and in particular to Carol Harrison, the series editor, for her many suggestions and careful reading of my manuscript.

I am also in debt to the many scholars whose works I have consulted over the years and who have informed and challenged me in my thinking about North African Christianity and Tertullian. In a book of this nature, designed for a more general audience, it has not been possible always to acknowledge my reliance upon the vast amount of scholarly literature available. My original bibliography for this volume included over 230 items.

Even at the last minute, as I prepare to send the manuscript to the publishers, I am making a great number of corrections and improvements. Although many imperfections must have slipped through undetected thus far, I hope that in years to come I can look back at my first book with great fondness.

Geoffrey D. Dunn
March 2004

Part I

INTRODUCTION

1

LIFE AND WORKS OF TERTULLIAN

Modern scholarship has made Tertullian a most accessible subject for the student and researcher. The critical editions of the Latin texts of all his treatises are available in two convenient volumes (*Corpus Christianorum*, series Latina 1 and 2). A concordance of Tertullian's vocabulary was prepared by Gösta Claesson (Claesson 1974, 1975). Timothy Barnes has written what will long be the standard biography in English, which, in his inimitable style, revises many long-held notions about Tertullian's life and works (Barnes 1985). There is also the annual review of publications about Tertullian in the *Revue des Études Augustiniennes*. Most of these reviews now appear together as a separate volume (Braun 1999). A full-length treatment of his theology has recently appeared in English (Osborn 1997a). Surveys of the trends in scholarship on Tertullian have appeared (Siniscalco 1978; Sider 1982), although they are now in need of an update. There is even a website devoted to Tertullian studies (http://www.tertullian.org).

While the contemporary scholar is well served by these research tools, Tertullian's life remains hidden in obscurity. The traditional picture of it was painted at the end of the fourth century by Jerome, who elsewhere described him as a 'learned and zealous writer' (*Letter* 84.2; see also 70.5), in his *On Illustrious Men* 53. Here, we find him mentioned as a presbyter from Carthage, whose father was a proconsular centurion, who had an impetuous temperament, who was at his prime under the Severan emperors Septimius Severus and Caracalla, who was read daily by Cyprian (who referred to him as 'master'), who lapsed into Montanism, who wrote many works and who died in old age. To that must be added Eusebius' comment that he was skilled in Roman law at Rome (*Ecclesiastical History* 2.2.4).

That information was accepted as reliable by scholars (e.g. Quasten 1953: 246–7) until the publication of Barnes' biography, which is a sustained critique of this picture. He questions or dismisses the ideas that Tertullian's father was a centurion, that Tertullian was a presbyter, that he was a jurist and that he lived a long life. Some scholars, possessed of the same revisionist spirit, have also questioned his legal background (Fredouille 1972; Bray 1977; Rankin 1997) and even whether his Montanism meant that he became a schismatic (Powell 1975; Rankin 1986, 1995; Trevett 1996: 69; Tabbernee 1997: 54–5). The question of Montanism will be addressed further below. Others, though, have not been convinced by all these arguments. A number of other writers, often not specialists on Tertullian, seem to have ignored this revision almost entirely.

Where does this leave a reconstruction of Tertullian's life? It seems to me that Barnes' scepticism about Jerome's sketch is well founded. In these few pages, I must rely heavily on the insights offered by Barnes, although without merely presenting a reduced paraphrase of his biography.

Tertullian's literary career was spent in Carthage. He made several references to the city in his writings. *On the Pallium* is addressed to the men of Carthage (1.1). The martyr Perpetua, who died in Carthage in 203, is mentioned in *On the Soul* (55.4). *To Scapula* was written to the proconsul of the Roman province of Africa (of which Carthage was the capital), calling upon him to stop persecuting Christians in order to spare the city and province from divine wrath (5.2–3).[1] In it are mentioned recent fires near the walls of Carthage (3.2) and the eclipse visible in the city of Utica, some 30 kilometres north-west of Carthage (3.3). The Pythian games under Septimius Severus in Carthage rate a mention in *Antidote for the Scorpion's Sting* (6.2; Barnes 1969: 125–8). Other references to Carthage are of a mythological or remote historical nature and tell us little about Tertullian in the city, except that it is not surprising for a local author to refer to his own city's past (*On Monogamy* 17.2; *To the Heathens* 2.9.13; 2.17.7). Unless he stated it merely as a rhetorical flourish, we know that he visited Rome at some stage (*On the Apparel of Women* 1.7.2).

Septimius Tertullianus grew up as a pagan.[2] That he converted to Christianity in response to some event, which led him to regret and reject his past life, is deduced from the opening of *On Repentance* (1.1) and from *On Flight in Time of Persecution* (6.2). He married, even though his treatise *To his Wife* tells us little about the relationship. Written early in their marriage (1.1.1), this work was not only for his wife but also for all Christian women (1.1.6). He advocated that a Christian (male as well as female – see *To his Wife* 1.6.1 and *On Exhortation to Chastity*, addressed to a man) should not seek remarriage after the death of their spouse (although this is modified in the second book of *To his Wife*). He described his wife, in the opening address, as joined with him in the Lord's service (1.1.1), so we may presume they were both Christians at this time. Whether it was the hyperbole of the argument or not is difficult to tell, but Tertullian seemed to demonstrate little interest in having children (1.5.1–2; 1.6.2). Despite the high moral standards he set for marriage, Tertullian confessed to adultery (*On the Resurrection of the Dead* 59.3). We do not know when his wife died.

That Tertullian could write meant that he belonged to an elite in terms of his education, if we accept the view that literacy in the ancient world was possessed by only about ten per cent of the population (Gamble 1995: 4–5). Tertullian himself acknowledged that most Christians were uneducated, even though that did not mean they were unwise (*Against Praxeas* 3.1). If we accept that Carthage had a population of up to 700,000 people in total (Duncan-Jones 1963; Norman 1988: 16), and if we accept the 'crude estimate' that in the year 200 about 0.35 per cent of the population was Christian (Stark 1996: 7), then we can reach the tentative conclusion that there were about 230 literate Christians in Tertullian's time in the city. Of course, if the population of Carthage was closer to one-quarter of a million then that figure drops to about eighty-five. As susceptible as these figures are to error, they give us some indication of Tertullian's potential for significance within the Christian community.

His education would have been thorough and there is no doubt that he progressed beyond grammar at a 'secondary' level to rhetoric at a 'tertiary' level.[3] He attended a declamation offered by the Carthaginian rhetorician Phosphorus (*Against the Valentinians* 8.3). We shall return to the influence of rhetoric in his writings below. He composed his treatises not only in Latin but also in Greek (*On Baptism* 15.2; *On the Military Crown* 6.3; *On the Veiling of Virgins* 1.1). A close relative wrote a literary piece based on Virgil (*On the Prescriptions of Heretics* 39.4). Tertullian himself knew the repertoire of classical literature, perhaps better than most of his generation (Barnes 1985: 196–206). It would seem likely that only someone from at least a moderately wealthy family could afford to be given such an education.

That Tertullian was not a priest may be inferred from some of the comments he made in which he contrasted himself and lay Christians with clerics on the topic of second marriage and found no contrast at all (*On Monogamy* 12.2; *On Exhortation to Chastity* 7.3). Indeed, Tertullian's claim to priesthood in *On Fasting* 11.4 is nothing other than the claim to the priesthood of all Christian believers found in 1 Pt 2:9.

We may even hazard a guess about his appearance and claim that he wore a beard, for he offers a stinging criticism of those who disfigure the way God created them by shaving (*On the Shows* 23.3). If he followed his own standards, we may conclude that he refrained from the stylish grooming that seemed to be the fashion, such as dyeing or setting the hair, depilating bodily hair, powdering the body and shaping the beard (*On the Apparel of Women* 2.8.2). He lamented the custom of the local population who abandoned the use of the pallium for the Roman toga (*On the Pallium*). Yet he remains a faceless figure, never the subject, as far as I know, of artistic representation.

Some of Tertullian's treatises reveal that he had much in common with Montanism (as we know it today), or the New Prophecy as he called it. To what extent, if at all, this meant that he joined a group that was schismatic (or, to put it another way, that he left the church) continues to be debated. This movement had emerged in Phrygia in about 165–170 with the oracles of Montanus, Maximilla and Priscilla. It was 'a prophetic renewal movement informed by the Holy Spirit' (Tabbernee 1997: 24), which can be characterized as charismatic, ascetic, enthusiastic, innovative, spiritualist, ecstatic and rigorous. We do not know much about early Montanism, and what we do know comes from Tertullian (and we do not know the extent to which he recast Montanism to suit his own inclinations), from some inscriptions or from sources that are both antagonistic and much later. Like most renewal movements within Christian history, Montanism went through phases and cycles, and it challenged the established authority (Trevett 1996: 146–9). Adherents attracted to this style of Christianity clashed with their more conventional Christians. Montanists claimed to be inspired by the Paraclete, which tended to give them a bad reputation with bishops, who wanted to be the sole source of authority within a community. They were considered to be élitist because of their more demanding and perfectionist notions of Christian life. They insisted on rigorous fasting, forbade remarriage and did not believe in the possibility of post-baptismal reconciliation of Christian sinners. They accepted women in positions of responsibility. Many of these beliefs attracted Tertullian, but the extent to which his own ideas about them or things like enthusiasm for martyrdom or eschatology derived from New Prophecy, or were projected upon it, remains unclear. The idea that Tertullian established an even more rigorous group when he grew dissatisfied with the Montanists (Augustine, *On Heresies* 86) has also been questioned (Barnes 1985: 258–9). The notion that Tertullian's Montanism meant that he ever left the church is one that does not seem sustainable today (Rankin

1995: 27–38). I think we can support the notion that the Christian community in Carthage contained a wide cross-section of opinion and practice, Montanists included. What we do find in Tertullian, I believe, is typical of those who join elitist movements: a tendency to become increasingly intolerant of the 'less committed' majority, particularly over the issue of whether or not the church (and who in the church) could readmit serious sinners to communion through a penitential process. By the end of his literary career, however, he certainly did not see himself as having anything in common with Christians who did not hold to his Montanist convictions (*On Modesty* 1.10), even if no group actually had been declared schismatic.

The date of his death is unknown but perhaps it was not long after his final treatise in the second decade of the third century (Barnes 1985: 59). His works were known in Late Antiquity, as indicated by Jerome's comments to Florentinus about Paul wishing to get his copy of them back from Rufinus (*Letter* 5.2).

There are thirty-one extant treatises generally accepted as being written by Tertullian.[4] A number have not survived.[5] When it comes to dating Tertullian's works, Barnes employs four criteria: allusions to historical events, references to earlier writings, doctrine and style (Barnes 1985: 32–54). From this, he produces a chronological table in which the works are dated between 196 and 212 (Barnes 1985: 55). The most distinctive feature is that all the Montanist works are dated from 206 to 211, and that after 206 there is no work that does not display characteristic Montanist indicators, except *To Scapula*, dated to 212 because of its reference to historical events. In his 1985 postscript Barnes makes a number of adjustments to that chronology. In particular, he accepts the likelihood that Tertullian's Montanist writings could have been written over a longer period of time than he first permitted, even up to the end of that second decade of the third century (Barnes 1985: 326–8).

The third criterion, concerning the appearance of Montanist references in Tertullian's treatises, is worthy of further comment. Any work that has one or more out of eight features is considered by Barnes to be from his Montanist period. Those features are: the naming of the three Montanist founders or their oracles, references to New Prophecy, promotion of ecstasy, reference to special spiritual gifts, reference to the Holy Spirit as Paraclete, first-person references to Montanists, second-person references to Catholics and abuse of Catholics as 'psychici'. This draws in a catch of the following treatises: *Against Marcion* (particularly books four and five), *Against the Valentinians*, *On the Soul*, *On the Resurrection of the Dead*, *On the Military Crown*, *On Exhortation to*

Chastity, On Flight in Time of Persecution, On the Veiling of Virgins, Against Praxeas, On Fasting, On Monogamy, and *On Modesty.* The first four have very limited references, whereas the last four seem to have the most strident abuse of those who do not support Montanism (placing them at the end of Tertullian's literary career).

There are several treatises that provide no indication of when they were written. Barnes places them in Tertullian's pre-Montanist phase, tentatively between 198 and 203 (Barnes 1985: 55). They are *To his Wife, On Baptism, On Prayer, On Repentance* and *On Patience.* It would be my argument, however, that Tertullian could have written a work in his Montanist years, as he did with *To Scapula,* which displays no signs of Montanism, particularly if its contents would not have been the subject of debate between Montanists and other Christians.

A comparison of Barnes' chronology with that offered by Fredouille reveals similarities, except for four treatises: *On the Shows, Antidote for the Scorpion's Sting, On the Pallium* and *On the Flesh of Christ* (Fredouille 1972: 487–8; Rankin 1995: xv). Even some of these differences can disappear. Given that in his postscript Barnes no longer insists on dating *On the Shows* and *On Idolatry* before *Apology,* the position of *On the Shows* in the table becomes more flexible. Also, the only point Barnes makes about *On the Flesh of Christ* is that it must follow *On the Testimony of the Soul* and precede *On the Resurrection of the Dead.* Thus, now that all the pre-Montanist works do not have to be before the first book *Against Marcion* in 207 or 208 (because its Montanist reference is likely to be a later addition), then there is nothing to stop moving *On the Flesh of Christ* from 206 closer to Fredouille's preferred date of 208 to 212.

The question of dating Tertullian's literary output, at least in relative terms, is important even if it is complex and open to much disagreement. He was a writer whose thinking about issues changed or intensified over the years, particularly with his increasingly Montanist perspective. In addition, he often revised material from one treatise and used it in another with some modifications. The other important point to note in interpreting his works is that sometimes it is not a question of him changing his mind over time but of writing with particular readerships in mind. In apologetic works written to imperial officials, he was not as critical of the Roman system as he was in works addressed to an exclusively Christian audience (Evans 1976: 21–2). As anyone trained in rhetoric would have known, telling the whole truth was not the best way to win arguments. Tertullian was selective and conscious of the occasion. One cannot refer simply to one passage in one text to demonstrate Tertullian's opinion on a matter. Instead, one needs to survey his output developmentally or comparatively, as well as rhetorically.

Even though Barnes divides Tertullian's literary career into two phases (pre-Montanist and Montanist), nowhere does he suggest that his later works are to be treated with suspicion as heretical. Thus, I have reservations about the implications behind the names of the divisions of Tertullian's works offered by Fredouille (Catholic, Montanist-influenced and Montanist), which suggest that his later works are to be mistrusted because they are no longer Catholic. No work of Tertullian is unorthodox. They may be unusual and extreme but they are not heretical. Christine Trevett writes that 'Tertullian the Montanist was Tertullian the Montanist catholic.' (Trevett 1996: 69). I am not inclined to see two distinct phases in his literary life. There was no dramatic or sudden catharsis. His ideas certainly became sharper over time, yet there is much that is Montanist in his writings, even before his 'Montanist period'. Again, Trevett's words are illuminating: 'More kindly one might describe Tertullian the spiritual high-flyer as a Montanist by instinct.' (Trevett 1996: 68). Or the question may well be less about how Montanism influenced Tertullian and more about how Tertullian's own personality is reflected in his writings and came to shape what is remembered as Montanism. So, even though specific references to Montanism do appear in his writings at a certain point (although he never used that term), we should not make too much out of this. 'Tertullian's adoption of the New Prophecy in mid-career should not be read as making a significant change of direction in his religious and theological orientation.' (Wright 2000: 1029).

Another way of classifying Tertullian's works is by their genre. Quasten grouped them into apologetic, controversial and disciplinary/moral/ascetic categories (Quasten 1953: 255–317). I think it can be said that every one of Tertullian's treatises is controversial, in the sense that in each of them there was a situation that he saw as a problem and to which he responded with a literary solution. Each of his works deals with some controversy. This is not to deny that many of his works are also controversial in the other sense of the word, in that they offer solutions that many Christians would find harsh and extreme, especially today. He did not preach (and I use the word loosely) simply to edify or extol a congregation. He did not engage in exegesis simply to unlock the meaning of Scripture. He did not write systematic theology simply to contemplate the mysteries of God. He preached, interpreted Scripture and wrote in order to argue. He was a pugilist with a pen. Sometimes the debate was with non-Christians (the apologetic treatises). Sometimes the argument was with Christian groups that he claimed were heretical (the doctrinal treatises). Sometimes the disagreement was with other Christians about practical matters (the disciplinary treatises). In everything he wrote, however, there was some point in dispute, some quarrel to be had and some error to be corrected.

What kind of person emerges from these texts? Scholars call him a firebrand, a puritan, a misogynist, a rigorist and label him as impatient, uncompromising, fiery, passionate, ardent, harsh, sarcastic and even cruel (e.g. Daly 1993: 3; Raven 1993: 156). It has been said that it is not easy to like Tertullian.

There is truth in all of this. His character will emerge with even greater clarity as we consider aspects of his thinking and writing in more detail and in reading his own words. No polemicist enters the fray seeking defeat, and Tertullian was no exception. Debate promotes the notion of 'us and them' and forces one not to seek the truth as much as to score points. There is no room for dispassion, no room for seeing both sides of the argument and no room for objectivity when one's object is to win. This was Tertullian's world, at least as he presented it in what he wrote. I am not suggesting that Tertullian was ever untruthful in what he wrote, but I think it must be accepted that he would either highlight or disguise reality to suit his argument.

Tertullian's Christianity had no room for tepidity or greyness. He had the enthusiasm and zeal of a fanatic, the rigour and clarity of the recently converted, and the intolerance and righteousness of the self-assured. He was a partisan and an extremist. Nothing less than perfection was the requirement for being his kind of Christian and, for him, there could be no other kind. There is a bluntness and directness in his writing, which sometimes verges on the obscure because of his brevity and reluctance to spell everything out.

The lasting importance of Tertullian is, principally, that he was the first Latin-writing Christian author whose works we still possess (leaving aside the question of when Minucius Felix wrote). He was responsible for much of the theological vocabulary of Western Christianity. Even if we cannot be sure that he was the first to use terms like *sacramentum, trinitas, persona, substantia* and *satisfactio* in their theological sense, it is to him that later Latin-writing theologians turned. His acerbic terseness, witty aphorisms and density of thought offer a style of Christian thinking that is not only eminently quotable but also the like of which has rarely been presented so starkly or so passionately. Further, Latin literature of any kind beyond Christianity from this period is almost entirely non-existent and Tertullian's place in its history cannot be denied and ought not to be neglected.

He enables us to see something of African Christianity in its earliest years and, through a comparison of his thinking with other Africans, like Cyprian and Augustine, we can build up a detailed picture of Latin Christianity in one part of the Mediterranean. Novatian, the mid-third-century Roman presbyter (and would-be bishop) and theologian notwithstanding, Tertullian helped make Carthage and North Africa the leading centre of Latin Christian thinking in late antiquity.

His writings are extensive enough for him to have made a contribution on just about every aspect of early Christian life and thought. His treatment of heretics and his Montanist sympathies are an important source of information for what we know about alternative Christian groups. His interaction with non-Christians marks the culmination of second-century apologeticism. In a most articulate manner that has rarely been surpassed since, Tertullian represents a strand of Christianity that endures to this day and continues to exert a powerful influence over many. Whether his example is to be avoided or imitated, there is much in Tertullian's writings that needs to be pondered today as Christians understand their relationships with each other and non-Christians alike.

2

NORTH AFRICAN CHRISTIANITY

In this section, I want to say something about the time and place in which Tertullian lived and wrote. Pre-Nicene Christianity was very different from that after the Council. North African Christianity had a different flavour to that in Italy, Asia Minor, Syria or elsewhere. Solid evidence for Christianity in North Africa comes with *Acts of the Scillitan Martyrs* in 180.[1] Scholars have been keen to find any glimpse of North African Christianity prior to that. Questions have been asked about whether Christianity came to the region from Rome (presumably from Christians of a non-Jewish background) or from the East with Jews who settled there, and when it arrived. Although no definitive conclusion can be reached, the various proposals can be summarized.

Those who argue for a Jewish origin for Christianity in Carthage put forward evidence to show a Jewish influence on the development of North African Christianity and attempt to find weaknesses in the suggestion that it came from Rome. North African Jews had developed a Latin religious vocabulary for those who could not read Hebrew or Greek, and the fact that Christians used some of these Latin terms is taken as an indication that the first North African Christians had been Jews.[2] The Old Latin version of the Scriptures in use in Africa shows the influence of the Hebrew text rather than the Greek Septuagint in some instances. Tertullian commented that the Jews called Christians 'Nazoraeans' (*Against Marcion* 4.8.1). Other examples of the appearance of Jewish expressions and oral traditions in early Christian North African writers can be found (Quispel 1982: 257–335). At the same time, it is claimed, Tertullian's writings were a reaction against the prevailing Jewish Christianity (Daniélou 1977: 139–76). Jews and Christians used the same cemetery outside Carthage (Frend 1965: 362). The practice in the North African churches of having lay elders (*seniores laici*) may also point to Jewish synagogue origins (Frend 1961: 280–4). This would have to have happened while Jewish Christians maintained a link to the synagogue.

In addition, against the idea that North African Christians came originally from Rome are the arguments that North Africa did not follow the Western practice of only few bishops, that Tertullian had little knowledge of the Roman church and never acknowledged any debt to Rome (as one would expect a daughter church would) and that the African Christians had been influencing Rome rather than the other way around (Telfer 1961: 512–17). The more Roman features of North African Christianity are claimed as a later graft upon its Jewish foundations.

On the other hand, while he sees no proof of Christianity coming to Carthage from Rome in what Tertullian wrote in *On the Prescriptions of Heretics* 36 (Barnes 1985: 64–7), Barnes does not find the evidence about the Jewish origins of North African Christianity convincing, particularly if Jewish communities were only established in the West after the capture of Jerusalem in 70 (Barnes 1985: 273–5, 330; Rives 1995: 217). Tertullian's reference to *seniores* (*Apology* 39.5) is probably to presbyters rather than to a group of lay elders (which really only emerges in the fourth century) (Shaw 1982: 207–26). Proof for Christian burial in the Jewish cemetery is lacking (Le Bohec 1981: 168–9). Some, myself included, are inclined to read a little more into Tertullian's statement about connections with Rome than Barnes (Rankin 1995: 16; Dunn 2001a: 408–10, 2003a: 12–15). Even if Carthaginian Christianity was a daughter church of Rome, it was now quite an independent one, as Tertullian's writings indicate.

If we accept that Apuleius referred to Christianity in Africa in *Metamorphoses* 9.14 then Christianity must have arrived there by the middle of the second century. The organization of Christianity, its spread into the countryside among local inhabitants and the fact that Tertullian could not be more explicit about its origins, suggest too that Christianity had been present for some time before it emerged into notice (Rives 1995: 223–5). It makes sense to think that Christians would have reached Carthage early, given that it was a major harbour in the Mediterranean.

Relying upon Tertullian for evidence of Christian origins in North Africa must remain of limited value. I think the most insightful comment comes from Telfer who suggested that 'African Christianity knew no single paternity, having resulted from the joining up of Christian groups with different origins' (Telfer 1961: 516). In a cosmopolitan trade centre like Carthage, it would not be a surprise to discover (if that were still possible) that both Christian Jews and Christian Gentiles arrived in Carthage from any number of other locations, sought converts from people from their own homelands and established quite a number of small and independent Christian communities that were probably language-based or based upon a city of origin. Which community came first or was most dominant seems to be something we shall never know. We also do not know when the various small communities became one Christian community under one bishop. As we shall note later in this introduction, many versions of Christian thinking came to Carthage and found a home. Montanism was embraced by Tertullian; the ideas of Valentinus, Marcion, Hermogenes and Prodicus, however, were the object of Tertullian's opposition.

In July 180, six or twelve Christians with local names were brought from a neighbouring town to be tried in Carthage before the proconsul, P. Vigellius Saturninus.[3] They had in their possession copies (presumably in Latin) of Paul's letters. Although given every opportunity by the magistrate to escape punishment, this group of women and men persisted in affirming their Christianity and in refusing to swear by the genius of the emperor. They asserted that they lived good lives and were no threat to the empire, even though they claimed not to recognize its powers. They were condemned to death and were beheaded immediately because they confessed to having lived according to Christian rites and refused to participate in Roman religious rites (*Acts of the Scillitan Martyrs*). We should accept this account as an official but incomplete record of their trial (Birley 1992: 39).

We do not know exactly where these martyrs were buried, but there was a basilica dedicated to them somewhere just outside the city limits. The fifth-century Christian, Victor of Vita, recorded the Vandals as handing over to the Arians the *Basilica Scillitanorum*, perhaps also known as the *Basilica Celerinae* (*History of the Vandal Persecution* 1.9), which may simply mean that Celerina was buried in the same basilica. Augustine preached in it on occasion.[4]

We do not know what had happened to bring them to the attention of the authorities but we read nothing about popular agitation against Christians. In the absence of any information to the contrary, it would seem that Christianity returned to obscurity in North Africa after this for the next quarter of a century. This document provides us with an insight into what appears to be, at least according to the surviving records, a characteristic attitude of North African Christians. They were eager for martyrdom. Even though they were obedient to civil authority, it was divine authority that mattered to them.

Reaction to persecution rather than theological dispute was always to be an issue of the utmost importance to Christians in this part of the Mediterranean. Martyrs were the role model.

In March 203, a small group of newly initiated Christians, who had been baptized while under house arrest, and their catechist met a grizzly end as public entertainment in the amphitheatre of Carthage. We still possess an edited account of their imprisonment and execution (one in Latin and another in Greek), which contains material recorded by two of the victims (the catechist Saturus and a young wife and mother from a respectable family, Vibia Pereptua), known as *The Passion of Saints Perpetua and Felicitas*. It is a possibility, although a very remote one in some scholars' opinions, that Tertullian was the editor of this *passio*. This is an enormously important document and has been used to gain insight into social, political and religious history, as well as feminism and psychology.

We find in it evidence for the catechumenate as a means of initiating those attracted to Christianity. In this group, there were both men and women, all of whom are described as young (Perpetua being twenty-two years old). They came from across the social spectrum: Perpetua was well-born, whereas Revocatus and Felicitas were both slaves (*Passion* 2). Although Perpetua and an unnamed brother were both catechumens, the rest of the family were probably not. Her Christianity angered and perplexed her father (who most definitely was not Christian) so much so that they were barely on speaking terms (*Passion* 3), yet he pleaded with her to avoid bringing shame on her family and to think of her new-born child (*Passion* 5–6). The group was moved from house arrest to prison after their baptism and the rest of the Christian community tried to take care of their needs through the deacons Tertius and Pomponius (*Passion* 3). Their catechist had not been arrested with the others but surrendered himself to the authorities to join his former catechumens (*Passion* 4).

Both Perpetua and Saturus made a record of visions they received while imprisoned, an indication of their literacy and status. In her first vision, Perpetua follows Saturus up a booby-trapped ladder, treading on the head of a dragon on the way (a possible reference to Ps 90 [91]: 13). At the top of the ladder was a garden, and old shepherd who gave her sheep's milk to drink, which she interpreted as a prediction of passion (*Passion* 4). In her second vision, her dead younger brother Dinocrates was revealed to her to be in suffering, from which he was delivered after Perpetua prayed in her next vision (*Passion* 7–8). In the fourth vision, Perpetua was escorted to the amphitheatre by the deacon Pomponius, where she fought naked with an Egyptian, in the guise of a man and won a branch for her victory (*Passion* 10). In Saturus' vision, he and Perpetua were led after death into a bright light and a garden where they received the homage of angels and met other martyrs. Outside the garden, alone, were Optatus the bishop and Aspasius the presbyter, who fell to their knees and begged the martyrs to restore peace between them. Perpetua spoke to them in Greek and the angels admonished them to settle their quarrels and quell the factions that divided their community (*Passion* 11–13).

In their trial, before the procurator Hilarianus, we are told that Perpetua refused to offer the sacrifice for the emperor's welfare and that the procurator asked her whether she was a Christian (*Passion* 6). Her positive answer was enough to secure her condemnation.

The rest of the *passio* is a graphic account of the death. In prison, they had secured the conversion of their warden (*Passion* 16). The martyrs are described as joyful in the face of death. They refused to be dressed in the robes of pagan priests. The spectacle involved them being pitted against wild animals like bears, leopards and boars. Perpetua and Felicitas faced a wild heifer. After being mauled, they were finished off by the sword, Perpetua guiding the sword of her inexperienced executioner into her own throat (*Passion* 18–21).

This all occurred while the emperor Septimius Severus was in Africa, probably at Lepcis (Birley 1988: 153–4). Other persecutions occurred during his reign (193–211). This raises the frequently asked question of the authenticity of a general edict against Christianity being issued by Severus, as is asserted in some of the ancient literature (Eusebius, *Ecclesiastical History* 6.1.1; [Aelius Spartianus], *Augustan History – Life of Severus* 17.1). Although both sides of the argument have not proven their cases convincingly, I would conclude that it seems unlikely that such an edict existed. The persecutions remained too sporadic and Christian literature too positive about Severus (Tertullian, *To Scapula* 4.3–6) to believe that it did. If Perpetua was arrested under it then why was her brother not arrested as well? We do not know why this group was arrested in the first place, but it does seem that they had not been sought out as part of a coordinated campaign. Persecutions, when they did occur, were sporadic and localized.

The martyrs were buried in the *Basilica Maiorum* to the north of the city on top of a small, grassy hill between what is now the American war cemetery and the beachside suburbs of northern Carthage. Today, the site is barely recognizable and is not sign-posted. It is a tragedy for one of the truly remarkable women of early Christianity (Ennabli 1982).

A generation or two after Tertullian, we know that there were numerous bishops scattered throughout the provinces of North Africa. The area was highly urbanized, with hundreds of cities and towns, even though many of them were quite small (about 2,000–3,000 people). Yet many people lived outside these urban settlements in the countryside, many on the vast agricultural estates that provided the agricultural lifeline upon which Rome depended, in situations where they benefited little from town amenities.

3

SCRIPTURE AND TERTULLIAN

Scripture was authoritative for Tertullian. Although he did not write commentaries on biblical books, he used Scripture as his primary source material in almost every chapter of every work (the only exception being his apologetic works that were designed for pagan readers). In this, he was no different from most other early Christian writers. Most books of both Old and New Testaments,[1] including the Apocrypha or deutero-canonical books, were cited by Tertullian. The exceptions are Ruth, Obadiah (only Melito of Sardis among first- and second-century Christian writers made use of these two), 1 Chronicles, Esther, 2 Maccabees, 2 John and 3 John. He was aware that *Enoch* was not accepted as belonging to the Hebrew Bible by some because something written supposedly before the Flood could not have survived. He defended it as genuine, claiming that Noah could have rewritten it from memory (*On the Apparel of Women* 1.3.1) and he made use of it (*On Idolatry* 4.5; *On the Resurrection of the Dead* 32.1). The Christian additions to Scripture were the authentic writings of the apostles and their associates (*On the Prescriptions of Heretics* 36.1). Thus, the Gospels of John and Matthew had a priority over those of Mark and Luke (*Against Marcion* 4.2.4). When he wanted to make use of the Letter to the Hebrews, which he ascribed to Barnabas, Tertullian felt the need to make some comment by way of justification; Barnabas was an associate of Paul and the letter was more widely accepted than *The Shepherd of Hermas* (*On Modesty* 20.2). Even though the latter was itself widely accepted, it was particularly disliked by Tertullian (*On Modesty* 10.11; *On Prayer* 16.1–2). Also rejected by him was *Acts of Paul* (*On Baptism* 17.5).

The reference in *Acts of the Scillitan Martyrs* 10 to Speratus carrying books and letters of Paul is taken as proof that Latin versions of at least parts of the New Testament existed before Tertullian. By the middle of the third century, it is clear that Cyprian, in Carthage, and

Novatian, in Rome, were using well-established Latin versions of the Scriptures. In the surviving manuscripts of Latin translations of the Bible that were made before or independently of Jerome's Vulgate and which date to between the fourth and thirteenth centuries (known as *Itala,* or in the Old Latin *Vetus Latina*), there seem to be two forms of the texts: one African and the other European. The Greek text they translated seems to be the Western text (as in the fifth-century Codex Bezae) of the New Testament and Lucian's version of the Septuagint. Given the fact that so many individuals made their own translations, the family similarities can be explained by adaptations based on earlier versions (which explains African traits in European versions) or on a shared Christian Latin vocabulary. The African versions of the Old Latin seem to be earlier than the European.

Tertullian's quotations from the Scriptures constitute the earliest extant Latin witness. The question of what version of the Scriptures he used has long been debated. Did he translate from Greek to Latin himself or did he make use of an already existing Latin text? If he had a Latin text, are we able to detect it in one of the surviving later versions of the Old Latin? Finding the answer requires the highly specialized skills of textual critics and the conclusions that they have reached are painstaking, complex, difficult to follow and, not surprisingly, not uniform.

We can find statements from scholars that Tertullian did not have any access to Latin New Testament manuscripts. Thomas O'Malley, on the other hand, concludes that 'there is no doubt but that Tertullian is in contact with Latin renderings of some parts of the Scriptures' (O'Malley 1967: 62). In the 1930s, Aalders investigated Tertullian's use of the gospels. In one article on Tertullian's use of Luke's Gospel outside the context of the Marcionite controversy, he compared 121 instances of Tertullian's quotations from Luke with several Old Latin versions. His conclusion was that there are many examples in which Tertullian's text was quite distinct from the Old Latin versions, indicating that he was offering his own translation. In other, fewer instances Tertullian has a translation that agrees with one or other of the African Old Latin versions. Not all of these instances were judged to be coincidence. However, in some of these cases, Tertullian did not depend upon his Old Latin text slavishly; sometimes he corrected or improved the Latin, obviously with his eye on a Greek text.[2] Further, he often quoted from memory and not always accurately (Aalders 1937: 279–82). Barnes seems to have misread Aalders when, based upon that research, he writes of Tertullian that '[a]lthough he sometimes chose to provide his own spontaneous translation of scriptural texts, he more often employed an already existing translation' (Barnes 1985: 277).

What complicates matters is that in his treatise against Marcion, Tertullian made use of Marcion's version of Luke, the only gospel that Marcion accepted. His principle was to use Marcion's own version of Luke back against him (*Against Marcion* 4.6.1–2). This heretic and schismatic had come to Rome from Pontus in the middle of the second century. He believed that there were two gods: the inferior creator god of the Old Testament and the superior God of the New Testament. For Marcion, only Luke's Gospel was free from Judaizing tendencies, at least after some editorial adjustments. Here the question is whether Tertullian had Marcion's gospel in Greek and made his own translation or had it in Latin already. Some scholars accept that Tertullian had such a Latin translation, which was probably made in Rome (e.g. Higgins 1951),[3] whereas others argue for direct translation from Marcion's Greek text, although with an eye to existing Latin translations of Luke (Quispel 1943).

The consensus would seem to support the position endorsed by O'Malley; Tertullian generally made his own translation from the Greek but, where a Latin translation existed (not all the scriptural books having been translated into Latin at the same time), he made some use of it. The debate is about the degree of that 'some use'. With Marcion's version of Luke's Gospel, he depended, to some extent, upon an already existing Latin translation.

If these comments say something about the complex question of what texts of the Scriptures Tertullian used, the next issue to be addressed is about how he interpreted those texts. We can begin by considering what he had to say about it himself. First of all, Scripture belongs to the church and not to heretics who had no right to use them (*On the Prescriptions of Heretics* 15.3). They not only altered the text but also its meaning to suit themselves. A Christian should not enter into debate with a heretic about the meaning of a passage of Scripture because both sides would claim to be right and a third party would not be able to distinguish orthodox from heterodox interpretation (*On the Prescriptions of Heretics* 17.2–18.3). What guaranteed the validity of the Scriptures was their conformity with the rule of faith (*regula fidei*). We may understand this as a kind of oral credal summary (Countryman 1982). It became the criterion by which the Scriptures could be evaluated, for it was the faith that existed before the written record (*On the Prescriptions of Heretics* 19–21; 37). Those who had handed on and received the faith would be those who possessed true Scripture. We find in Tertullian the priority of Tradition over

Scripture (to use the language of the sixteenth-century Reformations) because Scripture is a record of Tradition. What the heretics claimed as Scripture was only the record of their own novel opinions (*On the Prescriptions of Heretics* 38.6).

On this point, Tertullian often failed to follow his own principle. His treatises against heretics are full of debate about the meaning of scriptural passages. Without this, Tertullian would have been reduced to silence in his engagement with the Marcionites, the Valentinians, Praxeas and Hermogenes.

The second thing to say about Tertullian's stated hermeneutic was his belief in the simplicity of Scripture. It could interpret itself, he claimed at one point, and had a method of its own, such that all apparent inconsistency could be explained (*Against Praxeas* 18.2). Indeed, the principle he put forward was that one text of Scripture must always be interpreted in the light of a greater number of texts (*Against Praxeas* 20.2), and that later texts must agree with earlier ones (*Against Praxeas* 20.3), principles with which he did not always conform.

How then are we to understand this variety of interpretative methods in Tertullian's treatment of Scripture? Waszink (1979: 17) sees this as a problem needing to be explained. I would see it as a deliberate rhetorical technique employed to win a variety of different arguments, each technique being used depending upon what an opponent had first put forward. Thus, at times Tertullian could argue for an allegorical or typological or spiritual interpretation of a scriptural passage (*Against Marcion* 3.5.3; 3.14.5, 7; 3.24.2; 4.17.12; 5.4.8; 5.7.11; *Against the Jews* 9.20; *On the Soul* 35.2; *On Modesty* 8.11; *On the Resurrection of the Flesh* 37.4), whereas at others he would support a more literal or obvious interpretation (*On the Resurrection of the Dead* 19–20; 26.1; *Against the Valentinians* 1.3; *Against Praxeas* 13.4; *Antidote for the Scorpion's Sting* 13.4). Parables, for example, obviously had a spiritual meaning, even though that meaning could be sometimes very obvious (which did not stop heretics from misinterpreting it), yet one should not go looking for allegory everywhere (*Antidote for the Scorpion's Sting* 11.4) (see O'Malley 1967: 145–58). *Against the Jews* is littered with examples of Tertullian's typological reading, from the opening interpretation of God's promise to Rebekah in Gen 25: 23 (1.3–4) to the closing interpretation of the two goats in Lev 16: 5–29 (14.9).

Just as anyone with an oratorical education would know how to argue in support of a strict interpretation of a law or a document or a less strict one, more in accord with the spirit or intention of the law

(Quintilian, *Oratorical Instruction* 7.6.1–12), so too Tertullian knew how to argue for or against allegory, depending upon what his opponent had already advocated. A good debater will find a way to contradict and undermine what the person from the other side has said. Tertullian would support whatever method of using the Scriptures would win his argument for him.

Scripture was an important source of evidence for Tertullian. I shall return to this in the section of this introduction that deals with Tertullian and philosophy, for logical argument makes up another block of material that he used as evidence. To take but one example, a threefold pattern of blocks of evidence forms the basic structure to *On the Veiling of Virgins*. The arguments are from Scripture, from reason or nature and from ecclesiastical teaching. As I stated at the beginning of this section, there is barely a chapter in Tertullian that is not a discussion about the proper interpretation of a binding scriptural passage, even though he did not write exegetical commentary as such.

4

RHETORIC AND TERTULLIAN

The first assessment of Tertullian's rhetorical ability was offered by the first writer ever to mention his name: his fellow North African Christian, the rhetorician Lactantius, who rose to prominence about a century after Tertullian under Diocletian and Constantine.[1] He claimed that Tertullian 'was skilled in literature of every kind; but in eloquence he had little readiness, and was not sufficiently polished, and very obscure' (*Divine Institutes* 5.1.21). It is sometimes claimed that Tertullian was a rhetorician, a teacher of rhetoric (Kennedy 1994: 264). I do not believe there is any evidence to support this claim. Quasten wrote that '[i]t is not right to represent Tertullian as a lawyer and rhetorician with a leaning towards sophism' (Quasten 1953: 248). We need not assert that he was a teacher of rhetoric, only that he had been a student of it.

One cannot over-emphasize the importance of rhetoric to the educated and literate in Roman society and its influence on much surviving Roman literature. Today the word 'rhetoric' often has the adjective 'mere' attached to it, and for many the word is a pejorative term to describe flashy but empty speech. It has to be admitted that at some stage in classical antiquity this association had already been formed. Tertullian lived in an age that, in very broad and loose terms and in places influenced by Greek culture, has come to be called the Second Sophistic. Anderson tentatively characterizes this particularly Greek phenomenon as follows: 'we are dealing with established public speakers who offered a predominantly rhetorical form of higher education, with a distinct emphasis on its more ostentatious forms' (Anderson 1993: 1). Sophists came to be understood as those who practised how to speak eloquently and with style, but who were so concerned with form that they neglected content. There is exaggeration in this, yet when we read things like Philostratus' *Lives of the Sophists*, Alciphron's *Letters*, Lucian of Samosata's *The Fly* and Marcus

Cornelius Fronto's *Eulogy of Smoke and Dust*, we have examples, not all of them strictly Sophistic, of how so much time and effort could be expended preparing and polishing speeches and texts about quite irrelevant matters. At its worst, by Tertullian's day, rhetoric represented the victory of style over substance. Students of rhetoric did not practice oratory in order to prepare for careers in law courts or political assemblies as much as to delight an audience with their skill. Practice became an end in itself and declamation, the practice of speeches, became more and more fanciful and less and less practical.

Rhetoric had not started that way. It emerged in the Greek city-states of the fifth and fourth centuries BC as an increasingly organized and structured way of being a successful public speaker. Success was measured in terms of persuasion; in the law courts one needed to persuade a jury about questions of guilt or innocence and in the assemblies one needed to persuade citizens about which course of action ought to be taken. Despite Plato's objections that, while philosophy and dialectic sought the truth, rhetoric and speech-making sought merely to flatter and win arguments, many, including Aristotle, composed handbooks setting out the rules for persuasive speaking.

The Romans adapted Greek rhetoric for their own oratory and from the writings of the anonymous author of *To Herennius*, Cicero, the elder Seneca, Tacitus, the younger Pliny, Quintilian, Fronto and the *Rhetores Latini Minores*, to name only the more obvious, we know a good deal about the Roman perspectives on the rhetorical arts and its changing relevance in Roman life.

Rhetoric was a complicated and intricate series of systems that varied from each other often only in nuance or in presentation and which took many years to master. Briefly, it was commonly held that there were three types of oratory: forensic (for use in law courts and which sought to persuade about past events), deliberative (for use in assemblies and senates and which sought to persuade about future events) and epideictic (which by then had lost its persuasive element and which sought to praise an individual while entertaining the audience, particularly when one was encouraged not to focus on the subject matter but on the person speaking). Persuasion could be achieved through the rationality of the argument, through the character of the speaker and through an appeal to emotion. In addition to persuading, orators saw their task as one of teaching and pleasing. It was believed that there were five functions of an orator: invention (the discovery of the arguments to be used), arrangement (the sequencing of arguments), style (the choice of words), memory (skills involved in moving from the creation of a speech to its presentation) and delivery (voice production and bodily gesture). A speech, especially a forensic one, could be divided into a number of sections: introduction (*exordium*, setting the mood), narration (*narratio*, telling the basic story), proposition (*propositio* or *partitio*, setting out the point in dispute and one's own position), confirmation and refutation (*confirmatio* and *refutatio*, arguments in support of one's position and arguments against one's opponent's position) and conclusion (*peroratio*). Style was a well-developed part of the art and much was written about the techniques of embellishment. It became the chief concern of the declaimers and was the principal cause of rhetoric's ultimate demise. In a forensic speech or piece of writing, there was most typically a basis or issue around which the case was constructed. It was generally considered that there were four main bases: conjectural (arguments about whether or not something happened), definitional (arguments about how to define something that happened), qualitative (arguments about the characteristics of something) and competency (arguments about a court's authority to hear a case).

One of the reasons why figures like Tacitus and the younger Pliny complained about the contemporary state of oratory and the art of rhetoric was because of the political situation. Being a persuasive public speaker was important when the affairs of state were directed by democratic or oligarchic assemblies. However, when one was a member of an assembly under increasing autocracy (as a traditionalist like Tacitus sought to persuade through the only medium left open to him, writing history), the need to persuade gave way to the need to flatter. Schools of rhetoric taught wealthy young men how to compose and deliver panegyric and encomium on set topics. Winning an argument became less important than appearing to be erudite, polished and sophisticated.

There is ample evidence that Tertullian had learnt oratory and was a skilled practitioner of the art. A number of scholars, most notably Sider and Fredouille, have recognized the importance of classical rhetoric in Tertullian. This is not to say that his works were originally speeches, even though this claim has been made about several of his works by some scholars. Yet what we have are what we would expect to find from someone who first committed what he wanted to say to paper. We know that *Against the Jews* was written because the speech on the same topic had not been able to be completed. In other words, his treatises were written as though they could be delivered as set speeches. These texts were not written merely as declamatory exercises, designed to impress the reader with Tertullian's linguistic dexterity and flair. The topics upon which he wrote were lively and

divisive ones in the Carthaginian Christian community and he turned
to rhetoric in order to achieve its original objective, persuasion. He
wanted to change opinion and convince others that he was right and
they were wrong. Yet what was the purpose of actually committing
his thoughts to writing? Did he intend them only for the small elite
who, like himself, could read, or did he intend for them to be available
to be read aloud for those who could not read for themselves? In a
society that was so oral, the oratorical qualities of Tertullian's writing
ought not be overlooked.

What is the significance of this for reading Tertullian? For one
thing, it provides us with a way of discerning the structure of what he
wrote, as Sider states: '. . . he frequently develops his thought not, as
we are often led to believe, in a random and haphazard fashion, but in
a nicely arranged sequence of topics with which his rhetorical training
had furnished him' (Sider 1971: 126). In other words, there is con-
nectedness and development in each treatise. Although modern and
post-modern literary criticism may decry the utility or even possibility
of knowing an author's intentions, it still remains, I believe, one way
in which readers can be guided to come to their own appreciation of
a text's meaning. Being aware of the traditional arrangement of parts
in a rhetorically influenced piece of writing also helps us appreciate
the adeptness that Tertullian had in being able to adapt and rework
that arrangement in creative ways as was needed, something he did
frequently, particularly in his more mature output. In other words, we
appreciate his originality as a writer.

More importantly, I think, an awareness of the rhetorical influences at work in his writings helps us to interpret what he wrote.
Even though there is structure and order to his writing, the fact that
rhetoric was so important to him means that we should probably not
consider his writings to be treatises as such, even though this is a term
I shall continue to use. This is the case if we understand a treatise as
a systematic and thorough investigation of a particular topic. This
Tertullian did not do, for he was not ultimately a systematic theologian. One should not turn to *On Baptism*, for example, hoping to find
a complete treatment on this sacrament. There was obviously much
about initiation practice and theory that was not controversial and
could thereby be passed over almost in complete silence. Tertullian
wrote this work because some 'Canaanite heresy' (*On Baptism* 1.2) had
denied the efficacy of washing with water for the forgiveness of sins
and he wished to respond (*On Baptism* 3.1).

I am convinced that most students who come to Patristic literature
for the first time read it at face value. In their essays, they write things

like 'Tertullian believed that' and then attach a brief (and hopefully referenced) extract from a tract, as though what Tertullian wrote was a string of facts. More familiarity with the author perhaps leads to the next stage, where one becomes aware that he could and did write contradictory things in different works, and one becomes locked in the struggle to figure out what he really believed. Such difficulties are only overcome when one realizes that he wrote from a rhetorical perspective. As I stated earlier in this introduction, in every instance Tertullian wrote in order to win arguments. He did not describe, he advocated. It was his overall position about which he was passionate; everything else was merely there to prove the point. Barnes states: 'Fallacious argument will always be a necessity for any orator. Even a valid case will have some weak points which need disguising.' (Barnes 1985: 217). So he could advance arguments that, in the context, helped his case but which were ones he personally would have found difficult to swallow. As the rhetoricians pointed out, for example, there were arguments that a forensic orator could put forward to defend the letter of the law, just as there were arguments that could be put forward to defend the spirit of the law and, no doubt, most forensic orators would have argued passionately and persuasively for one position at one time and then for the opposite in another case.

Having a rhetorical appreciation also helps evaluate Tertullian's limitations. Those who know the rules of rhetoric know what to expect and, in reading Tertullian, when what one expects does not materialize, it could well be because he was not able to do that due to the weakness of his position. What Tertullian did not say is very important for understanding what he did say. Sometimes he makes it appear as though he has quite a number of reasons to support what he is arguing yet which, upon closer examination, turn out to be variations on the one argument. That he resorted to such tricks suggests that he knew himself that his case was on shaky ground. He did not write treatises as much as he wrote position papers or advocacy reports. For every text he wrote, there is another text (perhaps never written or not surviving), which is the argument a skilled opponent could have produced. Perhaps we need to read Tertullian less like literary critics and more like judges and juries.

The use of rhetoric will help readers of Patristic texts to appreciate both the rhetorical situation that occasioned a text and the intertextual relationship between author and reader, which, in other words, necessitates giving attention to historical, literary and social questions.

5

PHILOSOPHY AND TERTULLIAN

Perhaps the two most oft-quoted lines from Tertullian are 'Therefore what of Athens and Jerusalem? What of the academy and the church?' (*On the Prescriptions of Heretics* 7.9) and 'I believe it because it is absurd (*credo quia absurdum est*)'. From this, it is only natural that he has often been considered as a fideist and opponent of philosophy rather than as a rationalist. The fact that what Tertullian wrote in Latin is actually *credibile est, quia ineptum est* (*On the Flesh of Christ* 5.4) should be enough to make us want to look more carefully at Tertullian's position with regard to the relationship between faith and reason and the broader issue of the relationship between Christianity and philosophy. As Osborn writes: 'Some writers take the passage by itself and find irrationalism, while others look at the context and find rational argument.' (Osborn 1997a: 48–9).

There is indeed much criticism of philosophy in Tertullian's writings. At the heart of the matter was his opinion that philosophy supported religious idolatry (*To the Heathens* 2.1.7). Philosophers are called 'patriarchs of heresy' (*On the Soul* 3.1). There was so much variation taught by philosophical schools, not all of which could be true, that it was simply an agent of spreading confusion and lies. On the other hand, what Christianity taught was the truth in all its simplicity (*To the Heathens* 2.1.12–14; *Apology* 47.4–10; *On the Soul* 2.6–7). Christian heretics distorted the truth because they depended upon the opinions of different philosophies (*On the Soul* 3.1; *Against Hermogenes* 8.3; *On the Prescriptions of Heretics* 7.3).

It was possible that the teaching of philosophy could coincide with Christian teaching, like a ship stumbling into a safe harbour during a storm (*On the Soul* 2.1; *On the Testimony of the Soul* 2.4), or could have borrowed from the Scriptures (*To the Heathens* 2.2.5–6). Yet, the method of philosophy was to distort the truth whenever it was grasped, so much so that Tertullian thought it better to ignore all philosophy, even though it might contain elements of the truth, because most people could not read it critically enough (*On the Testimony of the Soul* 1.4).

Tertullian also contrasted Christians and philosophers in terms of their practical morality. The philosophers based their ideas of goodness and virtue on mere human opinion. The obligation to live morally was based upon human authority for the philosopher. But just as human authority could be despised, so could human opinion be deceived (*Apology* 45.2). In contrast, Christian morality was based upon divine revelation and went much further in its demands (*Apology* 45.3). It also irked Tertullian that, while both Christians and pagan philosophers both were critical of the claims for the existence of the pantheon of gods, only the Christians were singled out for punishment for this view (*Apology* 46.4). Tertullian was not shy in naming philosophers and his points of disagreement with them. He devoted chapters two to six of the second book of *To the Heathens* to refuting the theories of what he described as 'physical philosophy'. Democritus, Thales, Socrates, Plato, Zeno, Epicurus, the Stoics and Varro are all mentioned.

Yet that is not the end of the matter. Tertullian did have a large debt to classical culture; it influenced his thinking and writing, it provided him with a language and a methodology and it furnished him with the material against which he could react and develop his own position. Recent scholarship has been reappraising Tertullian's use of philosophy without reaching a unanimous conclusion (Sider 1982: 247–50). If one may be permitted to generalize, it seems that some modern commentators are taking the approach that Tertullian was not so much anti-philosophical or anti-rational, but rather that he developed a philosophy based on revelation; he did not separate faith and reason, but developed a reason based on faith. Osborn is at pains to mention Tertullian's Stoicism throughout his 1997 monograph, particularly with regard to his concepts of the immanence of God, the balance between positive and negative theology, divine mutability, materiality, the two natures of Christ, rationality and ethics.

When we consider texts like *On the Shows* and *On the Veiling of Virgins*, in which we find Tertullian's rhetorical threefold arrangement of arguments, not only is Scripture an authoritative source of evidence but also truth or intellect. What is particularly interesting is that these two works are not addressed to pagan readers but to Christians, when one might have thought that an appeal to 'religiously neutral' arguments based on reason would have been superfluous. Whole chapters of these and other treatises are devoted to rational argument not based upon anything overtly Christian. As Guerra points out, Tertullian constructed arguments from reason as one of the building blocks of treatise writing, but it is not just a question of a choice between reason and faith because Tertullian used about five such building blocks (moral behaviour, tradition and spiritual testimony being the other three) (Guerra 1991: 109).

Tertullian opens *On the Testimony of the Soul* by acknowledging that non-Christians are more likely to be convinced by non-Christian evidence than by Christian evidence, no matter how overwhelmingly true the latter was. He pointed out that a number of Christian intellectuals had turned to philosophy and other pieces of non-Christian literature to demonstrate that there was nothing in Christianity that was contrary to philosophy at its best (*On the Testimony of the Soul* 1.1–2). Reason was a gift from God (*On the Soul* 16.2). Reason was to lead to what God has revealed in the Scriptures and reason could be judged by its conformity with the rule of faith (*On the Prescriptions of Heretics* 1–2). Osborn writes: 'The solution of the puzzle lies in the perfection of Christ; when the perfect is come, that which is in part, like philosophy, must be done away' (Osborn 1997a: 37).

We may witness this more positive mood in relation to classical culture in *On the Pallium*, a work of Tertullian's maturity. On one level of reading, it is a work that advocates the abandonment of the Roman toga for the Greek/Punic pallium (*On the Pallium* 3–4).[1] Yet, as Barnes has noted, many commentators have read more into it than that. Some have seen it as a work in which Tertullian displayed his rhetorical abilities, others as a work in which he turned his back on everything Roman (Barnes 1976: 13–4). Indeed it does in one sense. Those who wore the toga were proclaimed as the worst people in society: carriers of the dead, pimps and gladiator trainers (*On the Pallium* 4.8). Those who wore the pallium had renounced superstition and had a claim to having had an education (*On the Pallium* 4.10; 6.2). The pallium had long been a garment associated with philosophy and learning and now Tertullian claimed it for Christians (*On the Pallium* 6.2). On a deeper level, the implication is clear; Christianity was the new philosophy.

So what does Athens have to do with Jerusalem? It all depends on how one interprets the two urban referents. González (1974: 22) has argued that we cannot equate Athens simply with reason and Jerusalem simply with faith: 'To him, then, the question is not one of reason versus faith as sources of authority but is rather a question of two different sorts of reason.' The first argues about what is theoretically possible (when facts are made to conform with reason); the second argues about what has actually occurred (when reason is made to conform with facts).

The response to the paradox in *On the Flesh of Christ* is to understand that Tertullian was making use of a rhetorical topos, a little maxim whose very familiarity gave it a ring of truth. I take Tertullian's comment about believing because something is improbable or impossible to be nothing much more than saying that the truth (in this case, about the resurrection of flesh) is often stranger than fiction (an argument that appears again in *Against the Jews* 9.7–8). González (1974: 19–21) and Osborn (1997a: 48–64) offer a more sustained investigation of this passage.[2]

6

THEOLOGY AND TERTULLIAN

Many readers who pick up this volume would expect this section to be the most important part of this introduction. Although his theology is important, there are many dimensions to Tertullian's writings in addition to the theological. In recent years in the field of Patristics, there has been an increasing awareness of the importance of cultural, historical, sociological, psychological, literary and pastoral aspects. The writings of early Christians are pieces of literature even before they are statements of theology. That some researchers describe the field now as early Christian literature or, even more broadly, early Christian studies, rather than simply as Patristics, may be an indication of this awareness and shift.

Those who expect to find theology and little else discussed in this book may be disappointed not to find more. Until we know how to read Tertullian as literature, we shall fail to interpret his theology accurately and thoroughly. The form is important for understanding the content. This is why Tertullian the orator, Tertullian the philosopher and Tertullian the writer come before Tertullian the theologian. In this section, all I can hope to achieve is to sketch some of the areas of systematic theology about which Tertullian had something to say, even though it must be borne in mind that Tertullian was not a systematic theologian. If anything, he was an occasional or polemical one, in the sense that he wrote to correct erroneous opinions, not to offer a thorough exposition of a topic.

We shall begin with God and the question of the Trinity. Reference has already been made in the section of this introduction on Scripture to Marcion (and there will be further discussions in the section on Christians and Jews, below). He presented a particular challenge. There was not one God but two: the first, revealed in the Old Testament, who is the creator and who is responsible for evil in the world, and the second, revealed in the New Testament, who is the

Father of Jesus and who is compassionate and kind. Tertullian's response was to assert the oneness of God. If God is supreme, eternal, unbegotten, unmade, without beginning or end, then there must only be one (*Against Marcion* 1.3.2). Another opponent, this time one who had moved to Carthage and was a contemporary, Hermogenes, argued that God must have created the universe out of pre-existent matter for otherwise God would have created evil, which Hermogenes could not accept (*Against Hermogenes* 2.2–4). Tertullian responded that if God is one then the quality of eternity could be possessed only by one (*Against Hermogenes* 4.1–3) and that God was responsible for the creation of evil things (*Against Hermogenes* 16.3–4). Valentinus was a Gnostic heretic whose followers had developed a variety of opinions about a hierarchical Pleroma of divine emanations (aeons) from God (*Against the Valentinians* 7–8). So bizarre are these systems that Tertullian spent most of his time satirizing rather than refuting them.

Yet, his belief in the oneness of God was not the same as that held by Praxeas, which may well be a pseudonym for a Roman figure who advocated monarchianism (modalism or patripassianism), the doctrine that so insisted on the oneness of God that it blurred any distinction between Father, Son and Spirit because each was just God in a particular guise, such that, as Tertullian claimed, it was the Father who was crucified (*Against Praxeas* 1.1, 5). Tertullian countered that the way in which God has operated in human history, as recorded in the rule of faith preserved in the Scriptures, has been as Father, Son and Spirit (who are distinct not identical), which he calls the economy (*Against Praxeas* 2.1). The oneness of God is on the level of substance (*substantia*), whereas the distinctions are on the level of degree, form and aspect because the economy of God is a trinity (*trinitas*), a term we first find in *Against Praxeas* 2.4. Later, Tertullian would use the word person (*persona*) to describe the level on which Father and Son (*Against Praxeas* 7.9) and Spirit (*Against Praxeas* 11.7, 10) were distinct but not separate (*Against Praxeas* 9.1). Unaware of later controversies, Tertullian stated that the Father is the whole substance, whereas the Son is a derived and inferior portion of the whole (*Against Praxeas* 9.2).

From this trinitarian position flows Tertullian's Christology, for the Monarchians had asserted that the term 'Son' could be understood as the flesh who is the human Jesus, whereas the term 'Father' could be understood as the spirit who is the divine Christ (that is, God) (*Against Praxeas* 27.1). As far as Tertullian was concerned, this made Father and Son into two. Instead, he argued that the divine Word, without a transfiguration or change of substance, became incarnate and was clothed with flesh (*Against Praxeas* 27.6–7). The incarnate Jesus is not a mixture of flesh and divine spirit such that he is neither completely human nor completely divine (*Against Praxeas* 27.8). Indeed, he is one person in whom are conjoined two substances (*Against Praxeas* 27.11). What it means to be conjoined in one person was not something that was investigated here any further.

Some opponents (and Marcion was singled out for mention) appear to have held a Docetic position with regard to Christology, in that they rejected the idea that the flesh of the Christ was real (*On the Flesh of Christ* 1.2). What lay behind this was their denigration of the material world (*On the Flesh of Christ* 4.1–2). Tertullian pushed the idea that the flesh of Christ, which experienced death and resurrection, was real and that human flesh too will share in this resurrection. It was an occasion to stress the 'two substances' understanding of Christ (*On the Flesh of Christ* 5.7); both born and unborn, both fleshy and spiritual, both weak and strong, both living and dying.

Against Hermogenes, Tertullian argued that the human soul was not derived from pre-existent matter but from the breath of God (*On the Soul* 3.4). In this work, the whole range of philosophical opinion about theological anthropology came under fire. Against the Platonic idea of the eternal pre-existence of the soul, Tertullian reaffirmed Christian belief that it was created by God (*On the Soul* 4). Following the Stoics, however, he accepted that the soul had corporeal substance (*On the Soul* 5.2). He went on to explain that by corporeal he meant that it was real although spiritual, for something incorporeal could not give life to the corporeal body the way the soul does, and the Scripture records that souls can experience torment and, as the ultimate argument, this has been revealed in the vision of a Montanist woman (*On the Soul* 5.3–9.8). The mind is a faculty of the soul (*On the Soul* 12.1). In chapter 22, he summarized what he accepted to be Christian teaching. Much of the rest of the treatise examines the question of the union of body and soul. The idea that the soul is added to the fully formed body at the moment of birth is rejected in favour of the idea that both are formed together at the same time (*On the Soul* 25–27). The soul does not transmigrate but is transmitted from one's father (*On the Soul* 27.7–33.11). An embryo becomes human in the womb at the moment when its form is completed (*On the Soul* 37.2). Ultimately all souls were contained potentially in Adam and were thus unclean until born again in Christ (*On the Soul* 40.1). After death it would seem that the soul is sent to Hades unless it were the soul of a martyr or the soul of one already dead at the time of Christ's death, which would gain access to paradise, which is not heaven, for heaven will only be opened when the world passes away (*On the Soul* 45).

The human person has free will to do what God commands or not and hence one cannot blame either God or the devil for human choices (*On Exhortation to Chastity* 2.3–5). Ethics were extremely important for Tertullian and the source for ethical life was found in the pages of the New Testament. A person's conduct was a sign of their faith (*On the Prescription of Heretics* 43.2) and the kind of conduct Tertullian demanded, exemplified by fasting, modesty, chastity and martyrdom, needed the purest and most resolute kind of faith.

In *Apology* 39, Tertullian offers a description of the life of the church for the pagan reader. He described the communal liturgical life of the community, the appointment of tested elders, the collections for the poor and needy, and the moral character of its members. We see in a late work, *On Modesty*, Tertullian's understanding of the perfection of the church, which he described as a virgin free from all stain (*On Modesty* 1.8). Tertullian was concerned that too great an emphasis on God's mercy would undermine the concept of divine justice (*On Modesty* 2). Rankin (1995: 94–5) argues that Tertullian's perfectionist streak did not emerge only after his Montanist conversion; it is evident throughout his literary corpus. The forgiveness of sins was a theological issue about which Tertullian had much to say and which will be examined in the last section of this introduction but, in essence, we can say that for him membership of the church was a clear-cut issue; only those who were faithful and pure were Christian.

The rule of faith was transmitted to the church by the apostles (*On the Prescriptions of Heresies* 20.5–9). The validity of anything purporting to be Christian teaching must be measured against what is found in apostolic churches (*On the Prescriptions of Heresies* 21.4) because of the apostolic succession of bishops (*On the Prescriptions of Heresies* 32.1). Rome was such a church (*On the Prescriptions of Heresies* 32.2; 36.2–3), yet Tertullian did not have a sense of Roman primacy (Dunn 2001a: 407–8; Dunn 2003a: 13–15). Although Tertullian accepted that clerics were of a higher status than lay people (*On Baptism* 17.2; *On Flight in Time of Persecution* 11.1) and that bishops had the responsibility for celebrating or authorizing others to celebrate sacramental liturgies (*On Baptism* 17.1), he was not reluctant to criticize bishops who rested their authority upon their claim to apostolic succession instead of upon their spiritual obedience (*On Modesty* 21.17).

7

TERTULLIAN AND PAGANS

In this section, I wish to consider what Tertullian tells us about the relationship between Christians and the vast majority of those people, among whom they lived, who did not share their religious affiliation. In particular, I am interested in that relationship at an official or public level; the relationship between Christians and the Roman provincial government, as reflected in those treatises of Tertullian that touch upon this topic.

Perhaps Tertullian's earliest surviving work is the two-volume *To the Heathens*, written in 197. It is addressed to pagan society at large and responds to their criticism that there were an ever-increasing number of Christians and to their practice of bringing them to trial without knowing much about them. Following the standard apologetic genre of the second century, Tertullian indicated that there were no crimes associated with being Christian for if there were they ought to be brought to light and Christians could then rightly be punished for them. Rejecting pagan gods was something many pagans themselves did and Christians, even though they did not sacrifice for the emperor, were more loyal than many other peoples. In the second book, Tertullian made use of Varro's work on pagan religion to demonstrate this similarity between Christianity and some pagan self-criticism.

There is much in this work that is incomplete and unpolished. Indeed, several years later Tertullian reworked this material into a finely crafted treatise, which has remained his most enduring, *Apology*. This work is a forensic defence of Christianity against the pagan charges.[1] As Birley (1992: 41) notes, both *To the Heathens* and *Apology* were responses to what can be found in the younger Pliny and Tacitus. Addressing himself now more specifically than his earlier work to provincial governors, not only did he argue that Christians were innocent but also he stated that there were procedural anomalies that made the trials against them invalid (*Apology* 1–3). He goaded them with the thought that if they condemned Christians out of ignorance of what Christianity was all about then it was a sign that they knew what they were doing was unjust, as it would not be able to stand up to scrutiny. He taunted them with the assertion that those who looked into Christianity ended up joining and that it must be good because Christians were proud to profess it, made no excuses for belonging and were prepared to be condemned for it (unlike those involved with evil who liked to keep their activity secret). Louis Swift has observed how *Apology* seeks to rouse indignation through the typical arguments of forensic oratory (Swift 1968: 867–9). A skilled opponent could have responded that all this showed was that Christians were merely deluded in believing that something indeed evil was good. Others charged with the same kinds of offences, such as murder, incest, sacrilege or treason, were permitted to conduct a thorough defence and even when they confessed to crime the circumstances were investigated. When Christians pleaded their innocence with regard to particular crimes this was not investigated, and when they pleaded their guilt about being Christian neither was this investigated. Others were tortured to confess their guilt, while Christians were tortured to recant their confession. Others were interrogated when they denied the charges, yet Christians who denied their Christianity were released at once. Unwillingly perhaps, but here we find Tertullian providing us with some information about the differing degrees of commitment and endurance to the faith in the face of persecution.

Against the charges of murder, cannibalism and incest Tertullian offered a simple plea of 'not guilty' and employed rhetorical con-jectural arguments to strengthen his case (*Apology* 7–9). Here he stated that Christians sometimes were betrayed to the authorities by their slaves and that their gatherings were the subject of raids (*Apology* 7.3–4). With regard to the charges of atheism or sacrilege (*Apology* 10–28) and treason (*Apology* 29–45), Tertullian admits the charge but used rhetorical qualitative arguments to justify Christian action by examining motive (Sider 1971: 74–8). Christians did not worship pagan gods as they did not exist (*Apology* 10.2). With regard to treason, Tertullian assured his readers that Christians prayed for the safety of those in authority (*Apology* 30.1), even for the bravery of armies (*Apology* 30.4). In fact, it was the empire that preserved the world from final judgement (*Apology* 32). The emperor was appointed to his position by God, Tertullian suggested (*Apology* 33.1). Christians would not engage in empty flattery of the emperor as did many pagans. Tertullian gives evidence that many non-Christians found the behaviour of their Christian neighbours anti-social and perplexing (*Apology* 35.4–5). Yet the response from Tertullian was to state that Christians stood shoulder to shoulder with their neighbours, sharing in the everyday events of life (*Apology* 42.3), including the army, even if only by chance (*Apology* 5.6; 37.4). He wanted his readers not to get the impression that Christians were somehow a separatist sect, even though they refrained from involving themselves in pagan religious activities, affairs of state or the spectacles of public entertainment (*Apology* 37.5–6; 38; 42.4–7).

Writing to fellow Carthaginians in *On the Pallium*, not only did Tertullian urge them to adopt their more native dress by wearing the pallium instead of the toga but also he advocated that they become Christian, as they had adopted the pallium as their own vestment (*On the Pallium* 6.2). This sense that Christianity was the only option for those who recognized the truth comes in the conclusion to *On the Testimony of the Soul*. The soul, the neutral witness, possessed by pagan and Christian alike, acknowledges the truth that Christians assert and yet its pagan 'owner' resists this truth (*On the Testimony of the Soul* 6.3–6).

When we compare this with what Tertullian wrote when addressing a Christian readership, Evans' point become clear; that Tertullian 'suppresses the intramural arguments which he would and did have with other Christians and writes to his pagan readers marshalling all serviceable data to be garnered from widespread Christian belief and practice . . .' (Evans 1976: 25).[2]

Two such early works written for Christians address the question of how they are to live their everyday lives in an overwhelmingly pagan society. *On the Shows* seeks to prove to Christians, especially the newly baptized, that the spectacles of Roman entertainment, whether the theatre, amphitheatre or circus, were, contrary to the views of pagans and some Christians, not consistent with Christian faith (*On the Shows* 5–14), Christian teaching (*On the Shows* 15–19) or the truth (*On the Shows* 20–23). Games and shows had more than entertainment value; they had a religious element in that they were dedicated to the gods and to participate in them, even as a spectator, was to engage in idolatry or to be tempted to immorality and violence, the practice of which the Christian had vowed to abandon at baptism. Human perversity had corrupted the goodness of God's creation. The Christian knows better than does a pagan and Tertullian's solution was to avoid entertainment spectacles altogether. He demanded a clear-cut loyalty from Christians; to go to the shows was to abandon Christianity (*On the Shows* 24.4).

Even though Tertullian referred to the daily chant at the amphitheatre for Christians to be thrown to the lions (*On the Shows* 27.1), one does not get the sense from this treatise that he felt that Christians were participating in pagan spectacles out of a fear of being singled out and liable to victimization if they did not. Those Christians who did attend were driven by their desire for self-indulgent and salvation-destroying pleasure.

In *On Idolatry*, Tertullian argued for a definition of idolatry that was general enough to include all other crimes within it and specific enough for it to be found in other crimes (*On Idolatry* 1). Not only must Christians have nothing to do with the manufacture of idols used in religious ceremonies but also they must not devote any artisan skill to that which facilitates pagan worship either (*On Idolatry* 8). Astrology, school teaching (although not the studying of literature), trade based on a desire to acquire or in products which could be used in pagan festivals, and the training of gladiators were all considered unacceptable professions for the Christian. For Tertullian, there could be no comeback; Christians ought to have thought about that before joining the church and, besides, Jesus called his disciples to leave security and comfort behind (*On Idolatry* 12). There is an extremism here and even though he acknowledged that Christians had to live with sinners, it was only allowed provided that they themselves did not sin. Here he offered an aphorism; it was permitted to live with pagans but not permitted to die with them (*On Idolatry* 14.5). There was a division between secular and sacred, between what belonged to Caesar and what belonged to God. Christians were to be obedient to civil authority, except where idolatry was concerned (*On Idolatry* 15.8). Such rigidity led to casuistry; it was lawful to be at a ceremony where honour was given to a person through sacrifice (provided that one did not participate in the sacrifice), but not to be at one where it was given to an idol (*On Idolatry* 16). One could enter public life provided that one could do the impossible and avoid the idolatrous trappings of office (*On Idolatry* 18). More explicitly, military service, because it involved violence, was completely forbidden to a Christian (*On Idolatry* 19). Even borrowing money, which required the taking of an oath, was classed as idolatry (*On Idolatry* 23). It was not an easy thing for a Christian to live in a non-Christian environment as far as Tertullian was concerned, and he wanted his fellow Christians to be clearly distinguished from their pagan neighbours in the way they lived their lives. I must disagree with Barnes (1985: 100) and reject the idea that this was not Tertullian at his most rigorous. Despite the few concessions he made, his aim was clear; the church he envisaged was to be a church of saints, not of sinners.

To the Martyrs was written around the same time as these other works, probably before *Apology*,[3] and was addressed to Christians in prison awaiting trial and execution, intended as food for their spirits. Tertullian contrasted the prison in which they were incarcerated with the prison that the world, with its blindness and impurities, could be and concluded that those in prison were in fact free because the world was a far larger prison, containing a far larger number of prisoners awaiting a far more imposing judge (*To the Martyrs* 2.1–3). There was a sharp distinction between the world and the Christian; even those Christians not imprisoned behind bars like Tertullian himself were considered to have renounced the world as well (*To the Martyrs* 2.5). Here we can see the genesis of that expression that Christians were *in* the world but not *of* the world. Furthermore, those in prison were not even in the world; they had been rescued from having to deal with the ever-present paganism of gods, holidays, religious festivals, public shows, brothels, temptations, further persecution and even pagans themselves. This advantage for the spirit far outweighed the disadvantages caused to the flesh (*To the Martyrs* 2.7). The spirit was free in prison! Tertullian's arguments in *Apology* that Christians were not segregationalists is, as we have noted, not entirely convincing because of contradictory statements; here, writing to Christians who had shown the full commitment to their faith that a rigorist and extremist like Tertullian applauded, he reveals more of his true position.

Tertullian encouraged those prospective martyrs to consider their imprisonment as training and strengthening, like that undergone by a soldier or an athlete, in order that they might obtain an everlasting crown (*To the Martyrs* 3.2–4). Christian life was a warfare for God and, thanks to the policies of provincial administrators, Christians were given ample opportunity to grow in virtue through trials and hardships (*To the Martyrs* 3.5). The work ends abruptly with a note that many of noble birth have been put to death recently for their loyalty to the contenders for the imperial crown or for their disloyalty to the victor (*To the Martyrs* 6.2). Presumably, the inference was that the Christian, who followed the cause not of an emperor but of God, ought to be all the more prepared to endure persecution willingly. Tertullian's reference to the devil in the opening chapter reveals the reason he wrote this small work: fear that those in prison would backslide (*To the Martyrs* 1.5).

This fear dominated much of Tertullian's thinking about Christians in the world, as we have noted already. If imprisonment was freedom and martyrdom was victory, then was Christianity merely a sect of suicide-seekers? Were those who escaped persecution only second-rate

Christians? If denial of one's faith was unacceptable in the face of trial, was any form of evasion of arrest legitimate at all?

Christian resolve in the face of persecution was being undermined by the attitude of Gnostic Christians (in particular the Valentinians), who questioned the relevance of martyrdom (*Antidote for the Scorpion's Sting* 1.5–9). Some Christians had been subjected to fire, the sword and beasts; others undergo torture in prison; and others are hunted like rabbits (*Antidote for the Scorpion's Sting* 1.11).[4] The whole work is a plea for the Christian to recognize that martyrdom was the will of God and that every Christian was obliged to stand firm when faced with trial. Thus, while Tertullian could accept Christians dodging persecution early in his career (*On Patience* 13.6; *To his Wife* 1.3.4), in the light of this encounter with the Valentinians and his own developing Montanism, we find him writing in about 208 or 209 that even avoiding arrest was contrary to the will of God, a view that aroused a degree of opposition (*On Flight in Time of Persecution* 1.1). While this treatise tells us much about internal Christian issues, it is based upon a strident rejection of any compromise with the world around them, and what seems to us today to be an unnatural desire for confrontation with the political system and its resultant persecution.

On the occasion of a military donative issued in the name of several emperors, which would have had to occur before Caracalla murdered his brother Geta in December 211,[5] one Christian soldier refused to wear the garland that had been awarded. Other Christian soldiers wore theirs in order not to be the object of derision from their fellow soldiers and of disciplinary action from their superior officers (*On the Military Crown* 1.1–2). The dissident individual was criticized by his fellow Christian soldiers as well, for drawing attention to their religious identity (*On the Military Crown* 1.3). Among the arguments Tertullian brought forward in support of this soldier's defiance was not only that the wearing of the crown supported idolatry (*On the Military Crown* 10, 12–14) but also that by wearing the crown, soldiers were demonstrating their allegiance to the emperor when, in fact, a Christian could have allegiance to God alone. What is more, the whole occupation of being a soldier was contrary to being a Christian, even though a number of Christians had become soldiers (*On the Military Crown* 11).

Particularly with regard to the issue of being a soldier, we can note the difference between what he wrote in *Apology* and what we find in *On Idolatry* and *On the Military Crown*. I do not think it can be explained as 'his changed outlook to military service' (Gero 1970: 294). Instead, as Evans suggested, the questions of audience and rhetorical purpose change. Tertullian's personal view concerning the incompatibility of military service and Christianity was unchanging.[6]

At the end of his literary career, Tertullian wrote to the proconsul in Africa, Scapula, who was in office from 212 to 213.[7] Unlike the forensic defence in *Apology*, here Tertullian argued deliberatively for a change in provincial policy to end the persecution of Christians (*To Scapula* 5.3).[8] He advocated religious freedom (*To Scapula* 2.1–2) and pointed out how harmless Christians were in contrast with supposedly good pagans, who had proven themselves rebellious to the emperor (*To Scapula* 2.3–5). In fact, Christians prayed for the safety of the emperor (*To Scapula* 2.6–9) and restrained the anger of God against those who persecuted (*To Scapula* 2.10), even as the signs of God's intending punishment could be witnessed (*To Scapula* 3.1–3). Other proconsuls and legates who persecuted Christians had been punished by God (*To Scapula* 3.4–5) and the efforts of some provincial governors to protect Christians from unjust treatment was offered as a precedent for Scapula (*To Scapula* 4.2–3). Tertullian was certainly not appealing to Scapula's better nature but to his fear of personal consequences and political unrest, which could be caused by Christians in great numbers presenting themselves for martyrdom (*To Scapula* 5.1–2). He even suggested to Scapula that he consider becoming a Christian as the only way to avoid his fate (*To Scapula* 5.4).

8

TERTULLIAN AND JEWS

We know there was a Jewish community in Carthage from the funerary inscriptions at Gamart, a cemetery a few miles north of Carthage, close to the coast, which had been excavated in the 1880s by Fr Delattre. About one-half of all Jewish inscriptions found in Africa by the early twentieth century came from this cemetery, with its two hundred or so hypogea carved into the rock. Depictions of menorah and the Hebrew word *shalom* on inscriptions, most of which were written in Latin, would confirm the Jewish nature of these burials (Caplan 1921: 4–5, 12–14). Caplan's idea that Christians were also buried in this cemetery, based on non-Jewish imagery on the wall decorations and lamps, although dismissed by scholars (e.g. Le Bohec 1981: 168–9; Barnes 1985: 274), is supported by others such as MacLennan (1990: 122–5).[1]

If there is disagreement about what we can tell about the relationship between Christians and Jews in Carthage based on the archaeological evidence, the same is true with regard to the literary evidence. Barnes' 1970 statement that 'Judaism and Christianity had diverged and gone their separate and hostile ways . . .' (Barnes 1985: 273) may be an accurate response to the notion that Christianity in Carthage derived from Judaism, but it is modified somewhat in his postscript of fifteen years later: '. . . we should think of Jews and Christians in the western provinces during the second century as rivals and competitors rather than as parent and daughter communities' (Barnes 1985: 330). Even though he admits that he had earlier underestimated Tertullian's knowledge of Jews in Carthage, his concession that we should think of Tertullian '. . . fixing the Jews whom he saw on the streets of Carthage with a gloomy and baleful gaze, but not as engaging them in conversation, still less as seeking their company in social or intellectual gatherings' (Barnes 1985: 330) does not sit well with his comment that they were rivals and competitors. Why describe them as rivals and competitors unless there was some point of contact?

As I argue in the introduction to my translation of *Against the Jews*, the evidence of this text has not been taken seriously enough by scholarship because of the debate surrounding its authenticity. If a structural rhetorical analysis of the text puts it beyond any doubt that Tertullian was indeed the author of the whole treatise, then this piece of anti-Judaic[2] literature needs to receive much more attention. The idea in the opening statement that the writing of the treatise was occasioned by a debate between a Christian (possibly Tertullian himself) and a proselyte Jew about who were God's chosen people (*Against the Jews* 1.1) is sometimes considered merely to be a rhetorical commonplace, with no basis in reality, because the prior assumption exists that Jews and Christians had nothing to do with each other after Titus captured Jerusalem in 70. Instead, I believe that this text should be used, along with all the other evidence that is now being amassed by scholars, to challenge the validity of that assumption. I am prepared to take it at face value and see it as evidence of some form of contact. I shall argue that rather than revealing nothing about contemporary Judaism, *Against the Jews* reveals that just as Tertullian claimed that heretics had no right to make use of the New Testament, the issue in Christian minds about contemporary Judaism was still whether or not they had any legitimate claims to ongoing identity. It was an old debate, even stale and sterile by Tertullian's time, and the texts used at the heart of that debate (the Scriptures) were unchanging, but it was carried on with vigour, generation after generation, and concerned how to interpret the Scriptures. It could be conducted with Jews themselves (given that Tertullian counted the proselyte as a Jew) (*Against the Jews*), with other Christians (*Against Marcion*) or with pagans (*Apology* 21).

Here I wish to consider some of Tertullian's references to Jews in his other treatises. Tertullian tells us that the Jews were 'the seed-plot of all the calumny against us' (*To the Heathens* 1.14.2) and the Jewish synagogues were the 'fountains of persecution' (*Antidote for the Scorpion's Sting* 10.10). Are Tertullian's statements historically accurate or merely part of his inflammatory rhetoric? William Frend has argued that Tertullian's charges against the Jews were in reference to recent events (Frend 1958: 157; 1965: 334; 1970a: 294–6). Scholer (1982: 821–8), however, examines all the texts that possibly refer to Jewish persecution of Christians in Tertullian and concludes that they all refer to events in apostolic times.

David Efroymson has pointed out that the vast bulk of Tertullian's anti-Judaic references are to be found in *Against Marcion* (Efroymson

1979: 100). Marcion, who was originally from the Black Sea area but spent his latter years in the middle of the second century establishing a rival church in Rome, put forward a hierarchy of gods: a lesser one revealed through the Old Testament who was responsible for creation, who operated according to justice and who was responsible for evil entering the world, and a greater one who was revealed through the New Testament, who operated according to compassion and who was Father of Jesus. This Jesus was not the messiah of the Old Testament, who was to be a Jewish political figure, but a universal messiah who had come unexpectedly to rescue humankind from what the creator god had established. Furthermore, this Jesus was not human because all matter was corrupt. In the five books of *Against Marcion*, which appeared in at least three ever-expanding editions over the course of a number of years and which incorporated material from the earlier *Against the Jews*, Tertullian argued for the unity of God (book one), defended the Old Testament god as God (book two), identified Jesus as the messiah promised in the Old Testament (book three), even on the basis of Luke's Gospel, the only gospel Marcion accepted as canonical (book four), and Paul's letters (book five).

Tertullian insisted that the one God acted more harshly in the Old Testament than in the New because God had been dealing with a more difficult people, the Jews. As Efroymson puts it: '. . . the (admitted) "inferiority" of God's "old" law and/or cult cannot be due to any inferiority on God's part, but must be accounted for by the "inferiority" of the people with whom God was working at that time. Thus the God of the Hebrew Bible was "salvaged" for Christians precisely by means of the anti-Judaic myth' (Efroymson 1979: 101). The fact that the Jews (like Marcion) did not recognize Jesus as the promised messiah was no reason to doubt the veracity of promise or the God who made the promise (*Against Marcion* 3.7.1; 3.8.1). Efroymson's point is that the Jews were not the primary targets or partners in dialogue with Christians. They had been transformed into something symbolic that helped mainstream Christians sharpen their self-identity (Efroymson 1976: 62–3). He would consider that, as so much of *Against the Jews* appears in *Against Marcion*, the former treatise was really only a draft for the latter and that the Jews were mentioned only in so far as that through them Marcion might be attacked, not because there was real contact between them.

Tertullian was a supersessionist – the Christians had replaced the Jews because of the latter's infidelity, which would mean that the Christians had inherited their claim to being an ancient religion (and therefore worthy of greater pagan tolerance) (*Apology* 21). This is why Tertullian could not accept Marcion's rejection of Christianity's Judaic origins; to do so would be to eliminate one of the features that gave Christianity any respectability in the eyes of the Romans. Elsewhere, Efroymson has pointed out that in his other writings Tertullian turned Jews into a symbol of all that was wrong: 'Most of his writing is an exercise in rhetoric, in argument, in polemic, and a good deal of the polemic finds at least some room for an anti-Jewish reference. Briefly, it usually involves the argument or the suggestion that the adversary or the opposing position is in some way "Jewish", and therefore wrong' (Efroymson 1980: 25). To take but one example, in *On the Apparel of Women* 2.13.5–6, Tertullian stated that love of gold was something the Jews did because they abandoned God and that Christians were not to imitate that. I would suggest, in addition, that the symbol worked because the referent still had the potency to challenge and shock.

Given that the Jews had a negative symbolic value for Tertullian, are we able to conclude anything about his contact with Jews in early third-century Carthage? Tertullian's references to Jewish customs and social practices like daily ritual bathing (*On Baptism* 15.3), fast days celebrated outdoors (*On Fasting* 16.6), observance of circumcision and the sabbath (*Against the Jews* 2.10; *Apology* 21.1; *On Idolatry* 14.6) and the veiling of women (*On the Military Crown* 4.2; *On Prayer* 22.8) have usually been taken as derived from a reading of the Scriptures rather than from contemporary familiarity (Barnes 1985: 92; cf. Frend 1968: 192–3). It is precisely this opinion that Barnes was later prepared to modify. As Horbury (1972: 457–8) points out, in *On the Shows* 30.5–6 Tertullian displays knowledge of some contemporary criticisms of Christianity offered by Jews: that Jesus was the son of a minor official or that his body was stolen by a gardener. *Against the Jews* 3.4; 13.4 shows knowledge of the ban on Jews entering Jerusalem after the Bar Kokhba revolt of 132–5 (and possibly of the granting of an exemption by Antoninus Pius to Hadrian's total ban on circumcision). Claudia Setzer (1997: 190) argues that not all of Tertullian's comments (such as those concerning ritual bathing and veiling women) are biblically based.

If there was a debate about the interpretation of Scripture, who was Tertullian's audience? Whom was he trying to persuade with his arguments? Was he trying to convince Jews that they were wrong? Was he trying to reassure Christians that they were right? Did he want to steer monotheistically minded pagans in the 'right' direction? Scholarship has tended to divide into one of two exclusive alternatives. The first, which we may call social or historical, was championed by Simon in 1948 (Simon 1996) and believes that there was a competition between the two religions, particularly for converts, which meant that anti-Judaic literature was directed against the Jews. The second, originally put forward by von Harnack in the 1880s but defended in more recent years by scholars like Tränkle (1964), Barnes (1985), Ruether (1974), Rokéah (1982), Gaston (1986) and Taylor (1995), which we may call theological, believes that the Jews in the Christian literature were symbolic constructs designed to help Christian self-definition. Such exclusive alternatives are rejected by several scholars (Lieu 1996; Stroumsa 1996), who are more inclined to find a 'both-and' solution. As Judith Lieu argues, there is both an image (the theological construct) and the reality (the historical and social rivalry): 'Recognition both of the stereotyping and of evidence of real contact, even in the same author, means we must speak about "image and reality" in some form of interaction.' (Lieu 1996: 12). Although Taylor has explicitly rejected such a possibility,[3] I believe that the multidimensional answer is the most fruitful. Claudia Setzer puts it well, I think, when she writes, '. . . there is no either-or view of biblical Jews or of contemporary Jews, but rather a tendency to project one on top of the other, or to understand one in the light of the other' (Setzer 1997: 187). For Tertullian, the Jews he discovered in the pages of the Scriptures were the same Jews (in his mind) he encountered in Carthage; for him their thinking had not changed at all.

9

TERTULLIAN AND CHRISTIANS

Here, as I examine relationships and attitudes among Christians themselves, I can consider only the issues of Christian women, marriage and the forgiveness of sins. Many scholars have been content to take his statement that a woman is the 'gateway of the devil' because of Eve's responsibility in introducing sin into the world (*On the Apparel of Women* 1.1.2) as sufficient evidence that Tertullian was a misogynist. Yet, as Church points out, in every other instance when Tertullian commented on the Fall, the blame for it was placed equally on both Adam and Eve (Church 1975: 86–8). It cannot be denied that Tertullian had some harsh things to say about Christian women, but it should not be forgotten that he had harsh things to say about Christian men as well. Just as in this treatise he commented upon women's appearance, in *On the Pallium* he commented upon men's appearance. His attitude towards women was determined in part by how he reconciled what he read in the Scriptures with what Montanists did in practice. Indeed, Hoffman (1995: 214) recently has gone as far as to suggest that Tertullian was 'exceptionally positive toward women'.

On the Apparel of Women urges women to dress simply, without the ostentation of ornamentation. It was modesty that would lead to salvation (*On the Apparel of Women* 2.1.1) and women (and men for that matter, *On the Apparel of Women* 2.8) must not only be modest but must also appear to be so. Women who took too much interest in their appearance invited the lust of men. There is a degree of pessimism here in Tertullian. Fear is what leads to salvation and the thought that one could fail was more appropriate than the idea that one could not (*On the Apparel of Women* 2.2.2–3), so one should err on the side of caution in appearance. Rather than suggest that men needed to do something to bring their lust under control, the only solution that was offered was for women to conceal and neglect themselves (*On the*

Apparel of Women 2.2.5). Furthermore, to beautify the body was to seek praise, which was vain (*On the Apparel of Women* 2.3). Yet, there were limits. Squalor was not the object (*On the Apparel of Women* 2.5.1), nor was disfiguring what God had created through the use of dyes and cosmetics (*On the Apparel of Women* 2.6). The Christian woman was seen in public less than her pagan counterpart and therefore had little need for dressing up as much (*On the Apparel of Women* 2.11.1).

Despite his claims that women ought to be modest and almost invisible, it was obvious that a number were not. *On the Veiling of Virgins* was addressed to those unmarried women who dedicated themselves to Christ as virgins (mostly adolescent girls really) who, in an effort to distinguish themselves from married women, did not wear the standard head-covering when gathered together in the Christian assembly, presumably at liturgy. Unwittingly, perhaps, Tertullian lets us into some of the problems of the local Christian community: tensions between those who veiled and those who did not (*On the Veiling of Virgins* 3.4); pregnancies among the virgins (*On the Veiling of Virgins* 14.2); and married women also flouting the conventions of veil-wearing (*On the Veiling of Virgins* 16.3; 17.1).

Although virgins were considered to be married to Christ (*On the Veiling of Virgins* 16.4), Tertullian had little interest in those who were married only to other people, apart from the question of second marriages. In the earliest of his treatises on marriage, *To his Wife*, Tertullian advised his own wife that, in the event of his death, although he recognized her right to remarry (*To his Wife* 1.7.3), she ought not to remarry. Tertullian manages to tangle himself with his arguments: on the one hand marriage is good (*To his Wife* 1.3.2), whereas on the other Paul preferred abstinence (1 Cor 7:1) (*To his Wife* 1.3.2–3, 5), which could well be directed as much against first marriages as against second. So too with regard to his idea that people who marry a second time need only display greater strength of spirit to overcome their excuses that they were too weak to resist the sexual urges or wanted to improve their social position through marriage or wanted children (*To his Wife* 1.4.1–1.5.3), it can be replied that this is as much an argument against any marriage at all and not only second marriages. For Tertullian, to be a widow meant that one ought to be independent of the need to rely on a man (*To his Wife* 1.4.3; 1.7.2). Yet, he accepted that his wife, like other Christian women who found themselves without a husband after divorce or death, might well remarry (given that womanly weakness made it difficult for them to be heroic enough to remain a widow – *To his Wife* 2.1.2), so he commanded her (as Paul commanded) at least to marry another Christian

(*To his Wife* 2.1.3–4). On a very positive note, Tertullian ended the treatise with a rousing encomium on the positive dimensions of marriage (*To his Wife* 2.8.6–9).

Some years later Tertullian wrote to a widower and repeated the arguments he had used already, except without the indulgence he showed his wife. Although he still recognized that second marriage was lawful (*On Exhortation to Chastity* 8.1), he was more insistent that it should not be taken up. To those men who said they needed a second wife to manage their households, Tertullian replied that they should take in widows as spiritual wives (something akin to housekeepers) (*On Exhortation to Chastity* 12.2).

At the end of his literary career, *On Monogamy* is a more hard-line exposition of the same subject. He claimed that the once-only marriage policy had been revealed apart from the Scriptures by the Paraclete (*On Monogamy* 2), although without offering any kind of proof that the Spirit had revealed some further teaching on this, except that it was consistent with a strict interpretation of what is found in Paul.

The last issue that can be considered in this introduction is Tertullian's attitude towards the forgiveness of sins. Again, his attitude became less tolerant as he became older. Having repented once thorough baptism, a Christian was not to sin again (*On Repentance* 5.1). Yet the reality of Christian backsliding vexed the Christian community. Catechumens put off baptism in the realization that they would continue to sin even after it, which cheapened their desire and commitment to repentance (*On Repentance* 6.3). To know that repentance is required is to be obliged to it. With regard to the baptized, Tertullian was reluctant to even discuss the possibility of a second divine forgiveness in case it encouraged people to think that sinning after baptism was not unacceptable (*On Repentance* 7.1–3). Yet a second, and only a second, forgiveness was granted by God (*On Repentance* 7.10–11), after a lengthy and onerous period of public acknowledgement and restitution for sin (*On Repentance* 9–12).

Later, in his Montanist *On Modesty*, in response to an episcopal decree that adultery and fornication could be forgiven after repentance (*On Modesty* 1.6), Tertullian insisted that, just as people could only marry once, they could only be forgiven sins like adultery and fornication once (*On Modesty* 1.20–21). God's goodness is balanced by justice. Some sins could be forgiven after correction, others could not (*On Modesty* 2.12) and the two sins under consideration in this treatise fell into the latter category, as most of the treatise sought to justify. Such a rigid system could lead to the conclusion that one may as well leave the church if they sinned after baptism, for entering a process of repentance without the prospect of forgiveness seemed pointless (*On Modesty* 3). Tertullian's answer was that although such a person would have to be excluded from the church, this did not mean that God would not forgive them. Indeed, while it was possible for the Spirit to forgive, it was not possible for a bishop to do so (*On Modesty* 21.17). The attitude of the rest of the church, whom he called sensualists, was too lax and indulgent for Tertullian.

Part II

TEXTS

10

GENERAL INTRODUCTION TO
THE TEXTS

This series aims at making key selected texts by the major Fathers available in English. Just what is a key text? When I was deciding what texts to translate for this volume, I was guided by words that Timothy Barnes wrote back in 1969: 'Modern scholarship has been unjustly selective in its treatment of Tertullian. Some of his works . . . receive lavish and repeated investigation . . . Yet other works, ultimately of no less importance, suffer almost total neglect.' (Barnes 1969: 105). This has always been the case when we consider the vast number of manuscripts of *Apology* that survive compared with the few for most of the other treatises. A work like *Apology* is popular not only because it has information relevant to historians of Christianity but also, particularly, for what it may reveal about the Roman political world for the broader and more numerous body of historians of classical antiquity itself. History has always tended to focus on political rather than social or even religious themes, and on the famous rather than the unknown. This has contributed to Tertullian's *Apology* long being his best-known work. As our interest today shifts away from the political, which dominated scholarship in the second half of the nineteenth and the first half of the twentieth centuries, other treatises by Tertullian that reveal something of the internal life of Christians are taking centre stage.

Ever since the English translation of the complete works of Tertullian in the late nineteenth century in *Ante-Nicene Fathers*, more recent English translations have appeared in a number of series: Loeb, Fathers of the Church, Ancient Christian Writers, and Oxford Early Christian Texts. Yet there are still about half a dozen treatises that have received no complete English translation in the twentieth century. It is a truism of Australians that we are drawn to support the underdog and in this I am no exception. My scholarly interest is drawn to neglected texts. Are such texts really so unimportant and undeserving of attention? Why have they been relegated to obscurity?

One of the criteria in my selection of texts, therefore, was to choose from among those that had received no full English translation in the twentieth century. A more comprehensive picture of our author and his interests and the development of his thought occurs when we take into account not only his most popular works but also his lesser-known ones.

Another criterion was to select treatises that represent the three broad divisions found in Quasten. Rather than selecting *Apology* as representing Tertullian's interaction with non-Christians, I have chosen *Against the Jews*. The relationship between Christians and pagan political authority is an important one to scholarship, but so too (and increasingly so in recent decades) is that between Christians and Jews. Tertullian's *Against the Jews* has not yet taken its full place within the anti-Judaic Christian literature because of the controversy that has surrounded its authorship and integrity. Obviously, it is my hope that by including it in this volume its place in Tertullian studies and in the study of Christians and Jews will be recognized more fully. I have chosen *Antidote for the Scorpion's Sting* as representative of Tertullian's controversial treatises dealing with Christian heresy. This work not only pits him against the Gnostics but also provides us with insight into his belief about martyrdom, a topic of interest across many scholarly spectra. Finally, I have chosen *On the Veiling of Virgins* to represent his moral and disciplinary works. Interest in women in ancient Christianity has certainly been a field of scholarly interest in recent generations and Tertullian has received his fair share of feminist critique, as he wrote a number of works that had women in the spotlight. Perhaps because of its narrow subject (virgins rather than women in general, and then, more specifically, why virgins should be veiled) it has not received the attention that some of his other treatises have received.

In addition, these works span his literary career. *Against the Jews* may be dated early, *Antidote for the Scorpion's Sting* to his middle years, and *On the Veiling of Virgins* from his later Montanist years. The style of writing noticeably changes as well, from a verbose to a very terse one. In deciding upon my own style of translation, it was my wish to capture something of the flavour of Tertullian's Latin: sometimes aphoristic and witty, sometimes long-winded and disjointed, sometimes brief and obscure. I debated long and hard about whether to make the translation more 'user-friendly' but, in the end, decided that where Tertullian's Latin was just as ambiguous and capable of misinterpretation for its original readers it ought to remain so in English. The rule of thumb that context decides meaning does not always apply with Tertullian so if a reader of my translation does not follow the argument I can only hope that it is not because of a fault in the translating but because of the complexity of the original. Yet, I have included other comments in square brackets as needed to complete the sense of what Tertullian wrote. Sometimes Tertullian, quite deliberately I think, chooses his words or constructs his sentences in such a way that they are open to several different meanings. While his comments lack the usual indecency of *double entendre*, they often may be more pointed than they first appear to those who do not read too deeply and, on the other hand, could be explained away innocently to those who did read them at their most pointed. Furthermore, in translating I have avoided the use of gender-specific language about God. I have done the same with people unless it is very clear that Tertullian meant a specific sex.

I did not want to produce an expanded version of Stevenson's *New Eusebius* dedicated to Tertullian alone. The latest edition of that volume has twenty-two selections from Tertullian from nine different treatises (Stevenson 1987: 157–77). A third criterion in my selection was to offer complete treatises in translation. It is only with an entire text that one can appreciate an aspect of Tertullian that is central to understanding him as a writer – his rhetorical skill in constructing, developing and presenting an argument. One of my interests here has been to present these works as written pieces imbued with an oratorical perspective and to arrange them in such a way that their rhetorical structure shines through. Tertullian was a skilled debater and full texts are the only way to do justice to his ability.

The numbers is square brackets represent the pages in the Latin edition of Tertullian in the first two volumes of *Corpus Christianorum, Series Latina*. The division into chapters and sections follows the divisions in those volumes. While the texts in *Corpus Christianorum* form the basis for the translation, I have utilized other, more recent critical editions that have been published, together with translations in other modern languages, to emend the Latin text I used. It has not been possible in this volume to note all such technical matters.

11

AGAINST THE JEWS (*Aduersus Iudaeos*)

Introduction

Without a doubt, *Against the Jews* is one of the most controversial of Tertullian's thirty-one treatises. It is not too difficult to understand why. To begin with, there have been questions about the integrity of the text and its authorship. Much of the material from chapter 9 onwards is virtually identical with sections of book three of *Against Marcion*. From Augustus Neander in the middle of the nineteenth century onwards, a significant number of scholars (Quispel 1943: 61–79; Quasten 1953: 269; Kroymann (see Gerlo *et al.*)1954: 1338) have reached the conclusion that the second half of the treatise was not by Tertullian and that someone had taken the material from the earlier *Against Marcion* and rather ineptly attached it to the first eight chapters, which Tertullian had written. Efroymson called this the majority view among scholars today (Efroymson 1979: 116). Ernest Evans, who has translated Tertullian's *Against Marcion* into English, even questioned the authenticity of the first half of *Against the Jews*, believing that the early chapters lack much of Tertullian's usually forthright energy (Evans 1972: 1: xx). So the *Clavis Patrum Latinorum* lists *Against the Jews* as one of Tertullian's doubtful works (Dekkers 1995: 9). Frend considers it to be one of his less significant works (Frend 1968: 6).

The second factor that contributes to the neglect of this treatise concerns its subject matter. It is an early example of the anti-Judaic genre of early Christian literature. Some scholars have traced that anti-Judaism (or even anti-Semitism – scholars define these terms differently) to the New Testament (Ruether 1974). Other early Christian texts that have been understood as discussing Christian attitudes towards Judaism include *Epistle of Barnabas* and Justin Martyr's *Dialogue with Trypho*, as well as the lost *Dialogue of Jason and Papiscus* and Miltiades' *Against the Jews*. Those scholars who have examined this body of literature have been concerned chiefly with the question of the target audience: were these pieces meant to be read by Jews? Closely related to that was the other question: do these texts indicate that there was ongoing contact between Christians and Jews in the second century and beyond? The answer from many scholars has been a definitive 'no' to both questions. The words of George Foot Moore in 1921 are indicative of this view: '. . . in the apologies the Jewish disputant is a man of straw, who raises his difficulties and makes objections only to give the Christian the opportunity to show how easily they are resolved or refuted, while in the end the Jew is made to admit himself vanquished. This of itself shows that the authors did not write to convert Jews but to edify Christians . . .' (Moore 1921: 198; see also Ruether 1974: 181; Rokéah 1982). More recently, Miriam Taylor has renewed this criticism of what she describes as 'competitive anti-Judaism': 'The Judaism opposed in the Christian writings is somehow devoid of life and substance . . .' (Taylor 1995: 23). She understands the purpose of this literary genre to be one of Christian self-definition, having little to do with real social contact. This lack of real interaction with Judaism has been seen in Tertullian's *Against the Jews* in particular. Lukyn Williams could write about Tertullian that: '. . . he is very inferior to Justin Martyr in any personal knowledge of his opponents and their religion' (Williams 1935: 52). Tertullian's arguments, it is claimed, are only biblical and thus indicate nothing about his contemporary setting or his contemporary concerns, thus demonstrating that he had no contact with Jews (Tränkle 1964: lxxiii–iv; Barnes 1985: 91–93;[1] Gaston 1986: 163–4).

This is a view that needs revision. Some scholars have contributed to that over the years in various ways. Noeldechen argued that the entire *Against the Jews* was written by Tertullian, the first eight chapters being the more finished part of the text, that it was composed about 195–6, and that it was used by Tertullian in the writing of book three of *Against Marcion* (Noeldechen 1888: 46–51; 1894: 14–92). Säflund also accepted the whole work as genuine and dated it early in Tertullian's career, before *Against Marcion* (Säflund 1955: 128–208). Harnack suggested that Tertullian wrote the whole treatise, but he dated it after *Against Marcion*, which was used to create the final chapters of *Against the Jews* (Harnack 1904: 288–92). Other scholars also accept Tertullian's authorship of the entire treatise, the integrity of the text, and the priority of *Against the Jews* over *Against Marcion* (Tränkle 1964: liii–lxvii; Fredouille 1972: 254–5; Aziza 1977: 104–8; Barnes 1985: 53; Aulisa 1998: 43–55).

I have reached the same conclusion about the authorship and integrity of *Against the Jews* from a rhetorical analysis of the text (Dunn

1999a). I am also content with Barnes' date of 197 (Barnes 1985: 55). Given that we find a similar assessment of Judaism in *Apology* 21, it would not surprise me to find that in writing *Apology* Tertullian adapted material from the earlier *Against the Jews*, as he did from *To the Heathens* (see also Tränkle 1964: lxvi-lxvii). What we find in the treatise are comments in its early chapters about its structure, which are realized in the later chapters. This would indicate that whoever wrote the first half intended to write something that, structurally, at least, closely resembles what we have in the second half. I have suggested a structure for the treatise, based upon the conventions of classical rhetoric (Dunn 1998: 120, 143; 1999b: 317–20; 1999c: 245; 2000: 3–7, 12–13, 15–18). Yet, it cannot be said that this is a well-written treatise. It has a very unfinished and rambling quality about it: there are repetitions, digressions, jumps in the logic of the argument, and a tendency to be long-winded. There are sentences that do not read well or make complete sense.

At its heart, the treatise is an argument about whether the Christians are beneficiaries in God's plans. Tertullian's proof was to try and demonstrate that they were beneficiaries on the basis of the fact that the promised Christ had come. Not only that, he wanted to argue that the Jews had been disinherited and that this too had been promised by God. In style, the treatise is forensic in nature: it argues about the truth of a past event. In many ways it is an example of Roman *controversiae* (legal-like declamations much favoured as oratorical training exercises and show pieces), some of which, as we find in the elder Seneca, were concerned with developing arguments for contesting wills. Tertullian was an out-and-out supersessionist; for him, the Christians had replaced the Jews. A rhetorical perspective helps us appreciate this as being at the heart of the treatise.

The work begins with an *exordium* (1.1–3a), which here explains why this work came to be written. A lengthy debate between a Christian and a proselyte Jew had ended in a shouting match involving the audience and so Tertullian decided to put into writing the Christian case. The topic for that debate seems to have been the question of whether Gentiles could be admitted to God's law. Then follows a *partitio* (1.3b–2.1a)[2] in which Tertullian set out the basic question he was going to address: had God made a promise in the past that the Gentiles would replace the Jews as God's people? He offered his answer: yes, God had made this promise to Rebekah and the promise had been fulfilled with the conversion of the Gentiles and the idolatry of the Jews. In the main body of the treatise, Tertullian offered a *refutatio* (2.1b–6.1) of the Jewish argument that God had only made a promise and entered a covenant with one people through Moses. He did this by attempting to prove that God promised a new law (2.1b–10a), a new circumcision (2.10b–3.13), a new sabbath (4.1–11) and a new sacrifice (5.1–7), which were to include all people, not just the Jews. After a brief summary of the *refutatio* (6.1), Tertullian moved to the other section of the treatise: the *confirmatio* (6.2–14.10), in which he offered his positive arguments in support of his case. This was to be shaped by two questions: had there been a promise of a Christ to instigate that new law, and had that Christ come? (6.2–7.1). The first question did not delay him (7.2), although it gave rise to a digression about the universal spread of Christianity (7.3–8.1a). The second question was divided into three sub-questions (8.2b): the predicted times for the birth and death of the Christ, and the time of the destruction of Jerusalem and the fulfilment of those time predictions; other predicted signs and activities associated with the Christ; and events predicted to occur after the Christ. These three questions were taken up in turn. First, the prophecy in Daniel 9 about the seventy weeks was used to examine the question of the timing of the birth and death of the Christ and the destruction of Jerusalem, in order to show that only Jesus could have fulfilled the prophecy (8.3–18). Second, other general prophecies about the Christ were examined in order to show that only Jesus fulfilled them (9.1–10.19). Third, the prophecy in Ezekiel 8–9 about the destruction of Jerusalem was presented (11.1–9) in order to show that all of the events destined to follow after the Christ had occurred already: the conversion of the Gentiles (12.1–2), the desolation of Judaea (13.2–5a), the end of the possibility of anointing a messiah (13.5b–7), the destruction of Jerusalem (13.9–10) and the suffering of the Jews (13.11–29), with only the second coming of the Christ being still awaited, yet definitely predicted (14.1–10). Clearly out of place among these three sub-questions is passage 11.10–11, being more obviously suited to a position after 8.18. Finally, there is 14.11–14 (of which 14.11–12 is an almost verbatim repetition of 11.10–12.2), which I regard as an interpolation because of some of the telling differences where things are not verbatim. The treatise thus structured does not flow entirely smoothly. This has to do, it can be argued, with the work surviving in an unrevised draft form. Had it been submitted to the scrutiny of an editor or anonymous readers for peer review, I am sure that the repetitions would have been eliminated, the meandering logic reigned in, and the whole argument tightened and made more focused.

Much of the argumentation may be found in Justin's *Dialogue with Trypho* and Irenaeus' *Against Heresies*. Yet, sometimes Tertullian adds his own twist and creates some subtle variation in the pattern of debate. I do not have the opportunity in this volume to explore that dependence in any great detail.

Furthermore, the whole question of the relationship between and attitudes of early Judaism and early Christianity has been revisited in recent years. It is one of the key areas of interest in scholarship on Late Antiquity. This text needs to be reconsidered in the light of this renewed interest. More and more scholars are coming to the conclusion that Marcel Simon reached early in the twentieth century – that the parting of the ways between Christians and Jews has been dated too early (Gager 1985: 154, 164; Simon 1996; Boyarin 1999). The question is becoming less about whether Christians and Jews were in contact with each other, and more about when, how and why Christians and Jews saw themselves as distinct from each other and how they reacted to that. Rather than simply re-adopt the older 'conflict theory', these scholars are trying to find new and dynamic ways of understanding the ongoing relationship (MacLennan 1990; Lieu 1996; Stroumsa 1996), which accept valid insights from both approaches. Of course, questions of separation (or, more accurately, of distinct identities) are different from those about ongoing contact. A community can be concerned to forge its own independent identity *at the same time as* it has contact with other groups. I support the idea that these do not have to be mutually exclusive. As Guy Stroumsa writes: 'Polemics . . . serves multiple purposes. It does not intend only, or even mainly, to convince and convert, but also to strengthen the faith, or the self-confidence, of those who are already converted' (Stroumsa 1996: 18). In *Against the* Jews, I see no reason to disbelieve Tertullian's opening statement that there had been a well-attended debate between a Christian and a proselyte. Certainly, in Tertullian's mind, as represented by *Against the* Jews, Christians and Jews were distinct people. So to answer the question about the intended readership of this work, I would say that it need not be either Christian or Jew but could well be both Christian and Jew.

Tertullian's argument from Scripture (rather than from contemporary events) is not necessarily an indication that he had no contact with Jews in Carthage in his own day, but rather that the issue between Jews and Christians at the end of the second century in that part of the Mediterranean remained constantly about the proper interpretation of Scripture. The earlier debate that Tertullian mentioned had been about the correct interpretation of Scripture. That he employed arguments that were not always original does not mean that they were irrelevant to his own time. Anti-Judaic Christian literature became repetitious not simply because authors imitated each other but because the same challenge from the Scripture to the Christian belief in Jesus as the Christ was mounted generation after generation. What this treatise tells us is that the ongoing issue between Jews and Christians was about who understood Scripture correctly.

At the heart of the early Christian understanding of the Hebrew Scriptures is this question of the relationship between Christianity and Judaism. Tertullian's *Against the Jews* is a *tour de force* in christological exegesis. It is one of the most scripturally based treatises he wrote and it should be important to us for this reason alone. In fact, in chapter 9 Tertullian presents us with some comment on one of the hermeneutical methods of exegesis he employed (he could use whatever method best suited his purpose at any one time). He was quite adept at reading a passage figuratively and in context, as he does here, as he was at reading it literally and in isolation. One of the interesting things for the historian in this treatise is the chronological list of political rulers and dynasties from the Persian king Darius II to the Roman emperor Vespasian. Also, Tertullian offers us his calculation of the year in which Jesus was born (3 BC) as well as a precise date for Jesus' death (25 March, AD 29). This is an important treatise for tracing the emergence of Christian anti-Judaism and for recovering Christian attitudes towards and relationship with Jews. Tertullian's polemics against pagans (*Apology*, *To Scapula*, *To the Heathens*) are better known, their popularity reflecting scholars' interest in using them to obtain information about the Roman empire in the Severan age, yet this ought not make them necessarily more important.

This text has not been translated into English since the middle of the nineteenth century in the Ante-Nicene Library/Ante-Nicene Fathers series. I have based my translation on the Latin text of Kroymann in the *Corpus Christianorum*, as it is the most readily accessible. I have, however, incorporated many of the alternative readings and emendations offered by Tränkle in his German commentary. I have been able to note some of these. I have also been guided by Aulisa's recent Italian translation and, where the parallels exist, by Evans' English translation of Tertullian's *Against Marcion*.

Text

[1339] 1.1 It happened very recently that a debate was held between a Christian and a proselyte Jew. Through the tug-of-war exchange between them, they dragged the day into evening. Also, through the clamouring from some supporters of both individuals, the truth was being obscured as if by a cloud. Therefore, as a full explanation was impossible on account of everyone speaking at once,[3] it was decided to settle the questions that have been reconsidered in writing, after a more careful examination of the texts. 1.2 For the opportunity indeed of claiming divine grace, even for the Gentiles themselves, had a sure sign from this fact: that the man who resolved to lay claim to God's law for himself is from the Gentiles[4] and is not a Jew from the stock of the Israelites. 1.3 In fact, this is enough – that the Gentiles are able to be admitted to the law of God – for Israel not to pride itself still that the Gentiles are counted as a drop in the bucket or as dust from the threshing floor.[5]

However, we have the sufficient promiser and faithful guarantor, God actually, who promised to Abraham that in his offspring all the tribes of the earth would be blessed and that from Rebekah's womb two peoples and two clans were about to come forth.[6] They are, of course, the Jews – that is, Israel – and the Gentiles – that is, us.[7] 1.4 Therefore, each has been named both a people and a clan, so that from the giving of the name nobody dared to claim the privilege of grace for themselves. {1340} For indeed, God designed two peoples and two clans to come forth from the womb of one woman, not to separate grace on the basis of the name but on the order of the birth,[8] such that the one who would come forth from the womb first would be subjected to the younger – that is, the later. For thus God has spoken to Rebekah, saying as follows, 'Two clans are in your womb and two peoples from your womb will be separated. One people will rise above the other people and the elder will serve the younger.'[9] 1.5 And so, although the people or clan of the Jews is anterior in time and older, graced with the first honour in relation to the law, ours is understood accurately as younger in the ages of time. This is so, as in the final lap of our age we have grasped the notion of divine compassion. Without doubt, according to the decree of the divine utterance, the first, the elder people, namely the Jewish, inevitably will serve the younger. The younger people, namely the Christian, will rise above the elder. 1.6 For also, according to the records of the divine Scriptures, the Jewish people – that is, the more ancient – were devoted to idols, as they had deserted God, and were addicted to images, as they had abandoned the divinity. The people were saying to Aaron, 'Make us gods who may go before us.'[10] When the gold from the women's necklaces and from the men's rings had been melted in the fire by these people and an ox head had come forth for them, as they had abandoned God, all Israel delivered honour to this figure saying, 'These are the gods who brought us out from the land of Egypt.'[11] 1.7 For thus, in later times, when kings ruled them, they, together with Jeroboam, were cultivating in worship golden calves and sacred groves and sold themselves to Baal. From this, by means of the divine Scriptures, there is proof that they were marked out indelibly as answerable for the crime of idolatry. {1341} In fact, our people – that is, the later – having forsaken the idols to which previously we used to be devoted, were converted to the same God from whom Israel departed, as we mentioned above. 1.8 For thus the younger people – that is, the later – rose above the older people, while it was obtaining the grace of divine honour from which Israel has been divorced. 2.1 Therefore, let us come to the point and define by fixed limits the extent of the investigation itself.

For why is God, the founder of the universe, the governor of the whole world, the creator of humankind, the instigator of every clan, believed to have given the law through Moses to one people and is not said to have given it to all clans?[12] 2.2 For unless [God][13] had given it to all, there is no way [God] would have permitted even a proselyte from the Gentiles to have access to it. But, as is appropriate to the goodness and fairness of God, as creator of the human race, [God] gave the same law to all clans and, at certain definite times, directed it to be kept when, by whom, and as [God] wished.

For, in the beginning of the world itself, [God] gave the law to Adam and to Eve in order that they might not eat from the fruit of the tree in the middle of paradise because, if they had acted against the law, they would have died.[14] The law would have been enough for them if it had been kept. 2.3 In fact, in this law given to Adam, we recognize all the hidden commands that afterwards came forth when they had been given through Moses, that is, 'You shall love the Lord your God from your whole heart and from your whole soul',[15] 'You shall love your neighbour as much as yourself',[16] 'You shall not slay, you shall not commit adultery, you shall not steal, you shall not give false evidence, you shall respect your father and your mother'[17] and 'You shall not desire another person's property'.[18] 2.4 In fact, the original law was given to Adam and Eve in paradise as the source of all the commands of God. Further, if {1342} they had loved the Lord their God, they would not have acted against [God's] command. If they had been loving their neighbour – that is, each other – they would not have believed the opinion of the serpent, and thus they would not have committed murder among themselves. By acting against the command of God, they fell from immortality. 2.5 They would have refrained from robbery too if they had not eaten secretly from the fruit of the tree, nor would they have longed to take refuge under the tree from the sight of the Lord their God, or have been made partners in

falsehood with the deceitful devil by believing [the devil] that they
were going to be like God. Nor would they have offended the Lord
God in the role of Father, who had shaped them from the mud of the
earth as from a mother's womb, if they had not, out of a desire for
another's property, eaten from the forbidden fruit.[19] 2.6 Therefore, in
this general and original law of God, which God had decreed to be
observed in the case of the fruit of the tree, we recognize that all the
commands of the later law, which came forth when promulgated in
their own times, existed already in a particular expression. In fact, to
add a law afterwards is also the right of the same one who earlier had
put forward the command, seeing that to instruct afterwards is the
right of the same one who earlier had undertaken to fashion the just.
2.7 In fact, is it a surprise if the one who established the directive adds
to it, or if the one who began it finishes it?

Again, I contend that before the law of Moses was written on
stone tablets there was an unwritten law, which was understood
naturally and was kept by the ancestors;[20] from where was Noah
found righteous if the justice of a natural law had not come before the
law of Moses?[21] From where was Abraham counted a friend of God
if not from the fairness and justice of natural law?[22] From where was
Melchizedek called a priest of the most high God if there were not
Levites who were offering God sacrifices before the priesthood of the
levitical law?[23] 2.8 For indeed, thus was the law given to Moses, after
the above-mentioned patriarchs, in that time after they had departed
from Egypt, following the intervening passage of much time. [1343]
Briefly, after 430 years from Abraham, the law was given to Moses.[24]
2.9 From this we understand that the law of God was already in existence before Moses, as [it has been given] first neither at Horeb, nor at
Sinai, nor in the desert, but [it has been given] first at a more ancient
time – in paradise – then afterwards to the patriarchs. And thus also,
it has been given to the Jews at certain times when [God] wanted,
and has been reformed at certain times. The result is that now we do
not pay attention to the law of Moses in such a way as though it were
the first law, but as a subsequent one. At a certain time, God both
produced this law for the Gentiles, as had been promised through
the prophets, and has improved it, as [God] foretold would happen,
with the result that, just as the law has been given through Moses at
a certain time, so it may be believed to have been observed and kept
for a limited time. 2.10 Nor may we take away this power of God to
modify the commands of the law for human salvation, according to
the conditions of the time.

Finally, let the one who still asserts both that the sabbath should
be kept as a means of salvation, and that circumcision should be

observed on the eighth day on account of the threat of death, demonstrate that, in the past, the just kept the sabbath or practised circumcision and thus became friends of God.[25] **2.11** For if circumcision justifies men, since God made Adam uncircumcised, why did [God] not circumcise him even after he sinned? Certainly, when [God] settled him in paradise, [God] appointed an uncircumcised man as inhabitant of paradise. **2.12** Therefore, as God established Adam neither circumcised nor observing the sabbath, consequently also [God] praised Abel, Adam's offspring, as he offered [God] sacrifices, uncircumcised and not keeping the sabbath. [God] accepted the offering that Abel presented in simplicity of heart and rejected the sacrifice of his brother Cain who had not divided equally what he was offering.[26] **2.13** God freed Noah from the flood although [Noah was] uncircumcised and not observing the sabbath.[27] [1344] For from this world also [God] removed Enoch, a man most upright, but neither circumcised nor observing the sabbath. He had not yet tasted death in order that one already a candidate for eternity might show us that we too are able to please God without the burden of the law of Moses.[28] **2.14** Melchizedek also, the priest of the most high God, was selected to the priesthood of God uncircumcised and not observing the sabbath.[29] Lot too, the brother of Abraham, was pleasing in that he was freed from the fires of the Sodomites as a reward for his upright living without his keeping the law.[30]

3.1 'But Abraham,' you will say, 'was circumcised.'[31] But he was pleasing to God before he was circumcised. Neither did he observe the sabbath. In fact, he had received circumcision, but it would have been as a sign of that time, not as a guarantee of salvation. In addition, subsequent patriarchs have been uncircumcised, like the uncircumcised Melchizedek who, on his return from battle, offered bread and wine to the now circumcised Abraham.[32]

'But also the son of Moses,' you say, 'would have been suffocated by an angel at that time if Zipporah, his mother, had not circumcised the infant's foreskin with a pebble.'[33] It is on the basis of this that all the circumcised say, 'There is the greatest danger if anyone will not circumcise the foreskin of the flesh.' **3.2** However, if circumcision were to impart salvation in every case, even Moses himself, in the case of his son, would not have omitted circumcising him on the eighth day. It is agreed that Zipporah did it on the journey when forced by an angel. Thus, we consider that the forced circumcision of one infant was not able to prescribe and to establish, as it were, a law for all people out of this [single] order.[34] **3.3** For God, foreseeing that this circumcision would be given to the people of Israel as a sign, not as salvation, for this reason urged the son of the future leader, Moses, to be circumcised. The result [1345] was that, as [God] had begun to give the command of circumcision to the people through him, the people, seeing that example now having been honoured in the leader's son, would not reject it.[35]

3.4 In fact, circumcision continued to be given, but as a sign by which [the people of] Israel, in more recent times, was to be distinguished [from other people], when it was justly prohibited from entering the holy city,[36] as found in the words of the prophets who said,

> Your land is waste, your cities are consumed by fire, strangers shall devour your territory in your sight, and the daughter of Sion shall be abandoned, having been deserted and subverted by foreign peoples, like a hut in a vineyard and like a watchtower in a field of cucumbers and like a city that is being stormed.[37]

3.5 Why so? Because the following statement of the prophet censures them saying, 'I have reared and raised sons. However, they themselves have rejected me.'[38] And again, 'And if you will have stretched out your hands, I will turn my face from you, and if you will have increased prayers, I will not hear you, for your hands are full of blood.'[39] And again, 'Alas sinful nation, people saturated in sin, wicked sons, you have abandoned the Lord and have provoked to indignation the Holy One of Israel.'[40] 3.6 Therefore, this was the foresight of God who gave circumcision to Israel as a sign, by which they might be distinguished when the time came, as they were prohibited from entering Jerusalem on account of their above-mentioned faults. And because it was going to be, it was announced and because we see it accomplished, we recall it.

3.7 In fact, just as circumcision of the flesh, which was temporary, was initiated as a sign for a stubborn people, so one of the spirit was given as salvation for an obedient people, as Jeremiah says, 'Renew yourselves and do not plant among thorns. Be circumcised for God and circumcise the foreskin of your heart.'[41] And in another place it says,

> [1346] 'For behold, the days are coming,' says the Lord, 'and I will draw up a new covenant for the house of Judah and the house of Jacob. It shall not be such as I gave to their ancestors on the day I led them from the land of Egypt'.[42]

3.8 From this we understand that it was announced both that the first circumcision would cease and that the new law, not like the one [God] had given already to the ancestors, would appear. This was just as Isaiah proclaimed when he said that, in the last days, the mountain of the Lord would be made visible, as well as the house of God upon the summits of the mountains.[43] 'It shall be raised,' he says, 'on the hills and all clans shall come to it and many shall walk and say, "Come, let us go up to the mountain of the Lord and to the house of the God of Jacob."'[44] He did not say 'of Esau', the first son, but 'of Jacob', the following – that is, of our people – whose mountain is the Christ who has been shown according to Daniel as having been carved without the hands of the carvers and filling all the earth.[45] 3.9 Further, Isaiah announced that the new law would appear from this house of the God of Jacob, when he said in the following words, 'For a law shall go forth from Sion and the word of the Lord from Jerusalem and it shall judge between the clans' – that is, between us who have been called from the Gentiles – and he says, 'they shall refashion their swords into ploughs and their spears into sickles and one clan shall not take the sword against another and henceforth they shall not learn to fight.'[46] 3.10 Therefore, who is understood other than us, who, having been instructed in the new law, observe it, since the old law has been cancelled, whose future abolition he was demonstrating beforehand, by that very act? For the old law used to protect itself by the vengeance of the sword and used to tear out eye for eye and would pay back injury with revenge. However, the new law was pointing out clemency and was changing the previous savagery of sword and lance into stillness, and was reforming the previous conduct of war against rivals and enemies into the peaceful actions of ploughing and cultivating the land.[47]

3.11 Therefore, as we have shown above, just as the ceasing of the old law and circumcision of the flesh was declared, so too the observance of the new law and of circumcision of the spirit {1347} has shone forth in peaceful obedience. In fact, the prophets have announced 'a people that I have not known have been attentive to me and in the listening of the ear have obeyed me'.[48] 3.12 Now who is the people who was ignorant of God, if not us who never knew God formerly? And who, in the listening of the ear, has obeyed [God] if not us who, having left idols behind, have turned to God? 3.13 For Israel, which had been known by God and had been rescued by [God] in Egypt, having been led across the Red Sea and having been fed with manna in the desert for forty years, was given a taste of eternity uncontaminated by human sufferings or the food of this age, but was fed with the manna, the bread of angels. Israel, having been indebted to God by these kindnesses, has forgotten its Lord and God[49] and said to Aaron, 'Make gods for us who may go before us, for that Moses who brought us out of the land of Egypt has deserted us, and we do not know what has happened to him.'[50] And because of this we, who were not formerly the people of God, have been made [God's] people by accepting both the new law mentioned above and the new circumcision proclaimed earlier.

4.1 And so it follows that, in so far as the abolition of the circumcision of the flesh and of the old law is shown to have been cancelled in its own times, so the observation of the sabbath is also shown to have been temporary. For the Jews say that from the beginning God sanctified the seventh day by resting on it from all the works that [God] made,[51] and this was the reason Moses also said to the people, 'Remember to sanctify the sabbath day. You shall not do any servile work on it, except so far as life is concerned.'[52] 4.2 From this we understand {1348} that we ought always to observe a sabbath from all servile work, not only on every seventh day but also for all time. And on account of this we ought to ask which sabbath God wishes us to keep, for the Scriptures describe an eternal sabbath and a temporal sabbath. For the prophet Isaiah says, 'My soul hates your sabbath.'[53] And in another place he says, 'My sabbath you have profaned.'[54] 4.3 From this we discern that the temporal sabbath is human and the eternal sabbath is reckoned divine. [God] announces this through Isaiah, '"And there shall be," he says, "month after month, day after day and sabbath after sabbath and all flesh shall come to Jerusalem to worship," says the Lord'.[55] 4.4 We acknowledge that this was fulfilled in the times of Christ when all flesh – that is, every Gentile – came to Jerusalem to worship God the Father through Jesus Christ his Son, as it was proclaimed through the prophets, 'Behold, proselytes shall go to you through me.'[56] 4.5 So, therefore, before there was a temporal sabbath, an eternal sabbath had been both foreshown and foretold, just as even before there was a circumcision of the flesh, a spiritual circumcision had been foreshown.

4.6 Further, let them teach, just as we have mentioned already, either that Adam observed the sabbath, or that Abel, when offering God a holy sacrifice, pleased [God] by reverence of the sabbath, or that Enoch, the one who was transferred [to heaven] was a keeper of the sabbath, or that Noah, the builder of the ark, observed the sabbath on account of the threatening flood, or that Abraham sacrificed Isaac, his son, in observance of the sabbath, or that Melchizedek received the law of the sabbath during his priesthood. 4.7 But the

Jews are going to say that from the moment this command was given through Moses then it ought to be heeded. And so it has been shown that the command was not eternal but temporal, as one day it would cease. **4.8** Further, so much so is this festival not to be celebrated in rest on the seventh day that Joshua, son of Nun, at the time he was subjugating the city of Jericho, said that a command [was given] to him from God that he should command the people that the priests {1349} carry the ark of the covenant of God in a circuit of the city for seven days and thus, when the circuit of the seventh day was completed, the walls of the city would collapse by themselves.[57] **4.9** Thus it happened that the walls of the city collapsed, just as had been foretold, when the course of the seventh day ended.[58] From this it is shown clearly that a sabbath day has occurred within the number of your seven days. In fact, it is necessary for seven days, wherever they began, to include within them a sabbath day. On this day, not only did the priests work but also, in the face of the sword, the citizens were taken captive by all the people of Israel.[59] **4.10** Nor is there doubt that they performed servile work when they dispatched the spoils of war by the command of God. For also, in the time of the Maccabees, they acted bravely in fighting on the sabbaths, they overcame their foreign enemies, and brought back their ancestral law to its former condition by fighting on the sabbaths. **4.11** Nor should I believe that they defended another law than the one in which it was prescribed that they should remember the sabbath days. It has been shown from this that commands of this kind had force for a time, and for the need of the situation then existing, and that God had not earlier given them a law of this kind for them to keep forever.

5.1 Thus we also show that sacrifices of earthly offerings and of spiritual sacrifices were foretold and indeed that, from the beginning, the earthly sacrifices of the elder son – that is, of Israel – were foreshown in Cain, and the other type of sacrifices of the younger son – that is, of our people – were shown in Abel. **5.2** For Cain, the elder by birth, brought gifts for God from the fruit of the earth, but the younger, Abel, [brought] offspring from the fruit of his flock.

> And God had regard for Abel and his gifts. For Cain and his gifts, however, [God] had no regard. {1350} And God said to Cain, 'Why is your face downcast? Surely you have sinned, have you not, even if you should sacrifice correctly, by not dividing it up correctly? Stop it! In fact, it [sin][60] is turning towards you, and you shall master it.' Then Cain said to his brother Abel, 'Let us go into the field.' He went away with

him and there he slew him. Then God said to Cain, 'Where is your brother?' And he said, 'I do not know. Am I the guardian of my brother?' God said to him, 'The voice of the blood of your brother cries out to me from the earth. For this reason the earth, which opened its mouth in order to receive the blood of your brother, is cursed. You shall be groaning and trembling upon the earth, and everyone who finds you shall slay you.'[61]

5.3 Therefore, from this event we notice that the double sacrifices of the two peoples were already foreshown from the beginning.

Finally, when the priestly law in Leviticus was being put together by Moses, we find the command for the people of Israel that sacrifices be offered to God in no other place than in the promised land, which the Lord God was going to give to their ancestors. This was so that sacrifices and burnt offerings would be celebrated for sins, as for souls, in that place, when Israel had been led in, and in no other place except the holy land. 5.4 Why therefore does the Spirit proclaim afterwards through the prophets that it would happen that sacrifices would be offered to God in every place and in every land? For example, [the Spirit] says through Malachi, [1351] one of the twelve prophets, 'I will not receive sacrifice from your hands, since from the rising of the sun through to its setting my name has been made famous among all clans,' says the all-powerful Lord, 'and in every place clean sacrifices are offered to my name.'[62] Likewise, in the psalms of David, 'Bring to God, homelands of foreigners.'[63] This is without a doubt because the preaching of the apostles had to go out to every land. 'Bring to God renown and honour, bring to the Lord a sacrifice to [the Lord's] name. Gather up a sacrificial animal and enter [the Lord's] courts.'[64] 5.5 Because it is not by earthly sacrifices, but by spiritual ones, that an acceptable offering is brought to God, thus we read as it is written: 'A contrite and humble heart is a victim for God'.[65] And elsewhere: 'Sacrifice to God a sacrifice of praise and offer your solemn promises to the most high'.[66] Thus, for this reason, the spiritual sacrifices of praise are marked out and a contrite heart is pointed out as an acceptable sacrifice for God. 5.6 And so, in the same way as carnal sacrifices are understood as having been rejected, Isaiah spoke about this saying, '"What do the great number of your sacrifices mean to me?" the Lord says,[67] because even, "If you bring," the Lord says, "the finest wheat flour for me, it is a worthless ceremony, it is utterly abhorrent to me."'[68] And also, '"Your holocausts and sacrifices and the fat of goats and the blood of bulls I refuse, even if you come to me. In fact, who has asked for these things from your hands?" '[69] So spiritual sacrifices are proclaimed acceptable, as the prophets announce. **5.7** In truth, sacrifices are carnal as {1352} I said above, about which it has been foretold, '"I have no interest in you," says the Lord. "I will not accept sacrifices from your hands, since, from the rising of the sun through to its setting, my name has been made famous among all clans," says the Lord.'[70] But about spiritual sacrifices the Lord adds '"And in every place, clean sacrifices are offered to my name." '[71]

6.1 It is clear that both a temporal sabbath has been shown and an eternal sabbath has been foretold. A circumcision of the flesh has been foretold and a circumcision of the spirit foretold beforehand. A temporal law and an eternal law have been announced. Carnal sacrifices and spiritual sacrifices have been foreshown. Therefore, because of this, it follows that, in the preceding time, when all those commands of yours had been given carnally to the people of Israel, a time would come in which the commands of the ancient law and of the old ceremonies would cease, and the promise of a new law, the acceptance of spiritual sacrifices, and the offer of the new covenant would come. This is because the light shining from on high has arisen for us, who were sitting in darkness and who were being held in the shadow of death.[72]

6.2 And so, because we have proclaimed a new law foretold by the prophets, and not such as had been given already to their ancestors in the time when [God] brought them out of the land of Egypt, it is incumbent upon us to show and prove that, as much as that old law has ceased, so too {1353} the promised new law now applies. And indeed, I need to ask first whether a proposer of the new law, an heir to the new covenant, a priest of the new sacrifices, a purifier of the new circumcision, and an establisher of the eternal sabbath is expected. This is the one who suppresses the old law, sets up the new covenant, offers the new sacrifices, represses the ancient ceremonies, suppresses the old circumcision together with its sabbath and announces the new kingdom, which will not decay. **6.3** For I ought to ask as well whether this proposer of the new law, the establisher of the spiritual sabbath, the high priest of the eternal sacrifices, the ruler of the eternal kingdom, has arrived yet or not, because, if he has come already he ought to be served, and if he has not yet come it should be endured until it is evident from his coming that the precepts of the old law are suppressed and that the introduction of the new law ought to arise. **6.4** It especially ought to be understood that the ancient law and the prophets could not cease unless the one had come whose coming was announced through the same law and the same prophets. **7.1** Therefore, let us take a position on this point of yours about whether the Christ[73] was announced as going to come, has come already or whether his intended coming is still awaited. Now in order that the issue itself may be proved, the timing, in which the prophets have announced that the Christ was destined to come, ought to be investigated by us. This is in order that, if we recognize him to have come during those times of your making, we may without doubt believe him to be the same one whom the prophets prophesied would come and in whom they announced we – that is, the Gentiles – would believe. And when it has been agreed that he has come, we may believe without a doubt also that the new law has been given by him and we may not deny the new covenant drawn up for us in and through him.

7.2 In fact, we know that even the Jews do not refute the fact that the Christ is going to come, in as much as they extend their hope to his coming. And we need not inquire about that in more detail as formerly, [1354] all the prophets have spoken publicly about it, like Isaiah, 'Thus says the Lord God to the Christ my Lord, whose right hand I have held in order that the Gentiles may hear him, "The bravery of kings I will smash. I will open the gates before him and cities shall not be closed to him."'[74] [We need not inquire] because we see now the prophecy itself having been fulfilled.

7.3 For whose right hand does God the Father hold if not that of Christ, his son, whom all clans have heard, that is, all clans have believed in him, whose preachers, the apostles, are revealed in the psalms of David, 'Their sound has gone out,' it says, 'to the entire earth and their words to the end of the earth.'?[75] 7.4 In fact, in whom else have the clans of the world believed if not in the Christ who has come already? For in whom have the other clans (the Parthians, Medes, Elamites and those who inhabit Mesopotamia, Armenia, Cappadocia, those dwelling in Pontus and Asia, Phrygia and Pamphylia, those remaining in Egypt and those inhabiting parts of Africa beyond Cyrene, Romans and foreign residents, then also Jews in Jerusalem)[76] and the remaining clans (as now the various Gaetulians and the many territories of the Moors, all [within] the boundaries of both Spains, the diverse tribes of the Gauls, and the region of the Britons that is inaccessible to the Romans but subject to Christ, and the Sarmatians, Dacians, Germans, Scythians, and the many concealed clans and provinces and islands unknown to us that we are less able to count) believed? 7.5 In all of these places the name [1355] of Christ, who is come already, reigns, in as much as the gates of every city have been opened before him and none has been closed to him, before whom iron bolts have been smashed and bronze folding-doors have been opened.[77] 7.6

Although those words of yours also ought to be understood spiritually – to the extent that the hearts of individuals besieged by the devil in various ways may be saved by faith in Christ – nevertheless, obviously even they have been fulfilled, in as much as the people of the name of Christ live in all these places. In fact, who could have reigned over all clans if not Christ, the son of God, whose eternal reign over all was announced?[78] 7.7 For if Solomon reigned, yet it was only within the boundaries of Judaea. The limits of his kingdom are marked from Beersheba to Dan.[79] If Darius truly reigned over the Babylonians and Parthians, he did not have further power beyond the boundaries of his kingdom, among every clan. If Pharaoh, or whoever succeeded him in his hereditary rule over the Egyptians, [reigned], only there did he possess the authority of his rule. If Nebuchadnezzar with his princes [reigned] from India to Ethiopia, there he had the boundaries of his kingdom. If Alexander of Macedon [reigned], he held no more than the whole of Asia and other regions that he had conquered afterwards. 7.8 If the Germans [reigned], still {1356} they are not allowed to cross over from their borders. The Britons have been enclosed within the ambit of their ocean. The Moorish clans and Gaetulian foreigners are contained by the Romans, lest they go beyond the boundaries of their own territories. What may I say about the Romans themselves, who fortify their empire with garrisons of their own legions, and who are not able to extend the force of their rule across those clans? 7.9 On the other hand, the name of Christ is extended everywhere, believed everywhere, honoured by all the above-mentioned clans. It reigns everywhere. It is cultivated in worship everywhere. It is assigned on an equal basis to everyone everywhere. No king has greater grace in his presence and no barbarian less joy. No dignity or birthright [is given] to anyone by the distinction of merit. He is fair to all, king to all, judge to all, lord and God to all. 8.1 Nor should you hesitate to believe what we claim, as you see that it is happening.

And thus the predicted times of the future birth of the Christ, of his suffering, and of the expulsion of the city of Jerusalem – that is, its destruction – must be considered. In fact, Daniel says, 'Both the holy city and the sanctuary are destroyed, together with the leader who is going to come, and the pinnacle is dismantled completely to the point of ruin.'[80] 8.2 And thus the times of the future coming of the Christ, the ruler, which we shall seek out in Daniel, must be considered. By having calculated these times we shall prove {1357} that he has come. Besides the ground of the fixed times, we will prove these things from relevant signs and from his activities, and from subsequent events that were announced as happening after his coming, in order that we may believe that everything anticipated now has been fulfilled.[81]

8.3 Therefore, Daniel spoke publicly about him in the following way, in order to show both when and in which time he was intending to free the clans, and how in the year after his suffering the city itself would be destroyed. **8.4** In fact, he speaks as follows,

> In the first year of Darius, son of Ahasuerus, from the stock of the Medes, who ruled over the kingdom of the Chaldeans, I, Daniel, became aware of the measure of the years in the books [of Scripture].[82] And while I was still speaking in prayer, behold Gabriel, the man whom I saw originally in a vision, was flying, and he touched me at about the hour of the evening sacrifice and made me understand, and he spoke with me and said, 'Daniel, I have come forth now to steep you with understanding. At the beginning of your entreaty a word was sent. **8.5** And I have come to tell you, as you are a man of longing: reflect on the word and understand the vision. Seventy weeks have been shortened concerning your people and the holy city. [This will last] until crime may be worn out, sins may be marked, injustice may have appeared, eternal justice may be introduced, vision and prophet may be sealed and a holy of holies be anointed. And you shall know and comprehend and understand that, from the sending of the word about the restoring and building of Jerusalem [1358] until the ruler Christ, there are (seven and a half weeks and)[83] sixty-two and a half weeks. It shall be both transformed and built in breadth and depth, but the circumstances shall be altered. **8.6** And after these sixty-two and a half weeks, anointing shall be abolished and shall no longer exist. Both the city and the sanctuary shall be destroyed, together with the coming leader. They shall be brought to ruin as in a flood until the end of the war, because it shall be brought to ruin until its [final] destruction. And he shall make a covenant among the many. In one and half weeks, my sacrifice and libation shall be put aside and in the sanctuary there shall be the curse of devastation constantly until the end of these times [when] there will be a finish to this devastation.'[84]

8.7 Therefore, let us take notice of the end-point in which he actually foretells that there are going to be seventy weeks in which, if they accept him [the coming leader] 'it shall be built in breadth and length, but the circumstances will be altered'.[85] **8.8** Moreover,

God, foreseeing what would happen – not only that they would not receive him but also they would both pursue and hand him over to death – recapitulated and said that within sixty-two and a half weeks he would be born and a holy of holies anointed. Moreover, [God said] that when seven and a half weeks were completed he [the coming leader] had to suffer, and the city had to be destroyed {1359} after one and half weeks, by which time of course the seven and a half weeks have been completed. In fact, [God] speaks thus, 'Both the city and the sanctuary are destroyed together with the leader who is going to come. They shall be thrown down as in a flood and the pinnacle is dismantled completely to the point of ruin.'[86]

8.9 Therefore, now we will show that the Christ came within the sixty-two and a half weeks.[87] Well, we shall count from the first year of Darius, since the vision is revealed to Daniel at that very time. In fact, [Gabriel] says to him, 'Both understand and interpret that from the sending of the word I have said these things to you.'[88] Whence we ought to calculate from the first year of Darius, when Daniel saw this vision. 8.10 Therefore, let us see how the years are filled up until the coming of Christ. In fact, Darius reigned for nineteen years and Artaxerxes reigned forty-one years. Then king Ochus, who is known also as Cyrus, reigned twenty-four years. Argus reigned one year. Another Darius, who is known also as Melas, reigned twenty-one years. Alexander from Macedon reigned twelve years.[89] Then after Alexander – who had reigned over the Medes and Persians {1360} whom he had subjugated, and who had secured his kingdom in Alexandria when he named it with his own name – Soter reigned there in Alexandria for thirty-five years, to whom Philadelphus succeeded, reigning thirty-eight years. Euergetes succeeded him for 25 years. Then Philopator reigned for seventeen years. After this, Epiphanes reigned for twenty-four years. Then another Euergetes reigned for twenty-seven years. Then another Soter reigned for thirty-eight years. Ptolemy reigned for thirty-seven years. Cleopatra reigned for twenty years and six months. Cleopatra then reigned contemporaneously with Augustus for thirteen years. After Cleopatra, Augustus ruled for another forty-three years, for the total years of the *imperium* of Augustus were fifty-six.

8.11 Moreover, we see that in the forty-first year of the *imperium* of Augustus, who, after the death of Cleopatra, ruled for twenty-eight years, the Christ was born. And the same Augustus survived for fifteen years from the year in which the Christ was born. Until the day of the birth of the Christ in the forty-first year of Augustus, who lived for twenty-eight years after the death of Cleopatra, there is a total of

437 years {1361} and six months (whence sixty-two and a half weeks are complete).[90] **8.12** And 'eternal justice has been made visible and the holy of holies – that is, the Christ – has been anointed and the vision and prophet has been sealed and sins have been renounced', which on account of the name of the Christ will be granted to all who believe in him.[91] However, why is it that he says that 'the vision and prophecy are sealed'? As all the prophets were making announcements about him, that he was destined to come and had to suffer, therefore, as prophecy has been fulfilled through his coming, on that account he said, 'vision and prophecy are sealed,' as he himself was the sign of all prophecy, fulfilling everything that the prophets had announced previously about him. **8.13** In fact, after his coming and his suffering there is now neither vision nor prophet announcing the Christ as going to come. Further, if this is not so, let the Jews produce some volumes of the prophets after the Christ, or visible miracles of some angels like those the patriarchs saw in former times up until the coming of this Christ, who is now come. **8.14** From [the time of] his coming 'vision and prophecy have been sealed' – that is, {1362} have been settled. And the evangelist rightly says, 'The law and the prophets were until John the baptizer.'[92] In fact, when the Christ was baptized – that is, when he sanctified the waters in his own baptism – all the abundance of past spiritual gifts ended in the Christ who has sealed all visions and prophecies, which he has fulfilled by his coming. **8.15** Whence he says most truthfully that his coming seals vision and prophecy.

Therefore, having shown that both the number of years and the time of the sixty-two and a half weeks have been fulfilled, at the completion of which the Christ has come (that is, he was born), let us see in what events the other seven and a half weeks, which have been subdivided in separation from the former weeks, have been fulfilled. **8.16** In fact, after Augustus, who survived fifteen years after the birth of the Christ, they are made up [as follows]: Tiberius Caesar succeeded him and he held *imperium* for twenty-two years, seven months and twenty-eight days. In the fifteenth year of his *imperium*, the Christ suffered, being about thirty when he suffered. Then Caius Caesar, known as Caligula, [held *imperium*] for three years, eight months and thirteen days. Tiberius Claudius [held *imperium*] for thirteen years, seven months and twenty days.[93] Nero [held *imperium*] for eleven years, nine months and thirteen days. Galba [held *imperium*] for seven months and six days. Otho [held *imperium*] for three months and five days. Vitellius [held *imperium*] for eight months and twenty-seven days. Vespasian, in the first year {1363} of his *imperium*, given that he ruled for twelve years, conquered the Jews. The number becomes fifty-two years and six months. In this way, on the day of their capture, the Jews satisfied the seventy weeks proclaimed in Daniel.

8.17 Therefore, when these particular times also were complete and the Jews conquered, afterwards libations and sacrifices ceased there and they were not able to be celebrated there after that. For even anointing was eliminated there after the suffering of the Christ. In fact, it had been foretold that anointing was to be eliminated there, just as it was prophesied in the psalms, 'They have destroyed my hands and feet.'[94] 8.18 And the suffering of the Christ was accomplished within the time of the seventy weeks under Tiberius Caesar, when Rubellius Geminus and Fufius Geminus were consuls, in the month of March at the time of Passover, on the 25th of March, on the first day of unleavened bread on which they slew the lamb at evening, just as Moses had instructed.[95] And so the entire synagogue of the children of Israel killed him, saying to Pilate, when he wanted to release him, {1364} 'His blood be upon us and upon our children,' and 'If you release him you are not a friend of Caesar,' in order that everything might be fulfilled that had been written about him.[96] 9.1[97] Therefore, let us begin to prove that the birth of the Christ was announced by the prophets. {It is} just as Isaiah proclaims,

> Listen, house of David! The human struggle is not a trifle for you as God is responsible for the contest. On account of this, God gives you a sign: see the virgin will conceive and will bear a son, and you will call his name Emmanuel, which means 'God is with us'. He will eat butter and honey, as before the infant knows how to say 'father' or 'mother' he will receive the wealth of Damascus and the plunder of Samaria against the king of the Assyrians.[98]

And so the Jews say, 'Let us challenge that {1365} proclamation of Isaiah, and let us make a comparison whether the name that Isaiah proclaimed and the signs of him that he announced, corresponds with the Christ who has come already.' And, indeed, Isaiah proclaims that it is necessary for him to be called Emmanuel, and afterwards he is going to receive the wealth of Damascus and the plunder of Samaria against the king of the Assyrians. 9.2 'Further,' they say, 'that [Christ] of yours who has come has neither been spoken of under such a name [as Emmanuel] nor has engaged in any warfare.' But we, on the contrary, consider that they ought to be reminded to consider the context of this passage as well. For there is added an interpretation of

Emmanuel ('God is with us'), so that you should not only pay attention to the sound of the name, but the sense as well. For the Hebrew sound, which is Emmanuel, has an interpretation, which is 'God is with us'. **9.3** Therefore, inquire whether that word 'God is with us', which is Emmanuel, is employed afterwards with regard to Christ, since the light of Christ has begun to shine. I think you will not deny it. For those from Judaism who believe in Christ, from the time they believe in him, since they wish to say Emmanuel, they mean that 'God is with us', and in this way it is agreed that he has come already who was proclaimed Emmanuel, because that which Emmanuel means, that is 'God is with us', has come.

9.4[99] No less are they being led by the sound of the words when they accept the wealth of Damascus and the plunder of Samaria and the king of the Assyrians as indicating the Christ as a warrior. They do not take heed of what Scripture promises: 'Since before the boy knows how to say father or mother, he will receive the wealth of Damascus and the plunder of Samaria against the king of the Assyrians'.[100] **9.5** In fact, you must examine before all else the description of his age, whether that age can represent Christ as now a man, {1366} far less a commander. Do you suppose the infant was going to call to arms by his squalling, and give the signal for war not with a trumpet but with a rattle instead, and point out the enemy not from horse or wall, but from his nurse's or nanny's back or neck, and thus overcome Damascus and Samaria before [overcoming] their breasts? **9.6** It is another matter if the infants among you sally forth into battles. I suppose they are first oiled and laid in the sun, and afterwards outfitted in nappies[101] and paid with butter – these same who know how to launch a lance before they learn to lacerate {with their teeth}. Certainly, if nature nowhere permits this – to be a soldier before becoming a man – it follows that the statement 'to take up the strength of Damascus before knowing a father' must be seen as figurative.

9.7 'But also,' they say, 'nature does not permit a virgin to bear, and yet the prophet is to be believed.' And rightly so. In fact, he laid the groundwork for faith in an incredible thing, by saying that it was intended for a sign. 'Therefore,' he says, 'a sign will be given to you. Behold a virgin will conceive in the womb, and will bear a son.'[102] Now a sign from God, unless it had been some strange novelty, would not be seen as a sign. **9.8** Consequently, whenever in the hope of dislodging anyone from this divine proclamation, or whenever you long to convert those who are simple, you dare to lie that it is contained in Scripture not that a virgin but a young woman is to conceive and bear, you are disproved also, because no sign is able to be

85

seen in an everyday occurrence, certainly [not in] the pregnancy and childbearing of a young woman. Therefore, a virgin mother, having been set up as a sign for us, is rightly believed; but truly an infant warrior is not equally [believed]. 9.9 In fact, also no question of a sign is involved, but with the sign of the new nativity having been written down, {1367} immediately after the sign another part of the infant's upbringing is now made known, that he will eat honey and butter. Nor is this undoubtedly a sign; it is part of infancy. But going to receive the wealth of Damascus and the plunder of Samaria against the king of the Assyrians is an unusual sign. 9.10 Observe the limit set for his age and seek the sense of the prophecy. What is more, give back to the truth the things you are not willing to believe and the prophecy is understood as it is reported fulfilled. Let those eastern magi be believed who present gold and incense to the newly born infancy of Christ. Thus the infant will have accepted the wealth of Damascus without battles or arms. 9.11 For aside from the wealth of the East – in fact, that is, its strength – which is known by everybody, is usually valued in gold and spices, it is certainly possible from the divine Scriptures to make gold the wealth of other tribes as well; as it is said through Zechariah, 'And Judah will stretch out before Jerusalem and gather together all the vigour of the peoples round about, gold and silver.'[103] 9.12 For about the present of gold, David also says, 'And it will be given to him from the gold of Assyria' and again 'The kings of the Arabs and of Saba will bring him gifts.'[104] For the East, on the one hand, generally has had {1368} the magi as kings,[105] and on the other, Damascus used to be counted in Arabia, before it was transferred to Syro-Phoenicia after the dividing up of the Syrias.[106] It was then that the Christ received its wealth, by receiving its symbols, namely gold and spices; while as for the plunder of Samaria [he received] the magi themselves, who – when they had discovered him, and honoured him with presents, and had worshipped him as Lord and king by bending the knee on the evidence of the star that was their guide and leader – were made the plunder of Samaria – that is, of idolatry – because they believed in Christ.[107] 9.13 In fact, he branded idolatry under the name of Samaria, which was in disgrace because of the idolatry by which it had once revolted from God under king Jeroboam.[108] In fact, this is nothing new for the divine Scriptures to make a figurative use of the transference of names from a comparison of crimes. 9.14 For it also calls your rulers the 'rulers of Sodom' and your people the 'people of Gomorrah', when those cities have been extinct now for a long time.[109] And in another place through the prophet to the people of Israel, 'Your father was an Amorite and your mother a Hittite',[110] of whose tribe they were not begotten. But he named them this because of the same sort of impiety, although at another time [God] had even said they were [God's] own sons through the prophet Isaiah, 'I have reared and raised sons.'[111] **9.15** Thus also Egypt is sometimes understood to mean the whole world, when charged by him with superstition and abomination.[112] Thus also in our John, Babylon is a figure of the city of Rome, which, like Babylon, is equally great and proud in territories and victorious over the saints.[113] In the same way, Scripture describes the magi also by the title of Samaritans, because, as we have said, {1369} they were completely ruined by idolatry against the Lord, a thing they had in common with the Samaritans. **9.16** 'Against the king of the Assyrians' is understood to mean against the devil, who still thinks that he reigns, if he forces the saints away from the worship of God. This interpretation of ours will receive support while elsewhere the Scriptures also designate the Christ as a warrior on account of the names of certain weapons and words to the same effect, if the Jews are convicted from a comparison of the remaining senses. 'Gird your sword upon your thigh,' says David.[114] **9.17** But what do you read above [this] about the Christ? 'You are ripe in beauty above the sons of men, grace is poured forth on your lips.'[115] Moreover, it is extremely absurd if he was flattering, in the matter of ripeness of beauty and grace of lips, one whom he was girding for war with a sword, about whom he went on to say, 'Stretch forth and prosper and reign' and he adds 'because of gentleness and your uprightness.'[116] Who is going to produce these results with a sword? Will that not produce the opposite of gentleness and uprightness instead – that is, deceit and severity and lack of integrity, which naturally is appropriate to the business of battles? **9.18** Let us see therefore whether there is a different meaning for that sword, which has so different an activity – that is, the divine word of God, twice sharpened from the two testaments of the ancient law and the new law, sharpened by the fairness of its own wisdom, giving back to each according to their action.[117] **9.19**[118] Therefore, it was permissible for the Christ of God in the psalms, without war-like intent, to be girt with the figurative sword of the word of God – to which the foretold condition agrees with the charm of the lips – which was at that time {1370} girt upon his thigh, according to David, when it was announced that he was about to come to earth at the decree of God the Father. 'Your right hand,' it says, 'will marvellously lead you forth,' which means the strength of spiritual grace, from which is deduced the knowledge of Christ. 'The arrows are sharp,' the precepts of God, which fly in every direction, threatening the exposure of every heart, which both pierce

and transfix every conscience. 'People will fall down before you.'[119]
9.20 This is how Christ is a warrior and an armed man, this is how
he will receive the plunder, not only of Samaria but also of all the
Gentiles. Admit also that his plunder is figurative, whose arms too
you have been taught are allegorical. And so the Christ who has come
was not a warrior, because he is not declared as such by Isaiah.

'But the Christ,' they say, 'who is believed to be coming, is not
even called Jesus. Why therefore is he who is come named Jesus
Christ?' 9.21[120] But each name is evident in the Christ of God, in
whom the name Jesus is found as well. Learn here also the character
of your error. While Hoshea the son of Nun was chosen as successor
to Moses, certainly he is changed from his original name, and begins
to be called Jesus (Joshua).[121] Certainly, you answer. We say that this
former {name} was a figure of the future {name}. 9.22 Because Jesus
the Christ was going to bring the second people, because we are the
tribes previously dwelling in the wilderness of the world, into the
{1371} land of promise, flowing with milk and honey – that is, into
the possession of eternal life – than which nothing is sweeter, and
because this was going to be effected not through Moses – that is,
not through the teaching of the law – but through Jesus, through the
new law of grace, after we were circumcised with flint knife[122] – that
is, the precepts of Christ – for Christ was announced, in many ways
and figures, as a rock. Therefore, that man who was being prepared
in imitation of this mystery was also first established as a figure of our
Lord's name, being named Jesus (Joshua). For he who was speaking
to Moses was himself the Son of God, who is the one who was always
seen, for no one ever saw God the Father and lived.[123] 9.23 And for
that reason it is agreed that the Son of God himself spoke to Moses
and said to the people. 'Behold I send my angel before your face'
– that is, of the people – 'to guard you on the journey and to bring
you into the land that I have prepared for you. Pay attention to him
and hear him and do not disobey him, for he will not hide it from
you that my name is upon him.'[124] For Jesus (Joshua) was to bring
the people into the land of promise, not Moses. He said that he was
an angel because of the magnitude of the courage he was to produce,
which courage Jesus (Joshua) the son of Nun accomplished, as you
yourselves read – and because of his office of prophet in declaring the
will of God. Similarly, the Holy Spirit, speaking from the person of
the Father through the prophet, calls John the precursor of Christ, a
future {1372} angel: 'Behold I send my angel before your face' – that
is, of the Christ – 'who will prepare your way before you.'[125] Nor is it
new for those whom God appoints as ministers of his strength to be

called angels by the Holy Spirit. **9.24** For the same John is called not only an angel of Christ but even a lamp before Christ. 'For I have prepared a lamp for my Christ,' David foretells.[126] [This lamp] was Christ himself, coming to fulfil the prophets, who says to the Jews, 'He was the glowing and shining light,'[127] in as much as he not only prepared his ways in the desert, but by pointing out the lamb of God he enlightened human minds by his proclamation, so that they understand him to be the lamb that Moses announced was going to suffer. **9.25**[128] And thus he called him Jesus (Joshua) because of the mystery of his own future name. In fact, he [Jesus] confirmed his own name that he had conferred upon him [Joshua], because he had ordered him to be called in future not as angel or as Hoshea but as Jesus (Joshua). Thus, therefore, both these names are appropriate to the Christ of God, such that he was named both as Jesus and as the Christ.

9.26 And seeing that the virgin, from whom it is proper for the Christ to be born, as we mentioned above, ought to have traced her descent from the seed of David, the prophet clearly {1373} says in the following passages, 'And there shall be born,' he says, 'a twig from the root of Jesse,' – who is Mary – 'and a flower shall climb from the root and the spirit of God and shall rest on it: the spirit of wisdom and understanding, the spirit of knowledge and godliness, the spirit of counsel and courage, and the spirit of the fear of God will bring it to fullness.'[129] **9.27** In fact, there is no one in all humanity about whom the whole of spiritual testimony corresponds, except Christ, who was equated with a flower because of grace, yet was accounted from the stem of Jesse, through Mary, of course, who is thought to be from it.[130] For he was from the land of Bethlehem and from the house of David, just as, among the Romans, Mary, from whom the Christ was born, was registered in the census. Still I demand whether he, who was announced by the prophets as going to come when he was born from Jesse and as going to display all humility and patience and non-resistance, has come.

9.28 And indeed certainly this man, who is shown as such, will be the very Christ who comes. For about this Christ the prophet says, 'A man placed in affliction, and knowing how to bear weakness,' who 'has been led like a sheep to sacrifice and like a lamb itself in the presence of the shearer he did not open his mouth.'[131] Thus, 'neither did he struggle nor cry, nor was his voice heard out of doors, he who did not break the bruised reed,' the faith of Israel, 'nor extinguish the burning flax,'[132] which was the recently lit flame of the Gentiles, but made it shine more {1374} by the rising of his own light,[133] he cannot be any other than the one the prophet announced.

9.29 And so the activity of [God's] Christ who comes needs to be authenticated by the rule of the Scriptures, where, if I am not mistaken, it is distinguished as a twofold operation of preaching and of strength. But concerning each topic having been arranged thus, for that reason specifically we may revise the order I have undertaken,[134] teaching that the Christ was announced a preacher, as through Isaiah: **9.30** 'Cry out energetically,' he says, 'and do not hold back. Lift up your voice as a trumpet and announce to my people their crimes and to the house of Jacob their offences. They seek me from day to day and they long to know my ways, like a people who have enacted justice and who have not abandoned the judgement of God'[135] and so on. Moreover, [I shall demonstrate] the feats of strength he was going to perform from the Father: 'Behold, our God shall restore judgement, God shall come and shall make us well. Then the weak shall be cared for, the eyes of the blind shall see, the ears of the deaf shall hear, the tongues of the mute shall be loosened and the lame shall leap like the deer',[136] etc. **9.31** Nor are you denying that Christ has done these things, seeing that it is you who used to say that you were throwing stones at him, not on account of his works but because he was doing them on the sabbath.[137]

10.1[138] Certainly you are disputing the issue of his suffering, denying that the passion of the cross was prophesied of the Christ, with a further argument that it is not to be believed that God should have exposed [God's] Son to that kind of death, because [God] has said 'Cursed is everyone who has hung on a tree.'[139] Now the reason for these things [1375] precedes the meaning of this curse. **10.2** For [God] says in Deuteronomy,

> Moreover, if he has committed some offence in such a way that the sentence is death, he shall die and you shall hang him on a tree. His body shall not remain on the tree, but you shall bury him with a burial that same day, since cursed by God is everyone who has been hung on a tree and you shall not pollute the land that the Lord your God will give to you for your destiny.[140]

10.3 Therefore, [God] has not cursed Christ to this suffering, but has made a distinction, such that a person, who had [the sentence] of death for some offence and died hanging on a tree, would be cursed by God as one who, on account of the faults of his own offences, was hung on a tree. **10.4** On the other hand, Christ – who did not speak deceit from his own mouth and who has displayed all justice and humility, as we mentioned above were foretold about him – was exposed to that form of death, not on account of his own faults but in order that the things about to occur to him through you [Jews], which had been foretold by the prophets, might be fulfilled,[141] just as the same Spirit of Christ was already singing in the psalms in these words, 'They were repaying me evil for good'[142] and 'Those things I had not seized, then I was paying off'[143] and 'They destroyed my hands and feet'[144] and 'They put bile into my drink and in my thirst they gave me vinegar to drink'[145] and 'They cast lots over my clothes',[146] just as the other things that you were going to commit against him have been foretold. **10.5** Certainly, having endured all of these same things, he suffered not on account of any evil in his own actions, but in order that the Scriptures, from the mouth of the prophets, might be fulfilled. And[147] undoubtedly it had been necessary that the mystery of the suffering itself was uttered in prophecies. The more incredible it was, the more it would become a stumbling block if it were prophesied plainly, and the more {1376} splendid it was, the more it needed to be obscured, so that the difficulty of understanding might ask for a favour from God.

10.6 And so to begin with Isaac, when led by his father [to be] a sacrifice, he carried the wood and was indicating then the death of the Christ, who, when surrendered as a victim by his Father, carried the wood of his own suffering.[148]

Joseph himself is also a figure of Christ – this is only the best known, lest I delay my course – because he suffered persecution from his brethren and was sold into Egypt because of God's grace, just as Christ was sold by Israel, his brethren according to the flesh, when he was handed over by Judas.[149] **10.7** For Joseph is blessed by his father in these words, 'His glory is that of a bull, his horns are the horns of a unicorn. With them he will sift the Gentiles together, even to the end of the earth.'[150] He was certainly not intended to be a one-horned rhinoceros or a two-horned minotaur. Instead, the Christ was indicated in him as a bull on account of each arrangement: to some people stern as a judge, to others kind as a saviour, whose horns were to be the extremities of the cross. For in the yard-arm of a ship, which is part of a cross, this is what its extremities are called, while the unicorn is the post upright in the middle. **10.8** So then by this courage of the cross, and by being horned after this manner, he is even now sifting all the clans through faith, lifting them up from earth into heaven, as he will later sift them by judgement, casting them down from heaven to earth. He will also be found as a bull elsewhere in the same Scripture, where Jacob, when he extends a blessing on Simeon and Levi, prophesies about the scribes and Pharisees, {1377} for their origin is drawn from these. 10.9 For [the blessing] is interpreted spiritually thus, 'Simeon and Levi have perfected iniquity by their way of life'; that is, by which [way of life] they persecuted Christ 'let my soul not come into their council, and let my heart not rest in their assembly since in their indignation they have killed men' – that is, the prophets – 'and in their desire they hamstrung a bull'[151] – that is, the Christ, whom they killed after the murder of the prophets and they savaged his sinews by crucifixion with nails. 10.10 Otherwise it would have been pointless if, after the murder already committed by them, he rebukes others and not them for the slaughter.[152]

And again, why did Moses particularly only then, when Joshua was engaged in battle against Amalek, pray sitting and with outstretched hands, when in such critical circumstances he might have been expected rather to commend his prayer with bended knees, with hands beating his breast, and with face rolling in the dirt?[153] Was it not because on that occasion, when one was fighting who bore the name of the Lord Jesus, as our Lord himself was afterwards to fight against the devil, the appearance of the cross was essential, so that by it Joshua might gain victory? The same Moses again, after he had banned the [making of] a copy of everything, afterwards set up a bronze serpent on a tree in a hanging position and offered salvation to Israel by its display at that time when they were being destroyed by serpents after their idolatry.[154] Why was this, if not because here he was pointing out the Lord's cross, where the devil was being indicated as a serpent? To everyone wounded in this way by snakes – that is, by [the devil's] angels – salvation from the offence of their transgressions was effected, after they were turned to the mystery of the cross. For the one who was looking at that [tree] {1378} was then freed from the bile of the serpent.

10.11 Come now, if you have read the prophet in the psalms, 'The Lord has reigned from a tree',[155] I am waiting for what you understand by it, lest perhaps you think some woodcutter is signified as king and not the Christ, who, ever since his suffering on the tree, has been king through his conquest of death. In the same sense Isaiah says, 'Because to us a child is born and to us a son is given.'[156] What is new if he is not speaking about the Son of God? And, 'To us one is given, the beginning of whose government is placed upon his shoulder.'[157] 10.12 Which of the kings explicitly displays the emblem of his power upon his shoulder, and not rather a crown upon his head, or a sceptre in his hand, or the use of some new property? No, only the new king of the ages, Christ Jesus, has lifted up upon his shoulder new glory and his own power and majesty – that is, the cross – so that from thenceforth, as our previous prophecy stated, he did reign from the tree as Lord. For God even hints about this tree, through Jeremiah, that you were going to say, 'Come let us put a tree into his bread and let us eliminate him from the land of the living, and his name will be remembered no more.'[158] Certainly the tree was put against his body – in fact, Christ, whose body the prophet had of old announced as bread, has revealed it a such, when he named his body as bread.[159] 10.13 If you ask for further prophecies of our Lord's cross, you will be able to satisfy yourself with the twenty-first psalm,[160] which contains the whole suffering of the Christ, who was even then foretelling of his own glory. 'They pierced,' he said [1379] 'my hands and my feet,'[161] which is the particular atrocity of the cross. And again, when appealing for his Father's help, he says, 'Save me from the mouth of the lion', meaning death, 'and [save my] wretchedness from the horns of the unicorn',[162] which are the points of the cross, as I have shown above. 10.14 Now as neither David nor any king of the Jews had to suffer that cross, you cannot think the suffering of anyone else to be prophesied than his, who alone was so remarkably crucified by the people.

So now, if the hardness of your heart rejects and derides all these interpretations, we shall prove that it may be sufficient that the death of the Christ has been prophesied, in order that from this, although the manner of death had not been determined, it may be understood to have come about by a cross. Nor ought the suffering of the cross to have been considered of anyone other than of him whose death was foretold. 10.15 For I can show his death and suffering and burial by one word of Isaiah. 'By the villainy,' he says, 'of my people he was brought to death and I shall give the evil ones for his burial and the rich for his death because he has not committed crime nor has deceit been discovered in his mouth, and God wants to remove his soul by death,'[163] and so on. 10.16 In fact, he says also, 'His burial was raised up out of the midst.'[164] For he was not buried without having died, nor was his burial raised up out of the midst except by resurrection. And so he adds, 'Therefore he will have the many for an inheritance, and he will divide the plunder of the many,' (who, if not he who was born? – as we show above) 'because his soul has been handed over to death'.[165] For in this is shown the purpose of his grace, that it is to be a recompense for the insult of death. It is also shown that he will obtain these things on account of his death. [1380] He is to obtain them after death, at least after his resurrection. 10.17 For that which happened at his suffering, namely that the middle of the day became dark, the prophet Amos announced saying,

'And it shall be on that day,' says the Lord, 'the sun shall set in the middle of the day and the daylight shall grow dark over the earth, and I will turn your feast days into mourning and all your songs into wailing and I will place sackcloth upon your loins and baldness on every head, and I will make him like the mourning of a loved one, and those who are with him like the day of grief.'[166]

10.18 In fact, Moses also prophesied that you were going to do this at the beginning of the first month of the new [year], when he was foretelling that the whole crowd of the synagogue of the sons of Israel was going to sacrifice a lamb in the evening and were going to eat this solemn sacrifice of this day – that is, of the Passover of unleavened bread – with bitterness. He added that it was the Passover of the Lord – that is, the suffering of the Christ – because it was fulfilled in such a way that, on the first day of unleavened bread, you killed the Christ.[167] 10.19 And in order that the prophecies might be fulfilled, the day hastened to bring evening – that is, to produce darkness – which happened in the middle of the day, and thus God changed your feast days into mourning and your songs into wailing.

In fact, after the suffering of Christ, captivity and dispersion also befell you, having been foretold before through the Holy Spirit. 11.1 For on account of those faults of yours, Ezekiel announced your future destruction, and not only in that age which has already occurred but also in the day of retribution that will follow. [1381] No one will be exempt from this destruction except the one who will have been sealed with the suffering of the Christ whom you reject. 11.2 In fact, thus it is written:

And the Lord God said to me, 'Son of man, have you seen what the elders of Israel are doing, each one of them in darkness, each one of them in a secret room, because they have said, "The Lord does not see us. The Lord has abandoned the land"? And the Lord said to me, 'Now when you turn you shall see greater villainy that they are committing.' 11.3 And the Lord led me to the north facing entrance of the doorway of the house of the Lord and behold there were women sitting there and bewailing Tammuz. And the Lord said to me, 'Son of man, have you seen? Is it a trifle for the house of Israel to commit the villainy that they have committed? And yet you are going to see still greater [indications] of their character.' 11.4 And the Lord led me into the inner room of the house of

the Lord and behold within the entrances of the house of the
Lord, between the vestibule and the altar, about twenty-five
men who had turned their backs to the temple of the Lord,
and with their faces towards the east, were worshipping the
sun. 11.5 And the Lord said to me, 'Do you see, son of man?
Is it so insignificant to the house of Judah to commit the
villainy that they have committed here? Because they have
had their fill of lack of respect and behold, they themselves
are mocking as it were, I will act on my indignity. My eye
will not spare and neither will I have compassion. They will
cry out to my ears with a loud voice and I will not hear them
and neither will I have compassion.' 11.6 And the Lord cried
out with a loud voice into my ear saying, 'The punishment of
this city has drawn near.' And each one had the equipment
of destruction in his hand. And behold, six men were coming
from the road of the north-facing high gate, and {1382} the
double-edged weapon of destruction of each was in his hand.
11.7 And there was one man in the middle of them clothed
with a long priestly garment and a belt of sapphires around
his loins. They entered and stood near the bronze altar. The
brightness of the God of Israel, which spread over them in
the courtyard of the house, rose from the Cherubim. 11.8
And the Lord called the man clothed with the long priestly
garment who had the belt on his loins, and the Lord said to
him, 'Pass through the centre of Jerusalem and write the letter T on the foreheads of those men who bemoan and bewail
over the villainy that is committed in their midst.' And the
Lord said to them while I was listening, 'Go after him into
the city and destroy, do not spare your eyes, do not have pity
on either the elders, the young or virgins. Slay all the children
and the women so that they may be wiped out. However, do
not approach those on whom there is the letter T. Begin at
my sanctuary.' [168]

11.9 Now the mystery of this sign, in which life was prepared for
people [and] in which the Jews were not going to believe, was made
known in various ways, just as Moses was announcing in Exodus saying, 'You shall be thrown out of the land into which you will enter,
and among those tribes you shall not be at rest, there shall be no
stability for your footsteps, and God shall give you a tired heart, a
ruined soul and failing eyes, with the result that they do not see, and
your life shall be hanging on the tree before your eyes and you shall
not trust in your life.'[169]

11.10 And so, since the prophecies were fulfilled through {1383} the coming of Jesus – that is, through the birth that we have mentioned above – and suffering, which we have established clearly, on that account Daniel also said that vision and prophecy were sealed, as Christ is the sign of all prophecy, fulfilling everything that had previously been announced about him.[170] For after his coming and his suffering, there is now neither vision nor prophet. Whence he says most truthfully that his coming seals vision and prophecy. 11.11 Therefore, showing that both the number of years and the time of the sixty-two and a half weeks have been fulfilled, we have proven that the Christ has come – that is, he was born – at that time. As to the seven and a half weeks, which have been subdivided by being separated from the former weeks, we have shown that the Christ has suffered within that time, and thus, with the seventy weeks brought to an end and with the city destroyed, that both sacrifice and anointing have ceased from then on.[171]

It[172] is sufficient so far to have run through Christ's condition in these things in the meantime, such that it is proven that he is such a one as was announced. And so now from that accord of the Scriptures, by prior authority of the majority of instances, we have spoken out against the Jews. In fact, they may neither bring into doubt nor deny the Scripture that we have produced, so that from this {run through} also they may not deny parallels with the divine Scripture, with the result that the things that were foretold as going to be after the Christ are recognized as having been fulfilled. 11.12 These things would not be found fulfilled in this manner, such that now they are proven, {1384} unless he had come, after whom the things that were being announced had to be accomplished.

12.1 See how all the tribes after that time [of Christ] are emerging from the abyss of human error towards the Lord God the creator and [the Lord's] Christ, and, if you dare to deny that it was prophesied, immediately the Father's promise in the psalms meets you, saying, 'You are my son, this day I have begotten you. Seek for me and I shall give you the Gentiles for your inheritance and the ends of the earth for your possession.'[173] 12.2 You cannot claim that David is son rather than Christ,[174] or that the boundaries of the earth were promised to David, who reigned only over Judaea, rather than to Christ, who has now captured the whole world by the faith of his gospel. So Isaiah says, 'I have given you for a covenant of the human race,[175] for a light to the foreigners to open the eyes of the blind' – those who are in error – 'to loose from their bonds those who are bound' – that is, to set them free from offence – 'and from the house of the prison' – that is, death – 'those who sit in darkness'[176] – the darkness of ignorance. If these things are coming to pass through Christ, they cannot have been prophesied of any other than him through whom we consider them to be accomplished.

13.1 Therefore, as the children of Israel assert that we are mistaken in accepting Christ, who is come already, let us put forward to them from the Scriptures themselves that the Christ who was proclaimed has come already, although we have proven, from the times made known by Daniel, that the Christ who was announced has come already. It was proper to him to be born in Bethlehem in Judaea. 13.2 In fact, thus it has been written in the prophet, 'And you, Bethlehem, are not the least among the leaders of Judah. In fact, from you a leader shall come forth who shall feed my people Israel.'[177] However, if he has not been born yet, what leader was announced as going to come forth out of Bethlehem from the tribe of Judah? 13.3 For it was proper for him [1385] to come forth from the tribe of Judah and to come forth from Bethlehem. However, now we notice that no one of the clan of Israel has remained in the city of Bethlehem since the time when it was forbidden for any of the Jews to linger in the boundaries of that region of yours, such that this {word} also of the prophet has been fulfilled, 13.4 'Your land is forsaken, your cities are consumed by fire', which happened to them in a time of war, 'foreigners shall devour your country in your sight and it shall be forsaken and overthrown by an alien people,'[178] that is by the Romans. Thus the prophet says in another place, 'You shall see the king with his brightness' – that is, the Christ performing feats of strength in the glory of God the Father – 'and your eyes shall see the land from a distance.'[179] As you are prohibited from entering your land after the destruction of Jerusalem on account of your faults, it is permitted to see it only with your eyes from a distance. 'Your soul,' he says, 'shall think about terror,'[180] namely, what they suffered from the time of their own overthrow. 13.5 How, therefore, will a leader be born from Judah, and to what extent will he proceed from Bethlehem – just as the divine volumes of the prophets announce – when even now no one at all from Israel has been left behind there from whose stock he can be born?

On the other hand, if, according to the Jews, the Christ has not come yet, when he does come, where will he be anointed? 13.6 In fact, the law has taught that it was not lawful that the anointing with royal chrism be made in captivity. But if now there is no anointing there, as Daniel has prophesied – for he says, 'anointing will be abolished'[181] – therefore now there is no anointed because there is no temple where the horn was from which the kings used to be anointed.

13.7 Therefore, if there is no anointing, where will the leader be anointed who will be born in Bethlehem, or how will he proceed from Bethlehem when no one at all from the seed of Israel {1386} is in Bethlehem? 13.8 Let us show again finally that the Christ has already come in accordance with the prophets, suffered, and has now been taken back into heaven from where he is going to come in accordance with the proclamations of the prophets. 13.9 For after his coming, we read, in accordance with Daniel, the fact that the city itself has to be destroyed and we recognize that so it has been done.[182] In fact, thus Scripture says, 'Both city and sanctuary shall be destroyed at the same time with the leader.'[183] With which leader? Undoubtedly, it was he who was about to proceed from Bethlehem and from the tribe of Judah.

13.10 From this it is also clear that the city was due to be destroyed at the same time as when its leader was having to suffer in it, in accordance with the writings of the prophets who say, 'I have stretched out my hands for the whole day to a people who are stubborn and speaking against me and who walk not in a way that is good but after their own sins.'[184] Likewise in the psalms, 'They have destroyed my hands and my feet. They have counted all my bones. Moreover, they themselves have seen and considered me',[185] and 'in my thirst they have given me vinegar to drink.'[186] 13.11 David did not suffer these things in order to seem to have spoken correctly about himself, but the Christ who was crucified {suffered them}. Hands and feet are not destroyed except of him who is hung on a tree. Also from [the psalms], David himself was saying that the Lord would reign from a tree, for elsewhere even the prophet proclaims the fruit of this tree, saying, 'The earth has given her blessings.'[187] {1387} Certainly that virgin earth was not yet moistened with rain nor had been made fruitful by showers, from which a human being was first created back then and from which now the Christ was born according to the flesh from the virgin. 'And the tree has borne its fruit';[188] not that tree in paradise that gave death to the first human beings, but the tree of the suffering of the Christ, from where the life that hung there was not believed by you. 13.12 In fact, this tree was at that time a mystery, when Moses sweetened the bitter water, from where the people, who were dying of thirst in the desert, revived by drinking.[189] We who have been taken out of the calamities of the times in which we used to dwell, dying of thirst, do the same – that is, having been approved by the divine word – we have come back to life by the tree of the suffering of the Christ through the waters of baptism, drinking the faith that is in him. 13.13 Israel fell away from this faith, according to Jeremiah who says, 'Send! Ask thoroughly if such things are done, if the clans have exchanged their gods, and those gods of yours are not gods. However, my people has exchanged their glory, from which [exchange] nothing will come forth for them. Heaven grew frightened over that.'[190] And when did it grow frightened? Without doubt, it was when Christ suffered. 13.14 'And it shuddered thoroughly.'[191] And when has it shuddered thoroughly if not in the suffering of Christ, when the earth also shook and the sun grew dark in the middle of the day and the curtain of the temple was split and the tombs were broken apart?[192] He said, 'This is because my people have done two vile things: they have forsaken me, the fountain of the water of life, and they have dug worn-out troughs for themselves, which are not able to hold water.'[193] 13.15 Without doubt, by not receiving Christ, the fountain of the water of life, [1388] they have begun to possess worn-out troughs – that is, the synagogues among the scattering of the Gentiles. The Holy Spirit does not now remain in them, as it used to dwell in the temple in the past, before the coming of the Christ, who is the true temple of God. 13.16 For the prophet also proclaimed that they were going to suffer that drought of the divine Spirit, saying,

> Behold, those who serve me shall eat but you shall starve. Those serving me shall drink but you shall thirst and shall howl from an anguish of spirit. In fact, you shall give up your name for loathing by my chosen ones but the Lord shall kill you. However, those who serve me, to them a new name shall be given which will be blessed in the lands.[194]

13.17 Moreover, we read in the book of Kings of the mystery of this wood still being celebrated. For when the sons of the prophets were cutting wood with axes on the river Jordan, the iron leapt off and was plunged into the river. And thus, when Elisha the prophet had arrived, the sons of the prophets begged him to lift out the iron that had been plunged into the river. 13.18 And thus, as Elisha had taken and released wood at that place where the iron had been submerged, the iron floated at once, and the sons of the prophets recovered it when the wood was immersed.[195] From this they understood the fact that the spirit of Elijah had been made present to him. 13.19 What is more obvious by the mystery of this wood, than that the hardness of this age has been plunged into profound error, and by the wood of Christ – that is, by his suffering – is freed through baptism in order that what once had been lost in Adam on account of wood, could be restored through the wood of the Christ to us who have followed in place of the prophets, enduring in this present age those things that the prophets always suffered on account of divine religion? **13.20** For some they stoned, some they drove away. In fact they handed more over to death, which they cannot deny. And this wood, Isaac himself, the son of Abraham, carried for himself to the sacrifice when God had commanded him to become the victim for [God].[196] **13.21** But as these things were mysteries that {1389} were being preserved to be understood in the times of the Christ, Isaac with his wood was saved when a ram, which had got stuck by the horns in a thorn bush, was sacrificed, while Christ in his times carried the wood on his shoulders, clinging to the horns of the cross, a crown of thorns around his head. For it was proper for him who, 'has been led like a sheep to sacrifice and just as a lamb itself without a voice in the presence of the shearer, thus he did not open his mouth',[197] to become this sacrifice for all clans. **13.22** In fact, he said nothing when interrogated by Pilate. For 'his trial was endured in submissiveness'. In addition, 'Who will tell of his birth?'[198] Why? Because no one at all of the human race was aware of the birth of the Christ, at his conception, when Mary the virgin was discovered pregnant by the word of God and because 'his life was removed from the land'.[199] **13.23** Why so? Certainly after his resurrection from the dead, which was carried out on the third day, the heavens took him back, according to the prophecy of this kind uttered by Hosea, 'Before daybreak they will arise and say to me, "Let us go and return to the Lord our God as God will rescue and free us after two days on the third day."'[200] This is the glorious resurrection of him from earth into the heavens, neither whose birth nor whose suffering the Jews acknowledged. [God] took him back from where the Spirit itself too had come to the virgin.

13.24[201] Therefore, as the Jews maintain that the Christ has not yet come, whom in so many ways we have proved to have come, let the Jews recognize the end that, it was prophesied, they would bring upon themselves after Christ's coming, on account of their impiety in despising and killing him. {1390} In fact, first, since that day on which, as the word of Isaiah says, a person has thrown away their detestable objects of gold and silver that they made for worshipping empty and hurtful things – since, that is, we Gentiles, our hearts enlightened through the truth of Christ, have thrown away our idols – let the Jews also see that what follows has been accomplished. **13.25** 'For the Lord of hosts has taken from the Jews and from Jerusalem' – among other things – 'the wise architect[202] who is building the Church, the temple of God, and the home of the Lord'. As from then on the grace of God has ceased among them, and the commandment has been given to the clouds that they do not release rain upon the vineyard of Sorech, which means that heavenly benefits have been commanded not to spring up for the house of Israel.[203] 13.26 In fact, it had brought forth thorns, with some of which it made a crown for the Christ, [it had brought forth] not righteousness but the cry it had extracted from him on the cross. Thus the showers of spiritual gifts were withdrawn, and the law and the prophets ceased with John,[204] and the pool of Bethsaida stopped curing the illnesses within Israel with the coming of the Christ.[205] After that, by the continuation of their own rage, the name of the Lord was blasphemed through them, as it is written, 'For your sakes the name of the Lord is blasphemed among the Gentiles.'[206] For from them began that infamy and the time between Tiberius and Vespasian.[207] Since they had committed those infamies and had not understood the Christ who came in the time of the own punishment,[208] 'Their land was made desolate and their cities burned with fire, their country was devoured [1391] before them by strangers, and the daughter of Sion was left as derelict as a look-out in a vineyard or a hut in a cucumber patch',[209] since that time, in fact, when 'Israel did not know the Lord and the people did not understand him',[210] but forsook him more and provoked the holy one of Israel to indignation. 13.27 Thus also the conditional threat of the sword threatens them: 'If you are unwilling and refuse to hear me, the sword will devour you'.[211] From this we prove that the sword was Christ whom they refused to hear. Also in the psalm he demands of the Father their dispersion saying, 'Disperse them in your strength.'[212] Again through the guise of Isaiah, he says about their being burnt, 'These things have been done to you, you will sleep in sorrow.'[213] 13.28 It follows, as the Jews were declared as going to suffer these things on account of the Christ, and we find them having been suffered and we perceive that the Jews linger in dispersion, that it is obvious that those things happened to the Jews on account of the Christ, by the agreement of the sense of the Scriptures with the course of events and the order of the times. 13.29 Or, if the Christ has not yet come, the Christ on whose account it is prophesied that they are to suffer these things, it follows that when he does come they will suffer them. But where by that time will there be a daughter of Sion to be made desolate, who today is not in Judaea? Where are the cities to be burned with fire? They are already in ruinous heaps. Where is the dispersion of that clan? It is already in exile. Give back to Judaea its position that the Christ may find it so. Only this way can you claim that he who has come is a different Christ.

14.1[214] Now learn guidance from the totality of your error. We say that there are two conditions of the Christ set forth by the prophets, giving a prior indication of an equal number of advents: one of them, the first, in humility, [1392] when 'he was led like a sheep to sacrifice, and as a lamb itself is without a voice before the shearer, thus he did not open his mouth,[215] and he was not even respectable to look at'. 14.2 In fact, he says

> We have announced concerning him: [He is] like a little boy, like a root in thirsty ground. There was also no appearance nor glory to him, and we saw him, and he had no appearance or beauty, but his appearance was without honour, [he was] more rejected than the children of men, a man placed in affliction, and knowing how to bear infirmity.[216]

That is to say, [he was] set by the Father 'as a stumbling stone',[217] and 'made a little lower than the angels',[218] by the Father, declaring himself, 'a worm and no man, a human disgrace and the outcast of the people'.[219] 14.3 These marks of degradation apply to his first advent, as the marks of exaltation apply to the second, when he will become no longer a stumbling stone or a rock of scandal, but the chief cornerstone, taken back again after rejection and set on high at the summit, that rock in fact mentioned by Daniel, which was cut from the mountain, which will crush and crumble the image of the kingdoms of this world.[220] 14.4 Concerning this second advent the same prophet speaks

> And behold, one like a son of man coming with the clouds of heaven, came even to the Ancient of days and he was in his presence, and the attendants brought him forward, and there was given to him royal power and all the earth after its kind and all glory to serve him. His power that shall not be taken away is eternal, and his kingdom is one that shall not be corrupted.[221]

14.5 Then certainly he will have an honourable appearance, and unfading beauty, more than the children of men. For it says, 'Fairer [1393] in beauty beyond the sons of men, grace is poured forth in your lips; therefore God has blessed you for ever. Gird the sword upon your thigh, O most high in your suitability and your beauty',[222] while the Father, now that [the Father] has made him a little lower than the angels, also has crowned him with glory and honour and has put all things under his feet.[223] 14.6 Then they will know him whom they have pierced and will strike their breasts, tribe to tribe, because in fact they formerly failed to recognize him in the humility of his human condition. 'And he is a man,' says Jeremiah, 'and who will know him?'[224] Because also, Isaiah says, 'Who will explain his nativity?'[225] 14.7 So also in Zechariah, in the presence of Joshua, yes truly, in the mystery of its own name, the truest priest of the Father, Christ, is marked out for two advents by two styles of appearance.[226] He was at first clothed in filthy garments, which means the indignity of suffering and mortal flesh, when also the devil, who put it into the heart of Judas the traitor, and who had tempted him after his baptism,[227] was standing as his adversary. Afterwards, he was stripped of his previous filthy garments and dressed in priestly robe and turban and crown, which means his second coming, as he is shown obtaining glory and dignity. 14.8 Nor will you be able to call him the son of Jehozadak, who was never in a filthy garment but was always arrayed with the priestly garment and was never deprived of the priestly office. However, that Joshua is the Christ, the high priest of God the Father, who, in his first coming, came [1394] in the humility of suffering human form, even in the period before his suffering. He was even proven through everything a victim for us all, who, after his resurrection when he was clothed in a robe, is named priest of God the Father for eternity.

14.9[228] In fact, thus also let me make an interpretation of the two goats that were offered at the fast.[229] Do these not also show the two conditions of the Christ who is already come? They are indeed of the same age and appearance on account of the one and the same aspect of the Lord, because he will return in no other form, seeing that he has to be recognized by those from whom he has suffered injury. One of them, however, which was surrounded with scarlet, cursed and spat upon and perforated and punctured, was driven outside the city by the people to ruin, marked with obvious emblems of the suffering of Christ, who, having been surrounded with a scarlet garment, spat upon and knocked about with every physical violence, was crucified outside the city. The other, however, made an offering for offences, and given as food only to the priests of the temple, is marked with the proof of his second manifestation, because when all offences have been done away, the priests of the spiritual temple – that is, the church – were to enjoy as it were a feast of our Lord's grace, while the rest remain without a taste of salvation. 14.10 Therefore, seeing that the first advent was foretold under obscurity by many figures and destroyed by every sort of indignity, while the second was both clearly told of, and was worthy of God, they set their eyes on that one alone that they were able to understand and believe easily – that is, the second – which is in honour and glory, and thus were, as might have been expected, deceived about of the more obscure, admittedly less dignified – that is, the first. Thus even until this day they refuse to admit that their Christ has come, because he has not come in majesty, being unaware that he was first also to come in humility.

{1395} 14.11[230] It is sufficient so far to have run through Christ's condition in these things in the meantime, such that it is proven that he is such a one as was announced. And so now from that accord of the divine Scriptures, we may understand also that the things that were declared as going to be after the Christ may be believed to have been accomplished by reason of the divine arrangement. In fact, in no way would the things have happened that were declared as following on his coming, unless he had come after whom they had to be accomplished. 14.12 Therefore, if you perceive all the tribes after that time {of Christ} emerging from the depths of human error towards God the creator and {God's} Christ, a point you would not dare to deny as being prophesied, because immediately the Father's promise in the psalms, just as now we have mentioned already, meets you saying, 'You are my son, this day I have begotten you. Seek for me and I shall give you the Gentiles for your inheritance and the ends of the earth for your possession.'[231] Neither can you claim Solomon, the son of David, for that proclamation, more than Christ, the son of God, nor the ends of the earth having been promised to the son of David, who ruled only within Judaea, more than to Christ, the son of God, who now has enlightened the whole world with the light of his gospel. 14.13 Furthermore, an eternal throne agrees more with Christ, the Son of God, than with Solomon, who was in fact a temporal king who ruled in Israel only. For today, the tribes that did not know him are invoking Christ, and today the people are taking refuge in Christ, of whom formerly they were ignorant. Moreover, you are not able to contend {1396} that what you see is done will be done. 14.14 Either deny that these were prophesied, when they are seen openly, or that they were fulfilled, when they are read. Or if you do not deny either of these, they have been fulfilled in him for whom they were prophesied.[232]

12

ANTIDOTE FOR THE SCORPION'S STING (*Scorpiace*)

Introduction

The traditional understanding that *Antidote for the Scorpion's Sting* was written about 211 or 212 during Tertullian's Montanist period (Harnack 1904: 284 n. 3; Quasten 1953: 282; Frend 1965: 372; Frend 1968: 8; Braun 1977: 574) has been challenged by Barnes, who has redated it to late 203 or early 204 (Barnes 1969: 105–32; 1985: 34–5, 328–9). This has been accepted by some (Rankin 1995: xvi) but not by others (Fredouille 1972: 488). More recently, Azzali Bernardelli has defended the date of 212 at some length (Azzali Bernardelli 1990a: 51–84; 1990b: 10–11) through a comparison with two of Tertullian's other works concerning martyrdom: *On the Military Crown* and *On Flight in Time of Persecution*. She places it between the two, believing that there is a logical development and an enrichment of themes and modes of expression that would warrant this order. This would make it a Montanist work. She finds a reference to a promise in *On the Military Crown* 1.5, to write about the techniques used for obtaining confession from Christians, fulfilled in this treatise.[1]

Barnes (1969: 108–10) offers a rhetorical structure for the treatise that may be adopted here, with minor modifications. The work commences with an *exordium* (1.1–11), which includes a *narratio* (1.6–8). The *propositio* (1.12–2.2a) is that martyrdom is both necessary and good, and is commanded by God. This is restated in 8.1 and indicates that the treatise is forensic in nature. At the same time there is an underlying deliberative theme in that Tertullian was encouraging those Christians who had succumbed to the opponents' arguments to return to an authentic Christian understanding of martyrdom and embrace its possibility. The vast bulk of the treatise, as would be expected, is *confirmatio* and *refutatio* (2.2b–14.3). This consists of a lengthy collection of texts from the Hebrew Scriptures indicating that idolatry was forbidden (2.2b–14) and would be punished by God (3.1–7). It has to be said that this section seems rather tangential to the whole argument of this treatise, which is not about idolatry but about martyrdom. The connection is that the faithful must face martyrdom rather than surrender to idolatry (4.1). The *refutatio* runs from chapter 4 to chapter 7. The argument of the opponents was either that the command to martyrdom was issued by another inferior god (and Tertullian's reply to the Marcionites and other such heretics had already been given and need not be repeated), or that martyrdom was not the will of God. Tertullian's refutation was that having established that it was the will of God that the faithful should avoid idolatry, it was sufficient to establish also that it was the will of God that the faithful should face martyrdom (4.2–5). The second argument that was countered was that martyrdom was not a good thing but an evil one (5.1–6.11). Tertullian's response was to demonstrate that just as God is good, so too is God's will (5.1–2); that if idolatry is evil then martyrdom, its opposite, must be good (5.3–5a); and that just because martyrdom is painful and difficult this does not make it any less good (5.5b–6.11). The last response is illustrated with two analogies about how short-term pain leads to long-term benefit: one medical (5.6–13) and the other athletic (6.1–11). The third response was to the argument that God was a murderer (7.1–7). In a ploy typical of forensic oratory, Tertullian admitted the action but debated about its quality.[2] In other words, Tertullian found an extenuating circumstance to justify God's murders, which was that life came from death. What amounts to the *confirmatio* starts in chapter 8. The Hebrew Scriptures are full of honourable characters who endured persecution and martyrdom (8.1–8). The New Testament likewise was full of admonitions to and examples of martyrdom (9.1–14.3): from Jesus (9.1–11.8), from Peter (12.2–3), from John (12.4–11) and from Paul (13.1–14.3). Included in that is a digression (10.1–17) in which he responded to Valentinian opinion that the call to acknowledge one's faith and face martyrdom was to answered in heaven not on earth. The works ends with a *peroratio* (15.1–5).

Who are Tertullian's opponents in this treatise? At 1.5, Gnostics and Valentinians are mentioned, and Valentinus is mentioned at 10.1 and 15.6, along with Prodicus in the latter instance. Valentinus was an Egyptian of the early to mid-second century who had moved to Rome. He taught a full Gnostic theology deriving from Pythagorean cosmology: there is a higher spiritual world (Pleroma) made up of thirty spiritual pairs of powers (aeons), the youngest of which, Sophia, who splits from the Pleroma (there are two different accounts), is the mother of the Demiurge (who was identified with the Old Testament God, who created the material and hence evil world), and another of which, Christ, came to earth and united with the human Jesus in order to bring people the secret knowledge (gnosis) necessary to achieve salvation. People are divided into those who are spiritual because they have received this gnosis, those who are psychics, Christians without gnosis but still with faith, and the rest of humanity who have no hope of salvation. Tertullian dedicated *Against the Valentinians* to refuting this Gnostic theology, a work that depended heavily on Irenaeus' *Against Heresies*.

The view of the Valentinians against the simple faith of ordinary Christians was that martyrdom was unnecessary. This was the scorpion's poison that Tertullian believed infected ordinary Christians.

This text has not been translated into English since the middle of the nineteenth century in the Ante-Nicene Library/Ante-Nicene Fathers series. I have used the text by Reifferscheid and Wissowa in the *Corpus Christianorum*. I have made very few emendations to this text. I have consulted the Italian translation of Azzali Bernardelli (1990).

Text

[1069] 1.1 The earth discharges a great evil from the small scorpion.[3] [There are] as many venoms as kinds [of scorpion], as many injuries as species, as many sufferings as colourings.[4] Nicander[5] writes and portrays [them]. And yet, the one movement of ferocity in all [scorpions is] not from the mouth [but] from the tail, which is whatever is extended from the rear of the body and strikes.[6] [It is] just like [the missile launcher known as] 'the scorpion'[7] – that sequence of joints, [which has] an interior, venomous, slender small, vein, rising with the force of a bent bow, draws tight a hooked sting at its summit. 1.2 From [this analogy] about the scorpion they also name the war machine, the missiles [of which] are brought to life by having been drawn back. That 'sting' is also a pipe with a narrow aperture and where it pierces it pours forth poison into the wound. The usual time of danger [is] summer: the scourge sails on the south wind and the south-west wind.[8] For relief [there are] many natural substances; sorcery also provides a bandage to some extent. Medical science remedies with surgical knife and potion. 1.3 For some drink a preventative for hastening the cure,[9] but sleeping together drains [it] and they thirst [for it] again. For us, faith [is] a protection, unless it too is struck with a lack of trust by the need immediately to sign [ourselves with the cross], to entreat [God] and to anoint the heel [stung by] the beast.[10] 1.4 Finally, in this way we often assist the pagans,[11] as we have been gifted by God with that power which the apostle affirmed, when he spurned the bite of the viper.[12] Therefore, what does your pen promise [, Nicander,] if faith is kept safe according to its own [properties]? It has been kept safe according to its own [properties] in other circumstances as well when it suffers its own scorpions? With these [scorpions to the faith there is] also a bitter meanness and a variety of kind, and they are armed in a single way, and are stirred up at a certain time and in no other way than by inflamed passions. 1.5 This is the persecution among Christians. Therefore, when faith is stirred up and the church is ignited, according to the figure of the thorn bush,[13] then the Gnostics sprout up, then the Valentinians progress without being noticed, then all the opponents of martyrdom bubble to the surface, and they are roused to lash out, pierce and slay. For because they know [that] many [Christians are] simple and unpolished, and in this instance feeble – in truth [they know] a great many [are tossed about] in the wind and [are] Christians [1070] when it pleases them – they think [there is] never so great an opportunity for approaching than when fear has weakened the gateway to the soul, especially when some atrocity has already crowned the faith of the martyrs.

1.6 Therefore, [while] still dragging their tail, they first attach [it] with regard to the feelings or lash [it] as if into empty space. 'Are innocent people to suffer these [persecutions]?' [they ask], in order that you may think the brother or the pagan [to be] from the better [way of life]. 1.7 'Is a way of life that troubles no one to be treated thus [with persecution]?' [they argue.] From this time they thrust [their tail] in: 'People are lost without reason!' For to be lost and moreover without reason [is] the first puncture. After that, they make the kill:

> But these simple souls do not know anything concerning what was written [about] where and when and in the presence of whom [the faith] ought to be acknowledged, save only that [it is] not only simplicity but pointless, or rather madness, to die for God, as it is [God] who makes me safe. 1.8 If [God] slays, who will be bound to make [me] safe? Christ died but once for us,[14] but he was slain once that we might not be slain. If he demands the same in return, surely he could not expect salvation from my violent death? Or

does God demand human blood, especially if [God] objects to [the blood] of bulls and goats?[15] Certainly, [God] prefers repentance rather than the death of a sinner.[16] And why does [God] desire the death of [those who are] not sinners?

1.9 Whom will these [taunts] and, if [they exist], any other inventions of the heretical venoms not pierce with doubt if not with destruction or with anger if not with death? But you, if faith is vigilant, shall stomp on the scorpion immediately with a curse, instead of with your sandal, and shall leave [it] dying in its own purulence. 1.10 Otherwise, if it should engorge the punctured area, the poison flows in and rapidly fills the internal organs. Immediately, all the normal senses become sluggish, the blood of the soul freezes, the flesh of the spirit decays, the nausea at the [Christian] name increases. The mind seeks [a place] where it may vomit. In this way also infirmity, which has been stung once only, exhales its impaired faith either into heresy or into heathenism. And now, in the present state of things, it is mid-summer, the very dog days[17] of persecution, certainly from the dog-headed one itself.[18] 1.11 Fire has tested some Christians, the sword others, the beasts [have tested] others, and others hunger in prison for martyrdom, having become acquainted with clubs and claws in the meantime. [1071] We ourselves, like hares intended for the hunting spectacle,[19] are under attack from a distance, and heretics prowl about as is their usual practice.[20]

1.12 On that account, the present situation urged that I administer the antidote against the native little beasts in my usual manner with the pen to bring about a remedy. You who read, will drink. And the potion is not a bitter thing. If the eloquent words of the Lord are sweeter than honey or the honeycomb,[21] then they are juice. If the promise of God flows with milk and honey,[22] it tastes of its ingredients. However, 'woe betide the ones who turn sweet into bitter and light into darkness'.[23] 1.13 For in the same way as the ones who oppose martyrdoms, interpreting salvation as destruction, change sweet into bitter and light into darkness, they also substitute this most lamentable life for that most blessed [one] by preferring bitter instead of sweet as well as darkness instead of light. 2.1 But [we] ought not to learn about the good of martyrdom, without first [learning] about its obligation; nor about the usefulness of it, as much as about its necessity. Divine authority leads the way: God has willed and commanded this in order that they who deny the good may not become persuaded of its usefulness only when they have been overcome. It is right that heretics be compelled to duty, not

enticed. Stubbornness ought to be subdued, not sweet-talked. 2.2
And certainly it will be a completely sufficient preliminary judgement
because [martyrdom] will be shown [as] having been established and
commanded by God.

Let them hold back the gospels for a little while, until I articulate
their underpinning law, until I elicit from there the will of God, from
where I recognize God's very self who says:

> I am God, your God, who led you from the land of Egypt.
> There shall not be other gods for you besides me. You shall
> not make images for yourselves of the things either in
> heaven, on earth below, or in the sea under the earth. You
> shall not worship them nor be in service to them. For I am
> the Lord your God.[24]

Likewise, in the same [book of] Exodus: 'You yourselves have
seen that I have spoken to you from heaven. You shall not make
for yourselves gods of silver and you shall not make for yourselves
gods of gold.'[25] 2.3 Following these [passages, we find others] too in
Deuteronomy: 'Listen [1072] Israel, the Lord your God is one, and
you shall love the Lord your God from your whole heart and from
your whole strength and from your whole soul.'[26] And again

> You shall not forget the Lord your God, who led you from
> the land of Egypt from the house of slavery. You shall fear the
> Lord your God and be in service to [God] alone and adhere
> to [God] and take the oath in the name of [God]. 2.4 You
> shall not go after other gods from the gods of the foreigners[27]
> that encircle you, because God your God is jealous for you,
> lest an angered [God] be offended and wipe you out from the
> face of the earth.[28]

2.5 But laying before them blessings and curses [God] says,
'Blessings to you if you obey the commands of the Lord your God,
whatever I command you today, and if you do not stray from the path
I have mandated for you, such that departing you serve other gods,
whom you do not know.'[29] 2.6 About rooting [foreign gods] out in
every way [God] says

> You shall destroy completely every place on mountains and
> hills and under lush trees in which the tribes whom you
> shall possess by inheritance served their gods. You shall dig

out every altar of theirs. You shall overturn and smash their figurines and you shall mow down their sacred groves and you shall burn up with fire the carvings of their gods and obliterate their name from that place.[30]

2.7 In addition [God] adds, when they had entered the land of promise and had wiped out its tribes, 'Be on your guard lest you follow them after they had been wiped out from your sight, lest you ask about their gods saying, "Just as the foreigners do with their gods, let me also do likewise."'[31] 2.8 But [God] also says,

> If a prophet himself should arise among you, or one dreaming a dream, and should he give a sign or a portent to you, and should he come and say, 'Let us go and serve other gods' whom you do not know, do not listen to the words of that prophet or dreamer because the Lord your God is testing you, [to discover] whether you fear God from your whole heart and from your whole soul. You shall follow after the Lord {1073} your God and you shall fear [God] and you shall keep [God's] commandments and you shall obey [God's] voice and serve [God] and you shall be added to [God]. However, that prophet or dreamer shall die, for he has spoken to lead you away from the Lord your God.[32]

2.9 But in another section

> However, if your brother, [the son of your] father or mother, or your son or daughter, or the wife whom you love,[33] or the friend who is equal to your soul, asks privately saying, 'Let us go and serve other gods, whom neither you nor your ancestors know, from the gods of the foreigners that encircle you near and far,' do not be willing to go with that [person] and do not obey him [or her]. 2.10 Your eye shall not have mercy on that [person], neither shall you have feelings for, nor preserve, him [or her]. Declaring you shall denounce that [person]. Your hand shall be the first to slay him [or her] and the hands of your people the last. You shall stone and kill that [person] because he [or she] has sought to turn you from the Lord your God.[34]

2.11 [God] adds [comments] as well about cities that, if one of these had agreed with the advice of evil men to go over to other gods, then all inhabiting it would be slain and everything in it would come under a curse and all its plunder would be collected together into every outlet and would be incinerated by fire with all its provisions and all the people in the sight of the Lord God.[35] And [God] says, 'It shall not be habitable ever again. It shall not be rebuilt any more, nor shall you hold on to anything that is under a curse, in order that the Lord may be turned from the provocation of anger.'[36] 2.12 [God] has also combined a series of curses from the solemn oath about idols, 'A curse to the man who has made an abomination by carving or casting, a product of skilled hands, and who has erected it in a secret place.'[37] Indeed, in Leviticus [God] says, 'You shall not follow idols and you shall not make gods cast from molten metals for yourselves. I am the Lord your God.'[38] And elsewhere, 'To me the children of Israel [are] young domestic servants. They are the ones whom I have led out of Egypt. I am the Lord your God. You shall not make for yourselves hand-made [things] nor set up carved figurines for yourselves. Neither shall you place a chiselled stone in {1074} your land. I am the Lord your God.'[39] 2.13 And these things indeed, said first through Moses, are certainly relevant to all whom the Lord God of Israel will similarly have led out from the Egypt of a most superstitious world and from the house of human slavery. 2.14 But afterwards, the mouth of every prophet resonates with the words of the same God by adding to the same law of [God] a renewal of the same commands. [A prophet] does not denounce anything else as of greater importance than to guard against all manufacture and cult of idols. As [God says] through David, 'The gods of the foreigners are silver and gold. They have eyes but they do not see. They have ears but they do not hear, noses but they do not smell, a mouth but they do not speak, hands but they do not feel, feet and they do not walk. They are similar to those who make them and trust in them.'[40]

3.1 And let me not think that it ought to be discussed whether God is right to prohibit [the divine] name and honour being awarded to a lie, or is right to be unwilling to send back those again into Egypt who were torn away from the error of superstition, or is right not to suffer the departure of those who have been chosen for [God's] self. Thus, we are not required to re-examine whether [God] has intended the teaching that was planned to be instituted to be kept, and has taken a deserved revenge against the abandonment of that which was intended to be observed. This is because it would have been a pointless institution if [the teaching] had not been intended to be observed, and it would have been in vain that [God] wanted it to be observed if there was no wish to avenge [its abandonment]. 3.2 For it follows that I must show that these sanctions of God against superstitions are as known as they are also avenged, as the whole rationale for martyrdoms depends on these.

Moses was away with God on the mountain when the people, so impatient with his necessary absence, sought to produce gods for themselves that they should rather have destroyed.[41] **3.3** Aaron is pressured and orders that their women's earrings be melted together in the fire.[42] In fact, the true ornaments of the ears, the words of God, were going to be lost in their self-judgement. The fire of wisdom poured out the likeness of a bull calf, taunting them [with] having their heart where their treasure also is,[43] [which was] certainly in Egypt, which also consecrates [the likeness] of a certain cow, among other animals.[44] **3.4** For that reason, the 3,000 [1075] men killed by their closest relatives because they had so offended God, their closest relative, announced the commencement and the recompense of transgression.[45] In Numbers, when Israel had turned away [from God] at Shittim and had lusted, they went away to the daughters of Moab and were invited to the idols, such that they fornicated in spirit as well. Finally, they eat from their polluted [sacrifices]. Next, they both worship the gods of the clans and are initiated into [the rites of] Baal Peor.[46] **3.5** On account of idolatry also, the sister of adultery, [only the deaths of] 23,000 of their family, who were cut down by swords, appeased the divine anger.[47] When Joshua, son of Nun, died, they abandoned the God of their ancestors and served the idols of Baal and Ashtarath, and the angry Lord handed them over into the hands of the plunderers, and they were plundered by them and sold to their enemies, and they were completely unable to stand in the sight of their enemies.[48] **3.6** Wherever they went, the hand [of God] was on them with severity and they were greatly restrained. After these things, God established judges over them, whom we understand as censors.[49] But they did not persevere in obeying them. When any of the judges died, they tended to fail [even] more than their ancestors by going after other gods and serving and worshipping them. **3.7** For that reason the Lord [was] angry, asserting, 'Since even that clan has transgressed my covenant which I arranged with their ancestors and they have not listened to my voice, I will not direct my attention to the removal from their sight of the foreign people whom Joshua left when he died.'[50] And thus throughout almost all of the records of the judges and of the kings that followed, Israel paid for the anger of God with war and captivity and a foreign yoke, with the strength of the clans that surrounded [them] preserved, whenever they deviated from [God], especially into idolatry.

4.1 Therefore, if it is evident from the beginning that this [situation of idolatry was the case], both having been prohibited according to so many and such important commands, and never having been committed without punishment according to so many and such important warnings (nor [is] any crime in the presence of God to be counted so arrogant as a transgression of this kind), we ought to understand better the intention of the divine threats and punishments [1076] that even then defended martyrdoms, not only by not calling [them] into question but also by supporting [them] as well, as [God] had certainly created the opportunity by prohibiting idolatry. For otherwise martyrdoms would not have occurred. And, at any rate, [God] established [God's] own authority, intending [martyrdoms], for which the opportunity had been created, to occur.

4.2 For now we are being stung concerning the will of God, and the scorpion inflames the punctured area, denying this will [concerning martyrdoms] and complaining about it, such that it insinuates either [the existence of] another god, who did not have such a will, or denies the will of God altogether if it is not able to deny [God]. 4.3 We, however, having taken up the fight elsewhere about God and also about the remaining body of heretical doctrine about God,[51] now sketch certain lines [of attack] for one form of contest: we defend this will [of God as being] of no other god than that of the God of Israel, who has created the opportunity for martyrdoms. As idolatry has always been prohibited by the commands, so it has been punished by [God's] judgements. For if by observing the command I suffer violence, this will be, in some way, a command about observing the command, such that I suffer that violence by which I can observe the command, no matter how much it seeks to draw me away from avoiding idolatry. 4.4 And certainly the one who imposes the command exacts compliance. Therefore, [God] cannot but intend these things to occur by which compliance will be established. I am directed not to call anything else 'god, not even by speaking – no less with the tongue than with the hand[52] – [nor] to fashion or worship another god and only to venerate that one who so directs,[53] and whom I am ordered to fear, in order that I do not depart from [God], and [am directed] to love from my whole being, such that I may die for [God]. 4.5 I am challenged by the enemies [as] a soldier [committed] to this oath. If I do not surrender my hand to them, I am equal to them. I fight defending this [oath] in battle, I am wounded, I am cut down, I am slain. Who desired this conclusion for their soldier if not the one who sealed him by such an oath?

5.1 Therefore, you have the will of my God. It counteracts this punctured area. Now let us consider another strike [of the scorpion] about the nature of [God's] will. It would take too long for me to show that my God is good, which the Marcionites have already learnt from us.[54] Meanwhile, it is enough simply to mention [the word] 'God' [1077] in order to believe that [God] is unavoidably good. 5.2 For the one who puts it forward that God is evil will not be able to establish both points. He will have either to deny that the one whom he considers evil is God, or to declare that the one whom he proclaims God is good. Therefore, the will also is good of the one who, if not good, is not God.

5.3 The goodness of the matter itself – I mean martyrdom – that God intends will also prove this, because it is not good unless the good one wills [it]. I contend that martyrdom is good to the same God for whom idolatry is both prohibited and punished. For martyrdom resists and is opposed to idolatry. However, to resist and be opposed to evil is not possible unless [one is] good. 5.4 [It is] not as if I deny that there could be a rivalry between evil things themselves, as much as there is among good, but that is something different from what is under discussion here. For martyrdom does not contend with idolatry from some shared spitefulness but from its own regard, for it frees [one] from idolatry. Who will not proclaim [as] good that which frees from evil? What else is the opposition [between] idolatry and martyrdom than [that] of death and life? 5.5 Life will be as much calculated by martyrdom as idolatry by death. The one who declares life to be evil rather than good has death.

And this [is] human perversity – to shake off the beneficial, to support the pernicious, to seek out the dangerous, to avoid the remedy, or, in short, to desire to die sooner than to be cured. 5.6 For there are many who flee the protection of medical science, for many are foolish, many are afraid and falsely modest. And just as obvious is the severity of medical science owing to the scalpel, the hot iron and the fire of the mustard.[55] Nevertheless, to be cut and burned and stretched and bitten is not evil on that account, because it brings useful pain. It will not be refused because it only brings sorrow, but because it necessarily brings sorrow it will be employed. 5.7 The benefit excuses the horror of this work. Further, the one howling and groaning and bellowing will afterwards fill up the same hands of the doctor with the fee and will declare [them] the most skilled and will then deny the cruelty. Thus also martyrdoms rage violently, [1078] but for salvation. And it will be permissible for God to administer eternal life through fires and swords and anything sharp. 5.8 But you will be astonished indeed at the doctor as well in this regard, because he employs medicines that are almost of an equal character to that of the complaints, when he helps, as if incorrectly, by means of the assistance of those things through which [the complaint] is produced. For he even restrains fever by applying more heat, quenches a burning thirst by tormenting the thirst more, concentrates the excess of bile by each bitter small potion, and he restrains the flow of blood by draining other small veins. 5.9 You will judge even God guilty of jealousy if [God] wished to deal with the cause and to do good by emulating the injury – to abolish death by death, to scatter slaying by slaying, to shatter the instruments of torture by the instruments of torture, to dry tearful entreaty by tearful entreaty, to confer life by removing [it], to help the flesh by damaging [it], [and] to serve the soul by tearing [it] out. 5.10 That which you held up [to be] perversity is rational, because that which you judge [to be] severity is a favour. Thus, with God healing that which is eternal by these momentary things, exalt your God for your good [fortune]. You have fallen into [God's] hands, but you are fortunate to have done so. [God] also fell into your illness. The person always first provides business for the doctor, [because] in the end, people attract the danger of death to themselves. 5.11 [Adam] received from his Lord, as from a doctor, enough useful teaching for living according to the law, such that indeed he ate everything and refrained only from one shrub, which that very doctor had known to be unsuitable.⁵⁶ 5.12 [Adam] listened to whom he preferred and broke off his restraint. He ate what was not allowed and having been filled by the transgression he suffered terminal indigestion, certainly being most deserving to perish completely as that was his wish. But with the inflammation of the offence having been sustained until the time the medicine was concocted, the Lord gradually prepared the relief – all the teachings of faith, matching themselves to the failing, repealing the word of death by the word of life, diminishing the hearing of transgression by the hearing of devotion. Thus, even when that doctor prescribes death, [God] removes the torpidity of death. 5.13 Why is a person now annoyed to suffer from a remedy that which he or she was not previously annoyed to suffer from an offence? Is it displeasing to be slain for salvation [1079] for the one who was not displeased to be slain for destruction? Will [that person] who has longed for the venom be nauseous about the antidote?

6.1 But if, in the name of the contest [between good and evil that I mentioned earlier], God had proposed martyrdoms for us, through which we might have been pitted against the adversary, in order that [God] may now strike the one by whom a person willingly is struck, here too the generosity more than the harshness of God is present. For [God] wished to produce a human person, plucked from the devil's throat through faith, who now tramples on [the devil] through virtue, in order that [the person] might not only have escaped the enemy but completely vanquished it as well. 6.2 [God], who has called to salvation, loved to invite to glory also, so that we who have been freed may rejoice, [and] that we who have been crowned may exalt as well. With what favour the world celebrates those festive games, [those] solemn competitions and superstitious contests of the Greeks, [dedicated to] both worship of the gods and pleasure; now it is allowed also in Africa. Cities continue to pester Carthage by congratulating it, one after another, for the Pythian Games having been awarded [to it so long] after the stadium was constructed.[57] 6.3 Thus it has been believed by [this] age that [these games are] the most suitable [way] to test the result of studies and to evaluate the skills of bodies and voices according to [their] excellence, with the reward [being] the title, the spectacle [being] the judge, the pleasure [being] the decision. Where the combats are nude, there are wounds, fists fly, heels butt like rams, boxing gloves tear to pieces, whips lacerate.[58] 6.4 However, there will be no one [who] protests to the judge of the games because people are confronted with violence. Accusations of injury [are only made] outside the stadium. But however many bruises, gashes and swellings they may trade [with one another inside the stadium], [the referee] extends to them, of course, crowns and glory and gifts, public privileges, civic handouts, images, statues and the kinds of things the world is able to offer, eternity through renown [and] resurrection through memory. 6.5 The boxer himself does not complain of the pain to himself, for he wishes [for it]. The crown [of victory] presses down on the wound, the palm branch [of victory] hides the blood, he swells more with victory than with injury! You, will you consider him hurt when you see him happy? Not even the defeated contestant himself will complain to the supervisor of the games about his situation. 6.6 Will it be unbecoming for God to bring forth skills and teachings into public view, into this 'secular stage', as a spectacle for people and angels and the universal powers? [Will it be unbecoming] to test flesh and [1080] soul for their constancy and tolerance? [Will it be unbecoming] to give to this one the palm [of victory], to this one honour, to that one citizenship, to that one handouts, even to condemn certain ones and to remove the punished with disgrace? You will without doubt direct God about which times or means or places [God] may judge [God's] own dependants, as if it were not suitable for the judge to give a preliminary decision. 6.7 What now if [God] had exposed the faith to martyrdoms, not in the name of the struggle but also for its own benefit, would it not be proper that [faith] has some gathering of hope to which its zeal may focus and lift up a prayer in order that it may struggle to ascend as earthly offices also rise in steps? Or how [can there be] many dwelling places with the Father[59] if not in accordance with the variety of rewards? In what way also will a star differ from [another] star in glory if not in accordance with the diversity of brightness?[60] **6.8** Furthermore, if on that account some extension of fame is suitable for the height of faith, it ought to have been something of such effort that exists by great labour, torture, torment and death. But reflect upon the compensation when flesh and soul, than which there is nothing more precious in the human person, is given up: one [from] the hand of God, the other [from] the breath[61] – themselves having been paid for the effort of which it has been obtained, themselves having been obtained which are made for profit, the price [is] the same which also [is] the income. **6.9** God had also foreseen other weaknesses of the human condition – the snares of the adversary, the deception of affairs, the trap of the world, the faith that would be endangered even after ritual washing, and after salvation the majority, the sort who soiled the wedding garment,[62] who had not prepared oil for their little torches,[63] and who needed to be looked for in the mountains and ravines and needed to be carried back on the shoulders,[64] would be destroyed again. Therefore [God] established second atonements and the final defences, the contest of martyrdoms and the ritual washing with blood following after that. **6.10** David says about the happiness of such a person, 'Blessed are they whose iniquities have been let go and whose sins have been covered. Blessed is the one to whom God charges no fault.'[65] For in a proper sense nothing now is able to be reconsidered with the martyrs with whom, in the ritual washing, life itself is handed over. **6.11** Thus 'love covers a multitude of sins',[66] which certainly, while loving God {1081} from [its] whole strength, with which it fights in martyrdom, [and] from [its] whole soul, which is handed over for God, moulds a person [into] a martyr. You, will you call these things – relief, pieces of advice, decisions, even spectacles – the atrocity of God? Does God desire human blood? However, I may even dare to say [yes], if a person also [desires] the reign of God, if a person [desires] sure salvation, and if a person [desires] a second new birth. No compensation is hateful in which the reason [for] either grace or injury is the same.

7.1 The scorpion, still swinging [its tail], may sting, [claiming] that God [is] a murderer. I shall shudder thoroughly at the filthy breath of blasphemy from the stinking mouth of the heretic, but I embrace even such a God by confidence of reason, by which reason even God's very self has proclaimed from the person of [God's]

Sophia[67] by the voice of Solomon, that [God is] more than a murderer. [Solomon] says, 'Sophia has cut the throat of her children.'[68] Sophia is wisdom. Certainly she has cut their throat wisely, provided that [it is] into life, and reasonably, provided that [it is] into glory. 7.2 O the cleverness of family murder! O the skill of crime! O the proof of cruelty that has slain for that reason lest that one die whom she has killed! And therefore what follows? 'Sophia is sung with hymns at the gates,' in fact the death of martyrs is sung also. 'Sophia goes into the streets with firmness,' for she cuts the throat of her children for their well-being.[69] 7.3 However, on top of the walls, when she is filled with confidence, she says, exclaiming according to Isaiah, '"I am God's," and this one gives voice, "In the name of Jacob," and another writes, "In the name of Israel."'[70] O good mother! I wish also to be restored to her children in order that I may be killed by her. I wish to be killed in order that I may become her child. However, does she only cut the throat of her children or torture [them] as well? For I also hear God saying elsewhere, 'I shall burn them just as gold is burned and test them just as silver is tested.'[71] 7.4 At any rate [it is done] through the torments of fire and execution, through the examining martyrdoms of faith. The apostle knows also what kind of God he has written about when he writes, 'If God has not been sparing with [God's] Son, but surrendered him for us, how did [God] not present everything to us with him as well?'[72] You see in what way even divine Sophia has cut the throat of her own unique, firstborn and only-begotten Son, [who] certainly was going to live, or rather also was going to bring others back to life. 7.5 I am able to say with the Sophia of God, 'Christ is the one who surrendered himself for our offences.'[73] Sophia now has slaughtered herself as well. They know about a word not only by its sound but also by its sense, not only just with the ears {1082} ought they to be heard, but also with minds. The one who does not understand believes God {to be} cruel. Nevertheless, there is also a determination given for the one who does not understand, in order to control their rashness in understanding differently: 7.6 'For who knows the mind of the Lord? Who has been an advisor to [the Lord], who has trained [the Lord] or who has demonstrated to [the Lord] the way of understanding?'[74] But indeed in this present age it has been allowed that Diana of the Scythians or Mercury of the Gauls or Saturn of the Africans be appeased by human sacrifice[75] and Jupiter has been given a taste of human blood in the middle of the city in Latium[76] to the present day. Nobody reconsiders [it] or supposes [it is] not something rational or [is] the unfathomable will of their god. 7.7 If our God too had demanded martyrdoms for [the divine] self by claiming a personal victim, who would have reproached [God] about a deadly religion and mournful rites and the altar funeral pile and the undertaker priest and who would not have gone further and counted as happy the one whom God consumed?

8.1 Therefore, we insist on one position and on this alone we issue a challenge – whether martyrdoms have been commanded by God, in order that you may believe that they have been commanded with reason, if you recognize them as commanded, because God will have commanded nothing without reason. If indeed the death of the faithful has been honoured in the presence of [God], as David sings,[77] it is not the common death, I believe, to which everyone is destined – even though that too, [which derives] from the record of the transgression and from the merit of the condemnation, is disgraceful – but [it is] that [kind], which is addressed in this very work, [that comes] through the proof of religion and the battle of acknowledgement on behalf of justice and the oath [of baptism]. **8.2** [It is] just as Isaiah says, 'See how the just person perishes and no one takes it to heart, and just people are removed and no one takes notice. For from the face of injustice the just person perishes and will have honour with their burial.'[78] There too you have both the foretelling and reward of martyrdom. For from the beginning justice suffers violence. **8.3** As soon as God begins to be cultivated in worship, religion has received ill will. The one who has pleased God is slain and is so by a brother.[79] Impiety, from its own beginning by auguries, has finally pursued not only the truth of the just but also of the prophets as well, that it may more easily pursue foreign blood. David {1083} is harassed,[80] Elijah is driven away,[81] Isaiah is cut,[82] Jeremiah is stoned, Zechariah is slaughtered between altar and temple, leaving a permanent stain in his own blood on the stone pavement.[83] That one, with the ending of the law and of the prophets,[84] said [to be] not a prophet but a messenger,[85] with outrageous shedding of blood, is beheaded as the reward for a dancing girl.[86] **8.4** And certainly they who were being driven by the Spirit of God were directed by [the Spirit] to martyrdoms, in order that they might endure those things they had also foretold. Similarly, the three brothers together, when the dedication of the image of the king urged the mob to submission, were not ignorant of what faith – which alone in them had not been taken captive – demanded, namely dying in opposition to idolatry.[87] **8.5** For they too remembered the writing of Jeremiah to those to whom captivity was looming.

And now you will see that the gods of the Babylonians in gold and silver and wood are carried on shoulders, exposing to view the fear of the tribes. Therefore, be on your guard lest you too are the same as the foreigners and be seized with fear while you behold the mob behind and before them worshipping, but say in your soul, 'We ought to worship you, Lord.'[88]

8.6 And thus with confidence gained from God they spoke with great vigour of soul, they shake off those conditional threats of the king,

We have no need of responding to this your authority. For our God, whom we cultivate in worship, is able to tear us out from the furnace of fire and from your hands, and then it will become obvious to you that neither will we be in service to your idol nor will we worship your golden image which you have erected.[89]

8.7 O martyrdoms, perfected also without suffering! They suffered enough, they are burned enough, whom God protected on that account lest they were seen as having lied about his power. For certainly the caged and typically fierce lions would also have immediately devoured Daniel, who was a suppliant of no one except God and who, on that account, had been driven away and reproached by the Chaldeans, if the proper presumption of Darius about God had been due to deception. 8.8 For the rest, every preacher of God and worshipper who, having been summoned to idolatry, had refused submission, ought to have suffered, according to the nature of that reason too by which the truth ought to have been recommended both to those then there and to those following, in order that the suffering of its very defenders would affirm confidence on its behalf, because no one would have wanted [1084] to be slain in vain unless possessing the truth. Such commands and examples from the beginning show that faith [is] in debt to martyrdoms.

9.1 It remains, lest the ancient [covenant] perhaps had its own unique deposit, to review the Christian new [covenant] to see whether it is any different with regard to God and therefore [whether it is] also opposed [to the ancient covenant] with regard to its teaching, the Sophia of which does not know to cut the throat of her own children [it is claimed].[90] Obviously, the divinity, the will and the followers [would be] different in a Christ who has either not commanded any martyrdoms at all or [whose command] is going to be understood differently, who has exhorted no one to this kind of danger, [and] who promised nothing to those who suffered on his behalf because he does not wish them to suffer, and for that reason does he say at the beginning of his commands, 'Blessed are they who suffer persecution on account of justice, since the reign of heaven is theirs.'?[91] 9.2 This indeed [was said] in an absolute way for everyone. Then, exclusively for the apostles themselves [he says], 'Blessed will you be, when people shall have dishonoured you and shall have persecuted you and shall have spoken all evil against you because of me; rejoice and exult seeing that your reward is greater in heaven. For thus also their fathers did to the prophets[92] in order that it be foretold also that they themselves had to be slain, according to the example of the prophets. 9.3 Nonetheless, even if he had intended all this persecution for the apostles alone [as] a condition of that time, at any rate through them, with the total mystery [of faith], with the offspring of the name, [and] with the grafting of the Holy Spirit, he would have aimed it – by the teaching of [the need to] undergo persecution – at us too as disciples of the inheritance and as the shrub of the apostolic seed.[93] 9.4 For if he also directs himself again to the apostles – 'Behold, I shall send you like sheep among wolves,'[94] and 'Be on your guard against people, for they will hand you over to the assembly and they will lash you in their synagogues and you will be led to judges and kings for my sake as a testimony for them and their tribes,'[95] and so on – he then adds in addition, 'Moreover, brother will hand over brother, and a father [hand over] a son for death, and children will rise against their parents and cause them to die.'[96] Obviously he has foretold that iniquity, which we do not discover in the apostles, for others. 9.5 For none of them had suffered a brother or a father as traitor, as very many of us now [have]. {1085} Next he refers to the apostles, 'And you will be hated by everyone on account of my name.'[97] How much more [he means] us, [for] whom it is proper to be handed over by parents too? Thus, by arranging this handing over itself now for the apostles, now for everyone, he pours out the same end for everyone who bears the designation 'Christian', [for everyone] on whom the designation has settled with its law of hatred for him. 'However, the one who has endured right through to the end, that one will be saved.'[98] By enduring what, if not persecution, handing over, slaying? For to endure to the end is nothing other than to suffer an end. 9.6 And therefore it follows immediately, 'A disciple is not above the teacher, nor a servant above their lord',[99] because as the teacher and Lord himself endured persecution and handing over and slaying, by much more ought servants and disciples to pay the same price lest they are seen to be superior, having been exempted from iniquity when this itself ought to be sufficient glory for them – to be equal to the sufferings of the lord and teacher. Creating tolerance of these things, he warns them 'not to fear those who slay only the body but who are not able however to destroy the soul, but rather [they] ought to save their fear for the one who is able to slay both body and soul and do away with them in Gehenna'.[100] 9.7 Who are these murderers of the body alone if not the judges and kings mentioned above whom I believe to be men? Who also is the master of the soul if not God alone? Who is that one who threatens fire if not the one without whose will not one of the sparrows falls to the ground,[101] that is neither of the two substances of the human person, flesh or soul? [This is] because the number of hairs is recorded by [God].[102] 9.8 When he says above, 'Do not be afraid, you surpass many sparrows',[103] he promises in return they will not fall to the ground without reason, that is without advantage, if we choose more to be slain by people than by God. Therefore, 'all who shall have placed their acknowledgement[104] in me before people, I shall place my acknowledgement in them,[105] as well as before my Father who is in heaven, and all who shall have denied me before people, I shall deny them as well before my Father who is in heaven.'[106] The explanation and reason for the acknowledgement, as for the denial, is obvious, even if the arrangement is different. 9.9 The ones who acknowledge themselves as Christian {1086} declare themselves to be of Christ. The ones who are of Christ of necessity must be in Christ. If they are in Christ, certainly they will place their acknowledgement in Christ when they confess themselves to be Christian. For they are not able to be this unless they be in Christ. Further, by placing their acknowledgement in Christ they, who are in Christ himself, acknowledge Christ as well, while he too is in them in as much as they are Christian. For if you were to say 'day' you have shown the reality of the light, which constitutes day, even though you will not have said 'light'. Even if he would not have declared it directly [by saying] 'the one who shall have acknowledged me,'[107] the daily behaviour of acknowledgement is not different from the sense of the Lord's declaration. 9.10 The ones who acknowledge themselves for what they are, that is Christian, also acknowledge him by whom they are [Christian], that is Christ. As a consequence, the ones who have denied themselves [as] Christian have denied in Christ,[108] by denying themselves to be in Christ so long as they deny themselves [being] Christian. However, by also denying Christ in themselves while they deny themselves [being] in Christ, they will deny Christ too. Thus also the ones who will have denied [being] in Christ will deny Christ as well, and the ones who will have placed their acknowledgement in Christ will acknowledge Christ. And yet, it would have been enough therefore if the Lord had made only this declaration about acknowledging. 9.11 For, from the statement about acknowledgement it would have been possible already to have reached a determination about its opposite (that is, denial), that denial is repaid similarly by the Lord with denial, just as acknowledgement [is repaid] with acknowledgement. And therefore in the manner of the acknowledgement is understood the condition of the denial as well, it appears to apply not to another manner of denial about which the Lord has made some other declaration, than by saying about acknowledgement 'the one who shall have denied me' not 'the one who [shall have] denied [that they are] in me'. 9.12 For he had foreseen also that this violence, for the most part, in the assaulting of the name, would follow, such that the ones who had denied [being] Christian themselves were compelled to deny Christ himself too by blaspheming. And thus, not long ago, at the beginning of the disgrace,[109] we shuddered at those who struggled in this way against the entire faith of certain persons. And thus it will be a mistake to say, 'Even if I deny myself [as being] Christian, I shall not be denied by Christ, for I have not denied him.' 9.13 For from that denial so much will be grasped, because by denying themselves [as being] Christian, denying also that Christ [is] in themselves, they have denied him. However, there is more, because he also threatens shame with shame. 'The ones who will have been ashamed of me before people, [1087] I shall also be ashamed of them before my Father who is in heaven.'[110] For he knew that denial is formed above all by shame, that the state of mind is evident on one's face, and that the punctured area of disgrace is prior to [that] of the body.

10.1 [With regard to] the ones who truly believe that [it is] not here, that is not on the face of this earth, nor through this passage of life, nor before people of this shared nature, that [the requirement for] acknowledgement has been established, how much is [their] presumption contrary to the whole order of things that are to be experienced on this earth and in this life and under human power? Undoubtedly, when the souls have departed from their bodies, and have begun to be evaluated concerning the return through each level of the heavens and to be questioned about those secret mysteries of the heretics, they must offer acknowledgement before the true powers and true people, namely the Teleti, the Acineti, and the Abascanti of

Valentinus![111] **10.2** For they say, 'The Demiurge itself did not constantly approve our people, whom he counts as a drop in the bucket and dust on the threshing-floor,[112] and spittle and locusts,[113] and values the same as irrational beasts of burden.'[114] Clearly, it is so written. Yet for that reason we ought not to understand any other species of person except us, [a species] which, because it corresponds with reality, has been able to assume, with a sound acquisition, both the properties of species and [its own] individual [properties]. **10.3** For if life has been corrupted, such that having been sentenced for contempt it was united with contemptible things, [human] nature did not suffer immediately, such that another [species of person that the Valentinians advocate] might have been counted in its place. Rather nature is protected, even if life is stained. Nor does Christ know another people than those about whom he says, 'Whom do people affirm me to be?'[115] and 'in the same way you wish that people would do to you, thus also you do to them.'[116] **10.4** See whether he has protected the species, from which he expects also his witness and to which he orders the duty of justice. However, if I should demand that those heavenly people [the Valentinians advocate] be shown to me, Aratus would more easily sketch Perseus and Cepheus, Erigona and Ariadne among the stars [than show me their species of persons].[117] However, who prevented the Lord clearly determining also that the acknowledgement of the people ought to be made there [in heaven] where he openly declared his [people] were going to be, such that [, if the Valentinians were right,] he should have asserted thus, 'The one who has placed acknowledgement in me before the *heavenly* people, I shall also place my acknowledgement in them before my Father [1088] who is in heaven.'?[118] **10.5** He ought to have rescued me from that 'error' of [making] an earthly acknowledgement that he had not wished be undertaken, if he had taught a heavenly one [instead], because I know no other people except the dwellers of the earth, since no people themselves have been observed from then till now in heaven! Further, what kind of faith is it, such that I am tested there [in heaven], having been raised above after death, to where I would not be located if I had not been tested already, [and such that] there I was examined about my return, to where I would not be able to arrive if I had not been admitted [already]? **10.6** Heaven lies open to the Christian before the way [of getting there does] because [there is] no way into heaven if not for the one [for whom] heaven lies open, and the one who has reached [it] will enter. What gate-keeping angels do you affirm for me on a par with Roman superstition: a certain Carna, Forculus and Limentinus?[119] What powers do you appoint at the barriers? **10.7** If ever you have read in [the psalms of] David, 'Lift up your gates, rulers, and let the eternal gates be raised above and the king of glory will enter,'[120] if you have heard in Amos, 'The ones who build their way up to heaven and lay the foundation of their abundance on earth,'[121] know also that way was later made level by the footsteps of the Lord and the entrance was later opened by the strength of Christ, that no delay or investigation is going to occur at the border [into heaven] for Christians, who are not to be distinguished there but recognized, not interrogated but admitted. **10.8** For even if you think heaven is shut till now, remember that the Lord left his keys here to Peter and through him to the church,[122] which everyone here will carry with themselves after they have been interrogated and placed their acknowledgement. But the devil asserts boldly that acknowledgement ought to be located there [in heaven] in order that [the devil] may urge that denial ought to located here [on earth]. Clearly, I shall present excellent documents, I shall carry good keys with me, I shall have been esteemed by the forsaking of this [supposed] command *to fear* those who slay only the body yet can do nothing to the soul,[123] I shall stand firm respectably in the heavens, who, on earth, was not able to stand firm, I shall restrain the major powers who ceded nothing to the lesser, I shall certainly obtain admittance, having now been excluded![124] **10.9** It is enough to say the following, 'If acknowledgement ought to be placed in the heavens, also here there ought to be denial.'[125] For where there [is] one, there will be both. For rival things go together. It will be proper for persecution to be maintained in the heavens, which is a matter of acknowledgement or denial. And so, why do you delay, most bold heretic, [1089] to transfer into the heights [of heaven] every type of agitation against the Christians, and to place there, where Christ governs at the right of the Father,[126] in particular, the very hatred of the name? **10.10** Will you also establish there [in heaven] the synagogues of the Jews, the sources of persecution,[127] before whom the apostles suffered the whips, and [establish] the peoples of the tribes[128] there with their own circus, where even they willingly shout, 'For what reason does the third division[129] [of humanity] continue to exist?' **10.11** But you ought to produce in that same place [– heaven –] our brothers and fathers and sons and mothers-in-law and daughters-in-law and our family members, through whom betrayal has been arranged.[130] The same [goes for] kings, judges and armed powers, before whom the issue must be fought. Certainly, there will also be a prison in heaven, without light or unpleasant brightness, and perhaps with chains from belts [of

Orion], and for a rack the axis itself that turns [heaven around].[131] 10.12 But if a Christian has to be stoned [in heaven], hail will be present; if burned, lightning is at hand; if slaughtered, the hands of the armed Orion will be engaged; if finished off by the beasts, the northern sky will send the bears[132] and the zodiac [will send] bulls and lions.[133] The one who has endured these things to the end, that one will be saved! 10.13 Therefore, [is there] death and suffering and slaying and first acknowledgement in the heavens? And where [is] the necessary flesh for all this? Where [is] the body that alone has to be slain by people? A solid reason has entrusted these things to us [to be said] even in a sportive way; nor will anyone raise an objection to [the conditions for acknowledgement in heaven rather than on earth] I have just written about, in such a way that one is not compelled to transfer every wave of persecution, every powerful instrument that brings it about, there [to heaven] where acknowledgement shall have been given a forum. 10.14 If indeed acknowledgement is extracted by persecution, and persecution is perfected by acknowledgment, it is not possible to arrange both entrance and exit, that is beginning and end, not to follow one another. Furthermore, hatred of the name will be here, persecution erupts here, betrayal brings [people] forth here, interrogation compels here, torment rages violently here, and acknowledgement or denial completes this whole series here on earth. 10.15 Therefore, if these other parts of the series are here, acknowledgement will not be elsewhere. If acknowledgement [is] elsewhere, the other things will not be here. Certainly the other things are not elsewhere, thus neither [is] acknowledgement in heaven. Or if they wish that their method of heavenly interrogation and acknowledgement be different, it follows that they ought to construct their own order very differently from the arrangement that is noted in the Scriptures. 10.16 And we are able to say, 'Let them see whether this earthly order of interrogation and acknowledgement, which flows from the opportunity [provided by] persecution and public discord, [1090] is wholly safe by its own faith, [and whether] it should thus be believed just as also it is written, [and] should thus be understood just as it is heard.' Here [on this earth] we are maintaining the whole order [of events], as the Lord himself has selected no other region of the world. For what did he add after the end of acknowledgement and denial? 10.17 'Do not think that I have come in order to bring peace on earth, but a sword' certainly on earth. 'For I come to divide a man against his father and a daughter against her mother and a mother-in-law against her daughter-in-law, and a man's enemies are his own family members.'[134] 'And thus it is brought about, such that brother betrays brother to death, and father [betrays] son, and children rebel against their parents and cause their death.'[135] 'And the one who has endured to the end will be safe.'[136] To such an extent this whole order of the Lord's sword, not having been sent to heaven but to earth, established acknowledgement there as well, which, by enduring to the end, is about to suffer death.

11.1 Therefore, in the same way we maintain that other expressions too are relevant to the status of martyrdom. 'The one who has made even more of their soul than of me is not worthy of me,'[137] that is, the one who would prefer to live by denying me than to die by acknowledging me, and 'the one who has found their soul shall lose it, the one who truly has lost [it] on my behalf shall find it.'[138] 11.2 For similarly, [the person] finds it [but only temporarily][139] who denies {it in order} to gain life, as [that person] shall lose {it} in Gehenna who thinks to themselves they have gained it by denying. On the other hand, [the person] shall lose it in the present, who is slain when they have acknowledged, but is also going to find it in eternal life. 11.3 Finally, judges themselves, when they encourage denial, say, 'Save your soul!' and 'Do not lose your soul!' How would Christ speak if not in the way a Christian should be treated? But when he prohibits planning a response to the tribunal,[140] he equips his domestic servants, he promises in return that the Holy Spirit is going to answer [for them],[141] and when he wishes a brother [or sister] to be visited in prison he orders care for the acknowledger,[142] and when he affirms that God will be making vindication for {God's} chosen ones he consoles their sufferings.[143] {1091} In the parable of the seed, after having made the soil dry, he represents the heat of persecutions.[144] 11.4 If these [expressions] are thus not accepted as they were uttered, [as they should be accepted,] without a doubt they suggest more than the sound they make. There is one thing in the sound and another in the sense, as with allegories, parables and riddles. Therefore, whatever wind of argument these scorpions may have taken hold of, wherever they may have thrust themselves with their point, there is now one line [of argument]: they shall be challenged on the facts themselves as to whether they be completed according to the Scriptures, 11.5 as [it would] then [mean that] another thing will be signified in the Scriptures if the thing itself would not be found to exist. For what is written must happen. Further, what is written then will happen, if something else does not. Behold, however, we are hated by all people because of the name, as it is written; we are betrayed by those closest to us, as it is written; we are brought before the powers, interrogated, tortured, place acknowledgement, and are slaughtered, as it is written. Thus the Lord determined. 11.6 If he determined these things differently, why do those things he determined not happen [any] differently, that is, in the manner he [supposedly] determined? Nevertheless, they do not happen differently than he determined. Therefore, just as they happen, thus he determined, and just as he determined, thus they happen. For neither would they have been permitted to happen differently than he determined, nor would he himself have determined differently than he wished [them] to happen. 11.7 Thus these Scriptures will signify nothing other than we recognize in reality. Or, if those things that have been proclaimed are not yet occurring, how are things occurring that have not been proclaimed? For these things that are occurring have not been proclaimed if the things that have been proclaimed are different and are not the things occurring. But now, because the things, which are believed [by the Valentinians] to have been said differently [from what is] in the words, are a reality, what would happen if the deeds should be found to be different? 11.8 But this will be a perversity of faith not to believe what has been proved, [and] to presume what has not been proved. To that perversity I shall make this objection too: that if these things that are thus occurring – just as they have been written – are not those which have been proclaimed, the others too ought not thus to be occurring as they have been written, lest they themselves also be in danger of being excluded by the example of these, as one thing is in the words, another is in the reality. It remains that the things proclaimed are not yet seen when they have happened, if [1092] they are proclaimed differently than they have to happen. And in what way will the things that have not been proclaimed be believed, because they were not proclaimed in the way they happened? Thus the heretics believe those things that have not been proclaimed by not believing those things that have been proclaimed as they have been proved.[145]

12.1 Who now should know the innermost part of the Scriptures better than the followers of Christ themselves? [They are] the ones whom the Lord adopted for himself as disciples, certainly who should be taught everything, and he set [them as] teachers for us, certainly to instruct in everything. To whom had he declared the meaning of his words more than to Peter, John, James and afterwards to Paul[146] (whom he also made a participant in paradise before martyrdom[147]), to whom he revealed the likeness of his glory? Or do they also write differently than they think, those teachers of deceit not of truth?[148]

12.2 Peter even says to those in Pontus, 'How great [is] the glory if you endure without being punished as offenders. For this is [God's] favour [to us]. In this also you have been called, since Christ also suffered for us, leaving you an example of himself in order that you may follow after his steps.'[149] 12.3 And again, 'Beloved, do not be terrified of the trial by fire that is set in motion among you, as if [something] new has happened to you. For in accord with what you share in the sufferings of Christ, rejoice in order that you may rejoice in the revelation of his glory with exultation. If you are dishonoured in the name of Christ, you are blessed because glory and the Spirit of God rest on you, provided that no one of you suffers as a murderer or a thief or an evil-doer or one who desires what is another's. If, however, as a Christian [one suffers], do not blush but glorify the Lord by that name.'[150]

12.4 John truly exhorts in order that we may lay down our souls on behalf of our brothers [and sisters],[151] denying there is any fear in love. 'For perfect love throws out fear, as fear has punishment and the one who fears has not been perfected in love.'[152] 12.5 What other kind of fear should we understand if not [the one that is] the author of denial? What perfect love does he assert if not the one that puts fear to flight and the one that stimulates acknowledgement? With what punishment may he punish fear if not that which the one who denies is about to repay with body {1093} and soul slain in Gehenna?[153] Even though he teaches dying on behalf of the brothers [and sisters], how much more for the Lord? This has been established sufficiently from his [book of] Revelation to persuade [us]. 12.6 For indeed the Spirit had given a commission to the messenger to the church of the Smyrneans [to say], 'Behold, the devil will hurl some from your number into prison that you may be tested for ten days. Be faithful up to death and I shall give you the crown of life.'[154] 12.7 Also [the messenger speaks] to the Pergameni about Antipas, the most faithful martyr, who was killed in the dwelling place of Satan.[155] Again, to the Philadelphians, [the Spirit attests] the fact that the one who did not deny the name of the Lord would be freed from the final trial.[156] 12.8 Next, to every victor [the Spirit] promises now the tree of life and pardon from the second death,[157] now the hidden manna with the white pebble and the unknown name,[158] now the power of the iron rod and the brightness of the morning star,[159] now to be clothed in a white garment and not to be blotted out from the book of life and to become a column in the temple of God, having been inscribed with the name of God and of the Lord and of the heavenly Jerusalem,[160] now to reside with the Lord on his throne,[161] which once was denied to the sons of Zebedee.[162] 12.9 Who [are] these blessed victors if not proper martyrs? For indeed, theirs [are] the victories, whose also [are] the fights, but indeed theirs [are] the fights, whose also [is] the blood. But also, in the meantime, the souls of the martyrs rest quiet under the altar and they nourish their patience with the assurance of revenge and, having been covered with long garments, they use the dazzling white [garment] of brightness until others also may fill the share of their glory.[163] 12.10 For the innumerable multitude clothed in white is revealed, distinguished with the palms of victory, no doubt triumphant over the antichrist,[164] as one of the elders affirms, 'These are the ones who are coming from that great affliction and have washed their clothing and whitened it in the blood of the lamb.'[165] For the attire of the soul is flesh. Even filth is washed away by baptism, but stains are truly made white by martyrdom. For Isaiah also promises whiteness like the snow and wool from the red and scarlet.[166] 12.11 Even the drunkenness of great {1094} Babylon, when it is described as drunk with the blood of the holy ones,[167] is, without a doubt, catered for from the cups of martyrdoms, the terror of which, since it is about to be endured, is equally shown. For among all the deceitful, or rather before [them] all, [are] the fearful. 'However, the lot for the fearful,' says [the author] – and then follows the others [in the list] – '[will be] in the pool of fire and sulphur.'[168] Thus fear, [as he says] in his letter, which love throws out,[169] has punishment.

13.1 In fact Paul, the persecutor turned apostle, who first poured out the blood of the church (afterwards changing the sword for the pen and converting the sword into a plough[170]) [and who first was] a greedy wolf of Benjamin[171] (but later himself carrying food just like Jacob[172]), how he commends the desired martyrdoms now also for himself! 13.2 When rejoicing about the Thessalonians he says, '. . . such that we boast about you in the ecclesial community of God in view of your tolerance and faith in every persecution and affliction, in which you manifest the right judgement of God in order that you may be held worthy of [God's] reign, for which you also are suffering.'[173] 13.3 Just as to the Romans [he writes], 'However, not only [that], but also exulting in afflictions certain that affliction brings about tolerance, and tolerance [brings about] trial, trial however [brings about] hope, and hope does not disappoint.'[174] 13.4 And again, 'Because if [we are] children [we are] heirs as well, heirs even of God, but co-heirs of Christ. Since we suffer with him, we are also glorified with him. For I calculate that the sufferings of this present time are not worthy of the glory that has to be revealed to us.'[175] And for that reason later he says,

Who will separate us from the love of Christ? Affliction or difficulty or hunger or nakedness or danger or the sword?

As it is written, 'For your sake we are killed the whole day; we have been counted as a flock for the slaughter.' But in all this we are overcome on account of him who loved us. For we are persuaded that neither death nor life, nor strength, nor heights nor depth nor [any] other circumstance is able to separate us from the love of God, which is in Christ Jesus our Lord.[176]

13.5 But also retelling his own sufferings to the Corinthians he certainly prescribed suffering, '. . . in my more abundant efforts, in my numerous imprisonments, [1095] and in my frequent [brushes with] death, five times from the Jews I received forty less one [strokes of the lash], three times having been struck with rods, once having been stoned . . .'[177] and so on. 13.6 If these misfortunes seem greater than martyrdoms, yet again he says, 'On account of this I count it as good [to be] in infirmities, in injuries, in deprivation, in persecutions, in difficulties for the sake of Christ.'[178] 13.7 [He says] as well in an earlier section, 'We are the ones who are troubled in everything but not confined, who are wanting but not in great need, who are hunted by persecutions but not forsaken, who are thrown down but not perishing, always carrying around the death of Christ in our bodies.'[179] 'But even if our exterior person is damaged' – the flesh no doubt by the force of persecution – 'yet the interior is renewed daily' – no doubt the soul by the hope of the promises. 13.8 'For our affliction in the present time, which is light and momentary, accomplishes step by step an eternal weight of glory, with us perceiving not the things that are seen, but the things that are not seen. In fact, the things that are seen are temporal' – speaking about misfortunes – 'the things that are not seen really are eternal'– promising rewards.[180] 13.9 Yet writing to the Thessalonians from his chains, he affirmed them certainly as blessed to whom it had been given not only to believe in Christ but even to suffer for him. He says, 'Having the same contest that you both have seen in me and now hear.'[181] 'For although I am offered as a sacrifice, I rejoice and rejoice with you all, as you also rejoice and rejoice with me in the same way.'[182] 13.10 You see how he defines the happiness of martyrdoms, for whom it becomes a solemn festival with mutual joy. When he finally came very close [to this happiness], he writes to Timothy as rejoicing about his prospects, 'For I am now offered up, and the time of separation is at hand. I have fought a good contest, I have completed the course, I have guarded the faith, the crown that the Lord will give to me on that day remains' – without a doubt [the crown] of suffering.[183] 13.11 He had roused [them] enough in the earlier [section], 'The word [is] faithful. For if we are dead with Christ, we shall also live with [him], if we have suffered, we shall also reign with [him], if we have denied [him], he shall deny us, if we do not believe, he is faithful {1096} [since] he cannot deny himself.'[184] 'Therefore, do not be troubled by the witness of our Lord nor of me his prisoner'[185] because he had earlier said, 'For God did not give us a spirit of fear but of bravery and of love and of a sound mind.'[186] 13.12 For we suffer with bravery from love of God and with a sound mind, when we suffer on account of innocence. But also if anywhere he prescribes tolerance for what more is he foreseeing it than for suffering? If anywhere he removes [people] from idolatry for what more is he removing them than for martyrdoms? 14.1 Plainly he warns the Romans 'to be subject to all powers because there is no power except from God'[187] and 'because he [the ruler] does not carry the sword without reason, because he is the attendant of God, but also the avenger for wrath to those who have done evil.'[188] For he had already said before, 'For rulers are not fearful for those who do good but for those who do evil. However, do you wish not to fear the power? Do what is good and you will receive back praise from it. Therefore, he is an attendant of God for your good. But you do what is evil, be afraid.'[189] 14.2 Thus he orders you to be subject to the powers that be, not as an opportunity for eluding martyrdoms but as a challenge to live well, and even [to live] with regard for those [in authority] as if [they were] aids of justice [and] assistants of divine judgement, who even here prejudge the guilty. Further, he also maintains the manner in which he wishes you to be subject to the powers that be, ordering, 'Give back tribute to whom tribute [is owed] and tax to whom tax [is owed],'[190] that is, 'To Caesar the things which are of Caesar and to God the things of God.'[191] The human person, however, [belongs to] God alone. 14.3 No doubt Peter had agreed that the king too should be honoured, such that he is honoured as king only when he pursues his own proper interests, when he is far from divine honours. And because brother, father and mother will be loved together with God, they will not be equal [to God].[192] It will not be permitted to love another above God, not even life.

15.1 Surely, therefore, the letters of the apostles are now well-known? 'And do we, simple souls and mere doves, make mistakes everywhere [in our interpretation of these letters] willingly?' [the Valentinians ask.] I believe [their mistake comes] from a desire for living. This may well be the case, with the result that they make their own interpretation of the letters. Nevertheless, we know the things the apostles suffered, the doctrine is clear. I become aware of

this simply by scanning Acts [of the Apostles], I do no seek it out.
15.2 The prisons there, the chains, whips, stones, swords, the attacks
of the Jews, the meetings of the tribes, the tribunes' [1097] records,
the hearings [before] kings, the tribunals of the proconsuls, and the
name of Caesar do not need interpretation. That Peter is struck,[193]
that Stephen is crushed,[194] that James is sacrificed,[195] that Paul is
dragged away,[196] has been written with their own blood. 15.3 And if
a heretic has [tried to] drag down the faith by [using] commentaries,
the public records of the empire will speak [for us], as do the stones
of Jerusalem.[197] We read in the *Lives of the Caesars* that Nero was the
first who stained the rising faith with blood at Rome.[198] Then Peter
is roped around the waist by another[199] when he is tied to the cross.
Then Paul obtains the birth of Roman citizenship when he is reborn
therewith the nobility of martyrdom.[200] 15.4 Whenever I read these
now, I discover suffering. It makes no difference to me which teachers
of martyrdom I follow, whether [it is] the thinking or the death of the
apostles, except that I also recognize the thinking in their deaths. For
they would suffer nothing that they had not known earlier they were
going to suffer. Although Agabus had foretold in gesture the chains
of Paul, the weeping and praying disciples had prayed in vain that
he not entrust himself to Jerusalem.[201] 15.5 For he says, having been
animated by what he had always taught, 'Why are you weeping and
saddening my heart? But I have wished not only to suffer chains in
Jerusalem, but even to die for the name of my Lord, Jesus Christ.'[202]
And thus they stopped by saying, 'Let the will of the Lord be done,'[203]
no doubt believing that sufferings belong to the will of God. 15.6 For
they had tried to hold [him] back, not by a council of dissuasion but of
love, as ones who yearned for the apostle, not as ones who dissuaded
from martyrdom. But if then, at that time, Prodicus or Valentinius
had been standing by, suggesting that acknowledgement ought not
be placed before people on earth who are less than truthful, – lest God
[be seen to] thirst for human blood or Christ [be seen to] demand
a recompense through [someone else's] suffering, as if he himself
were going to achieve salvation through [someone else's suffering]
– immediately he would have heard from a servant of God what the
devil had heard from the Lord, 'Stand back, Satan! You are offensive
to me.' It is written, "You shall worship the Lord, your God and serve
only [God]."'[204] 15.7 But even now he will be bound to hear [these
words], in as much as, long after he has spread them, those venoms
harm none of the weak, unless one of the faithful does not drink our
potion before, or even after, [being bitten by the heretic scorpion].

13

ON THE VEILING OF VIRGINS
(De Virginibus Velandis)

Introduction

Timothy Barnes dates *On the Veiling of Virgins* during Tertullian's Montanist period, after *On Prayer* (which is considered an early work), *On the Apparel of Women II* and *On the Military Crown*, to 208 or 209, or possibly later according to his revised chronology (Barnes 1985: 44, 46, 140, 328). Fredouille allowed a date between 208 and 212 (Fredouille 1972: 487–8), after *On Prayer* and roughly at the same time as *On the Military Crown*. In the most recent edition of the text, Schulz-Flügel places it after *On Prayer* (Schulz-Flügel 1997: 17), *On the Military Crown* and *On the Soul*, at the same time as *On the Resurrection of the Dead*, after 213, but before the writing of *On Monogamy* (Schulz-Flügel 1997: 44–6). There is some importance in establishing at least a comparative chronology, even if an absolute one is impossible, for some of the same issues are to be found in *On the Military Crown* 4 and *On Prayer* 21–2. Are we able to determine a sequence for these three treatises?

In *On the Military Crown*, Tertullian pointed to Jewish women who were all veiled and said that this practice was not prescribed anywhere (Rebekah veiling herself when she saw Isaac – Gen 24:65 – could not be taken as prescriptive for the Jews because it would be a precedent only for unmarried women – girls more realistically – when they were about to marry – *On the Military Crown* 4.2). It was custom that gave the practice the force of law (*On the Military Crown* 4.4–5). Tertullian's ultimate argument was that custom rather than explicit scriptural teaching was the force behind a Christian's refusal to wear the military garland. In *On the Military Crown*, Tertullian held out a positive estimation of the value of custom. In *On the Veiling of Virgins*, he held the opposite position. In both these treatises he was writing to that part of the Christian community that did not support his thinking. In one, he found that custom supported him; in the other, it did not (although he spent the early chapters of *On the Veiling of Virgins* arguing for apostolic custom against local custom). Interestingly, in *On the Military Crown*, he put the question of Christian women being veiled aside (*On the Military Crown* 4.2), quite possibly because he was aware that he was skating on thin ice – he knew that if he mentioned them his opponents could turn his appeal to custom (with regard to the military garland) against him and argue that the custom of not forcing virgins to be veiled should be upheld as a legitimate custom. It would seem to me that these two treatises ought to be dated to around the same time, for veiling and custom both seemed very much on Tertullian's mind and yet he had to be careful in what he said.

On Prayer 21–2 has many similarities with *On the Veiling of Virgins*. The question is whether Tertullian expanded or contracted from one to the other. It has generally been held that *On Prayer*, which does not show any signs of Montanist influence, must be earlier than *On the Veiling of Virgins*, which does. A contrast between the structures of the two relevant parts of the treatises would support this notion, namely that *On the Veiling of Virgins* is an expanded form of what appeared in the earlier and briefer *On Prayer*. *On the Veiling of Virgins* seems to me to have a smooth and flowing tripartite structure, whereas the material in *On Prayer* seems more jumbled and haphazardly arranged. Further, the attitude about veiling virgins is a little more relaxed in *On Prayer* (22.10), where it is granted that no one ought to be compelled to be veiled. Later, because some of the unveiled virgins wanted to 'liberate' their veiled sisters (*On the Veiling of Virgins* 3.4), Tertullian's attitude hardened – all female persons must be veiled from the time they reach puberty. It was this incident that was probably the occasion that prompted him to revisit this issue (twice – once in Greek and then in Latin) about which he had written in *On Prayer* some years previously.

There is indeed an evident rhetorical structure to the treatise. It begins with the *propositio*, the central argument, that virgins ought to be veiled from puberty (1.1a). As will become clear from the rest of the treatise, the reference is to the fact that virgins were appearing at the ecclesial gathering without being veiled. Then an *exordium*, an opening, follows (1.16–17). Here Tertullian contrasted custom with truth: our understanding of truth grows and develops and therefore must replace customs that are contrary to the truth, no matter how well established those customs might be. The custom of some Carthaginian virgins not being veiled in public, which seems to have been well established, fell into that category according to Tertullian.

God's truth is revealed only gradually (illustrated through the organic metaphor), but, now that the fullness of truth has been revealed through the Paraclete, custom must change. Tertullian announced that he was going to present arguments from the Scriptures, from reason and from ecclesiastical teaching or practical instruction. The *narratio* (2.1–3.5b) tells the story of the origins of the true custom of veiling virgins (which he traced to the practice of churches founded by the apostles or their associates) and the false custom of not veiling virgins (which has its origins in lustful desire).

The main body of the treatise is *confirmatio* and *refutatio* (positive and negative arguments supporting his position) (3.5c–15.3). This section is divided on the basis of the threefold pattern of argumentation: Scripture, nature and teaching, with the arguments for and against being presented in turn. He began with the scriptural arguments (3.5c–6.3). Here he first considered 1 Cor 11:5–16. The non-veiled virgins and their supporters had argued that Paul had directed only women to have their heads covered, and they defined 'women' as 'married women' only. As virgins, they considered that Paul had exempted them. Tertullian's response was to show that 'woman' is the genus that includes 'virgin' as a species. He turned to a passage like 1 Cor 7:34 (4.1–5), where Paul distinguished between virgins and women, to argue that, in 1 Corinthians 11, if he had wanted to make the same distinction, Paul would have been explicit about it, which he was not. He also turned to Gen 2:23–4 (5.1–5) to argue that Eve was called a woman when she was obviously still a virgin. Finally, he made use of Lk 1:26–8 (6.1–3), where Mary, though still a virgin, was called a woman.

After the arguments from Scripture come the arguments from nature or reason (7.1–8.4). The first argument here is that men were in authority over women. The implication is that women should wear something over their heads to indicate that there was someone in authority over them. If this applied to women, it must of necessity include virgins. Even though we find this argument in 1 Cor 11:3, Tertullian was not making an argument from Scripture, but, like Paul and following Paul, was appealing to what was commonly accepted as being the natural order of things. The second argument is that if women were not going to be veiled then they should cut their hair as men do. Yet it was against nature for women to have short hair. Even the long hair itself was a kind of natural indicator that women should be veiled. This is found in 1 Corinthians 11. Again, if this applied to all women, it applied to virgins. As Paul did in 1 Cor 11: 10, Tertullian stated that women should be veiled to prevent them tempting the angels (as well as being an indication of their submission to male authority). Although he claimed to be presenting arguments from nature, Tertullian's knowledge of what was natural is very much shaped by the Pauline presentation to the Corinthians. Even though we would probably want to classify everything from chapter 2 to chapter 7 as arguments from Scripture, it is clear that, by dividing them into arguments from Scripture and arguments from nature, Tertullian was attempting to make his case look more impressive and convincing.

In a digression involving Gen 6:1–2 (7.2b–4a) about the angels being tempted by virgins, Tertullian argued that virgins too must be counted as part of Paul's statement about women tempting angels. Next comes a typical rhetorical technique of developing an argument by considering the contrary position to what one had just said (8.1–4). This Tertullian did by considering the implications of men having short hair and not being veiled. The fact that no one insists on veiling boys, even though they are not mentioned as having the exemption that men did, comes from the fact that everyone understands that boys are included as part of the category 'men.' So too, virgins should be understood as part of the category 'women' and veiled.

The last of the three groups of arguments comes from ecclesiastical teaching (9.1–15.3). The first teaching comes from the Scriptures and is about women not speaking in the ecclesial gathering (9.1b), upon which Paul insisted in 1 Corinthians. Perhaps one may think that Tertullian ought to have included this in his arguments from Scripture. What he seems to have done is to have distinguished scriptural passages that have explicit disciplinary or instructional material from other types of passages where such material was more implicit. Tertullian's argument here only works if the reality was that no Christian woman spoke in the ecclesial assembly. If Tertullian's opponents were forced to concede that virgins did not speak in the ecclesial gathering, even though Paul had only mentioned women not speaking, then they would have to concede that virgins ought to be veiled, even though Paul had only mentioned women.

Tertullian next countered an argument that allowing virgins to be unveiled distinguished them from married women (9.1c) by stating that there were other ways to recognize them, if indeed they needed to be recognized. Similarly, giving them a seat with the widows (9.2–3) was inappropriate because the latter had proven themselves worthy of honour after many years of testing. Another contrary argument is offered in chapter 10: if female virgins were to be distinguished by not being veiled then male virgins ought to honoured (10.1–2a). Even further, all men ought to be more honoured than any woman because male sexual self-control was more difficult to maintain than (female) virginity (10.2b–4). That men were not honoured thus meant that virgins had even less claim to marks of distinction.

Tertullian responded to a further objection in chapter 11. The case had obviously been put that if virgins were to be veiled then that should be applied to all prepubescent girls as well. Their argument obviously was that if prepubescent girls were not to be veiled then neither should virgins. They could have pointed out that if Tertullian's earlier statement about 'woman' being the general term was true, then all females, even young girls, ought to be included. In response, Tertullian steered away from this flaw in his position and argued that it was only from the time of puberty that the law of veiling was necessary because at this age a girl was marriageable and had sexual self-awareness (11.1–2). So his position was that from the age of twelve a girl should be veiled not because she was a virgin but because she could be a wife and a mother (even though she was not – of course, girls from that age who were married were veiled) and because she was a temptation to men. Women who were engaged were veiled even though they were still virgins (presumably) because of that sexual self-awareness (11.3). When a girl became a woman she could no longer be classed as a virgin. She must dress like an adult and that included wearing the veil (11.4–12.2). Here Tertullian was not using 'woman' as the term for the genus but as equivalent to 'adult female person.'

Tertullian argued that these unveiled virgins were living a contradiction in that they were content to be veiled when out in public, in the glare of Christian and non-Christian alike, and only reserved the right to be unveiled when gathered together with other Christians in liturgy (13.1–14.1). The only reason Tertullian could adduce for this was their desire to gain the spotlight and to impress the men in the gathering. He would not accept their argument that they were glorifying God by their distinguishable dress. The trouble with impressing men was that it often led to pregnancy and to the contradiction of a young woman proclaiming her virginity by not wearing the veil while being pregnant (14.2–5). She was trapped because she could not suddenly start wearing a veil (to acknowledge that she was no longer physically a virgin) without drawing scandal upon herself. By way of contrast, true virginity does nothing to draw attention to itself; rather, it hides itself away (15.1–3).

The treatise ends with a *peroratio*, a conclusion (16.1–17.5). The threefold division of the treatise into arguments from Scripture, nature and ecclesiastical teaching is again mentioned (16.1–2). He then makes a series of direct appeals. The first is to all women to be veiled (16.3). Mothers are mentioned specifically. We are to take this as evidence that even some married women were seeking to avoid the duty of wearing the veil by wearing scarves that were too small, as he mentioned a little later (17.1–2a). The second appeal is to the virgins themselves to be veiled because they are married to Christ (16.4). In contrast with those women who wore the short scarves, Tertullian mentioned pagan practice of complete covering (17.2b–3a) and the revelation of a particular prophecy (17.3b). Those women who pretend to be covered by the smallest of scarves are no different than ostriches, which hide their heads (here Tertullian's simile breaks down a little I think) and think they are completely hidden (17.4–5a).

From these comments about the structure of the treatise we may turn to a few other questions. Just who were these virgins whom Tertullian was addressing? Were they merely rebellious and unruly, unmarried teenage girls or was it a group of consecrated virgins? We know that in Carthage in Tertullian's time there were women and men who were each constituted as an *ordo* of virgins (*On Exhortation to Chastity* 13.4), just as there was an *ordo* of widows (*On the Veiling of Virgins* 9.2). At the end of our treatise Tertullian refers to the virgins as being married to Christ (*On the Veiling of Virgins* 16.4). Unless we are reading this with too modern an understanding, one may conclude that there were virgins who dedicated themselves to remain as virgins for the rest of their lives (or perhaps only for a period of years, although there is no evidence to suggest this). On the other hand, Tertullian's position, announced at the beginning of the work (*On the Veiling of Virgins* 1.1), is that all girls be veiled from puberty. It would seem that his words must be taken as directed not only to those who had taken some vow of virginity (was such a vow taken at the age of twelve?) but to those who were simply still unmarried during their teenage years (and beyond). Further, in the section 11.4–12.2, Tertullian was concerned with those girls who were not married off at the start of puberty, as was most normally the case, because of some inexplicable reason on the part of their parents. The reference seems to be simply to unmarried female adolescents and young adults. What we need is more evidence about the age of girls marrying in the age of the Severan emperors and the percentage of those who did not marry, evidence not readily to hand. My conclusion, based on *On the Veiling of Virgins* 11.4 is that Tertullian was writing about Christian girls who had reached puberty and were not yet married as well as with those who had taken a vow of virginity (*continentiae uotum*) who could have been adolescent or adult (although such a distinction did not operate at this time).

What are we talking about when we mention veils? Perhaps today we think of the images of what we in the West would consider the more extreme form of a Moslem veil – something like a long hood that completely covered the head and reached down the body. This was not what Tertullian had in mind. In fact, he mentioned something very similar when he referred to pagan women of Arabia (*On the Veiling of Virgins* 17.2). The Roman mantle worn by all post-pubescent women outdoors perhaps was more of a shawl that was draped around the body, a little like the male toga, which could be pulled up over the head when needed (when out of one's own home) thus leaving the face exposed (Croom 2000: 87–8). It was the distinctive sign of the married woman and her modesty. Yet we do not know what adult unmarried women wore when in public. It may be that the push for not wearing the veil among unmarried females who had left childhood behind was not restricted only to the Christians, although there is no evidence to suggest this.

What was Tertullian's goal in writing this treatise? He certainly followed the Pauline tradition of accepting that women were inferior to men. I do not find him being any more extreme in his views than any other male, whether Christian or not, of the time. What I find interesting is that Tertullian's Montanism was a form of Christianity that valued women rather more highly than their mainstream fellow Christians – two of the founders of the movement had been women, and women prophets (who were presumably Montanist) did speak in the community, but only after the liturgical assembly had concluded (*On the Soul* 9.4). Could it be, given that Paul had insisted that any woman who prophesied with her head uncovered brought shame upon herself (1 Cor 11:4), that Tertullian wanted not only married but unmarried women to be veiled in the liturgical gathering, not so that they could simply be submissive to their menfolk but so that there could no hindrance to any woman exercising a prophetic ministry?

Who are these unveiled women? It would too simplistic to suggest that they were non-Montanist Christians who were of a more libertine persuasion, whereas the veiled were the more conservative Montanist virgins. There may be great truth in this, but it could also be that some Montanist virgins in particular were following their non-Montanist counterparts. If what I wrote above about Tertullian's desire to keep the virgins eligible to prophesy after liturgy is true, then this makes some sense; he would naturally be all the more upset about those who should be more interested in the gift of prophecy throwing away their opportunity, than those (non-Montanist) virgins, for whom prophecy was not such an issue. This would also make sense of the reference to the uncovered woman prophesying in 17.3b.

This text has not been translated into English since the middle of the nineteenth century in the Ante-Nicene Library/Ante-Nicene Fathers series. The text I have used is Dekkers in *Corpus Christianorum*. I have made very few emendations to this text. I have consulted the German translation of Stücklin (1974), the Italian translation of Gramaglia (1984), and the French translation of Mattei in Schulz-Flügel's *Sources Chrétiennes* (1997).

Text

[1209] 1.1 Since I have taken the particular trouble of [expressing] my opinion already [in Greek], I shall show in Latin as well that it is proper that our virgins be veiled from when they reach puberty.[1] [I shall show that] truth, to which nothing – either intervals of time, or patronages of person, or privilege of places – is able to object, demands this.

In fact, having begun from some ignorance or innocence, custom generally is strengthened by them into habit through repetition, and so is defended against the truth.[2] But Christ our Lord has named himself truth, not custom.[3] 1.2 If Christ is forever and prior to everything,[4] [then] equally truth is an everlasting and ancient thing. Therefore, let them, for whom what is old in itself is [taken as] new, take notice. It is not so much novelty as truth that restrains heresy. Whatever runs counter to the truth will be heresy, even if it is an old custom.

Besides, the one who does not understand anything does so through their own fault. However, what is thus not understood ought to have been asked about, just as what is understood ought to have been accepted. 1.3 Indeed, the rule of faith is entirely one, alone unchangeable and unalterable. Of course [the rule is] for believing in the only almighty God, the founder of the world, and in [God's] son Jesus Christ, born from Mary the virgin, crucified under Pontius Pilate, revived[5] from the dead on the third day, taken back into heaven, sitting now at the right of the Father, going to come to judge the living and the dead, even through the resurrection of the flesh.[6]

1.4 While this law of faith endures, other matters of teaching and conduct now allow the novelty of improvement, that is to say by the grace of God operating and making progress until the end. For how is it possible, while the devil is always operating and is daily adding to his abilities with regard to injustice, that the work of God should either cease or should stop progressing?

Therefore, when the Lord sent the Paraclete[7] [it was] in order that, as human inferiority was not able to grasp all things at once, teaching may be guided and arranged and brought to perfection gradually by that substitute of the Lord, the Holy Spirit. 1.5 'I still have many things to say to you,' he says, 'but you are not yet able to bear them. When that Spirit of truth has come, it will lead you into all truth and will declare to you the things to come.'[8] And indeed he made mention about this work [of the Spirit] earlier [in the gospel].[9] What then is the function of the Paraclete {1210} if not this: that teaching is directed, the Scriptures are made known, understanding is reformed, and that it is advanced towards better things?[10]

Nothing is without its time; all things await their opportunity. Furthermore, Ecclesiastes says, '[There is] a time for everything.'[11] Consider that creation itself is advanced gradually towards fruition. 1.6 The grain is first and from the grain the stem shoots and from the stem the shrub struggles forth. Then branches and leaves grow strong and the whole form of the tree is expanded. Then follows the swelling of the bud and the blossom is released from the bud and from the blossom the fruit is exposed to view. This [fruit] also, unripened for some time and oddly shaped, gradually directing its own generation, is brought to perfection into the sweetness of flavour. 1.7 Thus also justice – for it is the same God of justice and creation[12] – was first in a trial state, fearing God by reason of nature. From there it advanced to infancy through the law and prophets. From there it fermented into adolescence through the gospel. Now it is brought to maturity through the Paraclete.

Only [the Paraclete][13] will both be called and revered as teacher by Christ.[14] For [the Paraclete] speaks not from itself but the things commanded by Christ.[15] [The Paraclete] is the only instructor,[16] because [the Paraclete] alone is after Christ. They who have accepted this [Paraclete], prefer truth to custom. They who constantly, not [just] in the past, have listened to this [Paraclete] prophesying, cover up virgins.

2.1 But I do not wish at this stage to class this usual practice as truth. Meanwhile let it be custom, in order that I may contrast even custom with custom. Throughout Greece and a number of its foreign countries, many churches conceal their virgins. It has also been established under this sky [here in Africa] in various places, such that no one may attribute that custom to the pagans[17] of Greek origin or to foreigners. But it is I who has proposed those churches, which either

143

the apostles themselves or apostolic men established, [as a precedent] and I believe them before [I believe] certain others.[18] Therefore those [apostolic] churches also have the same authority of custom. They set before [us] the prevailing conditions and instructors to a greater extent than those later [churches] of yours.[19] 2.2 What shall we heed? What shall we select? We are not able to reject a custom that we are not able to condemn, as [it is] not a strange [custom] since it does not belong to strangers [but to those] with whom of course we share the law of peace and the name of fraternity.[20] [There is] one faith for us and for them, one God, the same Christ, the same hope, the same mysteries of the ritual bath, let me say once for all, we are one church.[21] So it is ours whatever belongs to our [brothers and sisters]. Otherwise you divide the body.[22]

2.3 Yet in this instance, just as is customary in various ways with all practices {1211} both problematical and uncertain, an examination ought to have been conducted about which of the two so diverse customs agrees better with the teaching of God. And surely that [custom] ought to be selected which encloses[23] virgins (who are known to God alone), for whom – besides [the fact that] celebrity ought to be desired from God and not from men[24] – also their own standing in the community itself now ought to be a source of shame. You may embarrass a virgin more by praising than by finding fault, since the appearance of the offence is more obstinate, since shamelessness has been produced from and in the offence itself.[25] For no one would have approved that custom which refuses [to become intimate with] virgins while [at the same time] displaying [them], unless some men had been of the same nature as the virgins themselves. 2.4 In fact, the eyes that will desire a virgin once seen, are the same kind as a virgin has who will desire to be seen. The same kinds of eyes desire each other mutually. To be seen and to see is of the same passion. Blushing upon seeing a virgin is as typical of a pure man as it is of a pure virgin if she is seen by a man.

3.1 But those most pure instructors[26] have not wanted to discern between customs. But still, among us until recently more tolerance was being shown for each custom. The matter had been entrusted to personal choice, such that each {virgin} had resolved either to be covered or to be exposed,[27] just as [the decision] to marry, which is also neither compelled nor prevented, [had been left].[28] Truth had been content to betroth itself with custom, in order that it might exist secretly, or at least in part, under the name of custom.

3.2 But seeing that the ability to discern had begun to develop, such that, by means of the freedom of practice of each [custom], an indication of the better option emerged, immediately that adversary of good people, and more particularly of their many good practices, set to work. In contrast with the virgins of God, the virgins of this world go around with foreheads distinctly uncovered, having been roused to a rash audacity. They are considered virgins who are able to ask anything from men, much less the following example, in order that their rivals (with so much more freedom as servants of Christ alone)[29] certainly are surrendered to them. 3.3 'We are scandalized,' the [virgins without veils] say, 'because the others go about differently [than we do],' and they choose to be scandalized rather than challenged. A scandal, unless I am mistaken, is not an example of a good situation but of a harmful one, creating an offence. Good situations scandalize nobody, except [those with] an evil mind. If restraint, reserve, aversion to the spotlight, striving to please God alone is good, let them who are scandalized by such goodness realize their own evil. 3.4 So what if those lacking self-control say that they are scandalized by those with self-control! Should self-control be revoked? Lest the polygamists be scandalized, must monogamy be [1212] objected to also? Why do these [virgins with self-control] not complain more that the petulance and shamelessness of ostentatious virginity is an offence to themselves?[30] Therefore, on account of the availability[31] of heads of this kind, must pure virgins be dragged into the church, being ashamed because they are recognized in public, trembling because they are uncovered, summoned as if to their defilement? For they are no less willing to suffer even this. Every confiscation[32] [of the veil] of a virtuous virgin is the suffering of defilement, and yet to suffer physical violence is less [terrible] because it comes from a natural bodily function.[33] 3.5 But when the spirit itself is violated in a virgin by her veil having been taken, she learns to cope with the loss of what she was guarding. O sacrilegious hands that have been able to remove the appearance[34] that was dedicated to God! What could some persecutor have done that was more evil if he had known this [appearance] had been chosen by a virgin? You have laid bare a girl by her head, and now she does not consider herself to be a complete virgin; she is made something else.

Therefore truth, arise![35] Arise and, as it were, break out from your patience! I want you to defend no custom, for now indeed that custom[36] under which you were existing is swept away. Demonstrate that it is you who covers virgins. Interpret your own Scriptures, which custom does not know, for, if it had known [them], it never would have come into existence.

4.1 However, in so far as it is the custom to argue against the truth from the Scriptures, immediately it is put to us that no mention of virgins has been made by the apostle [Paul in the place] where he makes a ruling about the veil, but that only women were named,[37] since, [it is argued,] if he had wanted virgins to be covered as well, he would also have written something about the virgins when the women were mentioned. In this way, it is said, in that [other] passage where he handles the issue of marriage, he declares what ought to be observed concerning virgins as well.[38] And thus [it is said by my opponents that] those [virgins] are not included in the law about the veiling of the head [in the former passage] as they have not been named in this law but, on the contrary, from this [law comes the practice for virgins] to be unveiled. They who are not named are not commanded by it.[39]

4.2 But we too can throw the same argument back. For he who knew how to make mention of both types at another time – I mean [mention] of virgins and of women (that is, of [those who are, by definition,] not virgins) – for the sake of distinction, in these [passages] in which he does not name virgins, he shows their shared situation by not making a distinction. Still, here too, he was able [if he had wanted] to establish a difference between a virgin and a woman, just as he says in another passage, 'There is a division between a woman and a virgin.'[40] Therefore, by saying nothing about those whom he has not divided, he has united [them] with the other [type].[41] However, because there is a division between woman and virgin in that passage [of 1 Corinthians 7, it does] not [mean that] here too [in 1 Corinthians 11] that the division be supported, as certain people want. In fact, how many sayings [present] elsewhere have no force [in those other passages] where [1213] the sayings certainly are not [present]? The only exception would be where the situation was the same in both cases, such that it was sufficient to say it only once. However, the former case – of a virgin and a woman – is vastly different form this case [in 1 Corinthians 11]. 4.3 [The former passage in 1 Corinthians 7] says, 'There is a division between a woman and a virgin.' Why? Because 'the unmarried [girl]' – that is, a virgin – 'considers the things which are the Lord's, in order that she may be holy both in body and in spirit.' The married woman, however,' – that is, one who is not a virgin – 'considers how she may be pleasing to her husband.'[42] This will be the interpretation of that division, which has no place in that [eleventh] chapter, in which [there is] mention neither about marriage nor about the life or the thinking of a virgin and a woman, but about the veiling of the head. The Holy Spirit, wanting there to be no discussion of this [veiling], has wanted 'virgin' – whom, by not naming separately, [the Spirit] has not separated from 'woman' – to be understood as included within the one noun 'woman'. Also, by not separating [them], [the Spirit] has [in fact] joined her [to the category 'woman'] from whom [the Spirit] has not separated [her].

4.4 Therefore, is it so unusual [to use] a designation's principal [term], while at the same time realising that other [terms are] nevertheless [included] in that [broader] designation, [especially] where there is no necessity for breaking the universal [term] down into its particulars? Naturally, brevity of speech is both welcome and necessary, as a verbose speech is both wearisome and worthless.[43] Thus, we too have been content with universal designations, which include the meaning of the particulars within them. Now therefore, [I want to say something] about the designation itself. The designation in nature is 'female'. Of the natural designation, that by genus [is] 'woman'. Also, of the general [designation], that by species is 'virgin' or 'married woman' or 'widow' or however many [designations] are needed to cover the various stages of life. 4.5 The particular is subject, therefore, to the general, because the general is prior, and the subsequent [is subject] to the antecedent, and the partial to the universal. It is understood in [the term] itself to which it is subject, and is signified in [the term] itself, because it is contained in [the term] itself.[44] Thus neither hand nor foot nor any member wants to be signified when the body is named. And if you say 'universe' it will mean both the sky and the things in it – the sun, the moon, the constellations and stars – as well as the earth and the seas and everything in the periodic table. You will have named everything when you have said that which is composed from all [those] things. Thus also by using the noun 'woman', [the Holy Spirit] named whatever pertains to a woman.

5.1 But since they use the name 'woman' in such a way that they do not consider that that [term] is suitable except for her alone who has submitted [to a man], it falls to us to prove the appropriateness of this designation to the [female] sex as such, [and] not to relate [it] to [one] category of the [female] sex, in order that even virgins may also be counted as belonging to it. When this second type of human being was made by God as man's helper,[45] that female immediately [1214] was named 'woman,' at that time happy, at that time worthy of paradise, at that time a virgin. 'She will be called woman,' he said.[46] Thus you have the name, not then a common [one] but I mean a proper [one], which was allotted to the virgin in the beginning.[47] 5.2 But some ingeniously want the saying [to be] about the future: 'She *will be* called woman,' as if she were going to be this when she had surrendered her virginity, as [the writer] also added, 'On account of this, a man leaves father and mother and will be joined together with his woman, and the two will be in one flesh.'[48] Therefore, let them show first, where that intricacy [of argument] exists, if she was named 'woman' owing to the future, what designation she will have accepted in the meantime. In fact, she is not able to have been without a designation of her present quality. Otherwise, what kind [of situation] is it, that she who would be called by that designated name in the future, would be named nothing in the present? To every animal Adam gave names and [he did so] to none from a future situation but from a present practice – a situation in which each would be subject to him, [each animal] having been addressed from the beginning by a [name] which he wanted.[49] Therefore, what was she called at that time? Instead, every time she is named in the Scriptures before [she became] a wife, she is addressed as 'woman', and never [addressed as] 'virgin' [even] while [she was] a virgin. This was the one name for her at that time, even when nothing had been said by way of prophecy. For when Scripture reports that the two were naked[50] – Adam and his 'woman' – this does not indicate the future, as if it said 'his woman' in anticipation of 'his wife,' but that [she was] his woman, even [when] unmarried, as [she was] from his substance. He said, 'This bone from my bone and flesh from my flesh will be called woman.'[51] 5.3 Therefore, from this time, by the unspoken awareness of nature, the divinity itself of the soul has given rise to the use of the word by ignorant people – just as elsewhere too we shall be able to show how many other customs and habits of speech [come] from Scripture – such that we call wives 'our women,' although granted that even we may utter certain [words] improperly. For the Greeks also, who use the designation 'woman' more frequently in the case of wives, have other proper designations for 'wife.'[52] But I prefer to put this use down to the testimony of Scripture. In fact, where two have been made into one flesh through the bond of marriage, the 'flesh from flesh and bone from bone' is called, in accordance with her origin, the woman of him from whose substance she begins to be considered as having been made his wife. Thus, 'woman' is not by nature a name for 'wife', but 'wife' is in this situation a name for 'woman'. Finally, also, she may be called a woman and not a wife; however, she cannot be called a wife and not a woman, because that cannot exist.

5.4 Therefore, by having established the name of the new female, which is 'woman', and by having explained what she was previously – that is, by the assigned name – [Scripture] turned to the prophetic reason, in order to say, 'Because of this, a man will leave father and

{1215} mother.'[53] To such an extent is the name separate from prophecy, even as much as from the person herself, such that [Scripture here] did not speak in fact about Eve herself, but about those future females, whom [Adam] has named in [she who is] the origin of the female population. Besides, Adam was not about to leave father and mother, whom he did not have, because of Eve. Therefore, it does not apply to Eve because that which was said prophetically does not [apply] to Adam either. In fact, the prediction [is] about the situation of husbands who were about to leave their parents on account of a woman, which was not able to happen to Eve, because [it was] not [able to happen] to Adam either. If this be the case, it appears [it was] not on account of the future that she was named 'woman', to whom the future did not apply.

5.5 To this [Scripture] adds that [Adam] himself gave a reason for the name. For when he had said, 'She will be called woman, because she has been taken from her man,'[54] he himself [was] still a virgin. But let us speak also about the name of the man in its own place. And thus let no one interpret prophetically the name ['woman'], which was derived from another explanation, especially as it is apparent when she accepted a name from a future [situation], in other words in that passage where she is named Eve, now [she is named] with a personal designation, because she already had a natural [one]. For if Eve is 'the mother of the living'[55], behold she is named from a future [situation], behold she is foretold as a wife and not a virgin. This will be the designation of the one about to marry, for the mother [is derived] from the married woman. Thus, this too is shown then having been named 'woman' not from a future [situation], who was soon about to accept the name of her future situation.[56] The response is sufficient for this section.

6.1 Now let us see if the apostle too maintains the particular meaning of that designation ['woman'] as it is found in Genesis, by considering it as a [general] reference to gender [rather than, as my opponents would have, as not applicable to virgins], thereby calling the virgin Mary 'woman', in the same way as Genesis also [called] Eve ['woman']. For instance, writing to the Galatians, he says, 'God sent [God's] Son, made from a woman,'[57] who, it is certainly agreed, was a virgin, although Ebion opposes [this].[58]

I recognize also that the angel Gabriel [was] sent to a virgin. But while he blesses her, he counts [her] among women not among virgins: 'You are highly regarded among women.'[59] The angel knew also that even a virgin is called a woman. 6.2 But also to these two [passages] someone has responded ingeniously, at least in their own mind, that, as Mary [was] indeed engaged, she [was] mentioned also as a woman both by the angel and by the apostle. For an engaged female [is] in some sense a married woman. Still, between 'in some sense' and the truth there is plenty of difference, at least in this instance, for in other instances, it certainly ought to be considered so. Now, in fact, they [(Paul and Gabriel)] mentioned Mary as a 'woman' not as if [she were] already a married woman, but as a female nonetheless, even if not a bride, as if [1216] she were called this from the beginning. In fact, it is necessary that he [Paul] decide beforehand that from which the term ['woman'] descended. 6.3 Otherwise, as far as this section is concerned, if this [term 'woman'] is equated with an engaged[60] person, such that Mary was said to have been a woman for that reason – not as a female but as a wedded woman – therefore the Christ was not then born from a virgin since [he was born] from an engaged female, who had ceased to be a virgin by this fact. Because, if he was born from a virgin – granted, [one] also engaged – one still unspoilt, recognize also that a virgin, even an unspoilt one, is said to be a woman. Without a doubt, nothing here can be regarded as having been said prophetically, as [though] the apostle named [someone who would be] a woman in the future – that is, a married woman – by saying 'made from a woman'. In fact, he was not able to name [one who would] later [be] a woman, from whom the Christ did not have to be born, – that is, [a woman] having experience of men – but she, who was present, who was a virgin and was being called a woman according to the proper meaning of this designation, which, in keeping with the original usage, has been maintained for a virgin and thus for the whole genus of women.

7.1 Let us turn now to the reasons themselves that need to be examined, by which the apostle teaches that it is proper that a female be veiled. [We shall do this] in order to establish from this common use of the designation ['woman'] by both virgins and non-virgins whether the same [reasons for veiling] are suitable for virgins too, while at the same time the reasons for the veil are discerned for both. If the head of a woman is a man,[61] certainly [he is head] also of a virgin, from whom comes that woman who has been veiled in marriage,[62] unless the virgin is a third division [of humanity], something strange with an origin of its own.

If it is a disgrace for a woman to be shaved or cropped,[63] [it is] especially so for a virgin.[64] Therefore, let the world, the rival of God, see whether it is just as mistaken for the appearance of a virgin [to have] cut hair, as it also is [mistaken] for a boy to be permitted [to have long hair]. 7.2 Therefore, just as it is not fitting for her either to be shaved or cropped, it is just as fitting that she be hidden [under a veil].

If the glory of a man is a woman,[65] how much more [is] a virgin, who is a glory to herself? If a woman [is] from a man and for a man,[66] that rib of Adam[67] was at first a virgin. If a woman ought to have [a sign of] authority on her head,[68] even more rightly [ought] the virgin, because she is responsible [to the one] to whom she belongs. In fact, if [it is] 'on account of the angels'[69] – we read plainly that they have fallen from God and from heaven because of their desire for females – can anyone presume that such angels have desired the already defiled bodies and the relics of human lust instead of being even more on fire for virgins, whose youthful freshness even excuses human {1217} lust?[70]

For Scripture also provides the following: 'As it happened, when human beings began to increase in number on the earth and daughters were born to them, now the sons of God, having seen the daughters of men, since they were beautiful, took wives for themselves from all whom they selected.'[71] 7.3 For here the Greek name of 'woman' has the sense of wives,[72] because marriage is mentioned. Therefore, when it says, 'the daughters of , when it could have said 'the wives of men', it obviously indicates 'virgins,' who to that point were counted with their parents – for married women are called by the name of their husbands.[73] Equally, it does not name the angels 'adulterers' but 'husbands' when they take the unmarried daughters of men, who, it was said above 'were born' – thus also it indicated [they were] virgins. Earlier [in the passage] they were born, here they were married to the angels. I do not know anything else other than that they were born and subsequently married. Therefore, a face which is so dangerous and which has cast scandals from here to heaven, ought to be shaded in order that, standing in the presence of God before whom it is accused of being responsible for the angels being banished, it may blush before the other angels also, and may restrain that former evil freedom of its own head, [a freedom] which now ought not be placed before the eyes of men. 7.4 But even if those angels had grasped after females who were already unclean, so much more the virgins ought to be veiled 'on account of the angels', as the sin of the angels would have been greater on account of [them being] virgins.

However, if the apostle also adds the precedent of nature, that cascading hair may be the honour of a woman, since hair is meant to be a covering,[74] certainly this is especially a mark of distinction for a virgin, whose adornment is properly this: that, by having heaped her hair together on the very crown of the head, she may cover up her highest point with a circle of hair.

8.1 Certainly the obverse of all these [arguments] means that a man may not veil his head, because he has not obtained by nature a great display of hair, because to be shaved or cropped is not felt to be a disgrace for him, because it was not on account of him that the angels deviated, because [he is] 'the glory and the image of God',[75] [and] because 'Christ [is] his head'.[76] And so when the apostle deals with man and woman – why it may be proper for the latter to be veiled but not the former – it is clear why he has said nothing about a virgin. Just as he has of course allowed a virgin to be understood in the [designation] 'woman', similarly has not [needed] to name a boy, though he would be counted in [the designation] 'man'; the whole class of each sex having been encompassed by the proper designations of 'woman' and 'man'. **8.2** For thus Adam, then pure, is named 'man' in Genesis. 'She will be called woman,' it says, 'since she has been taken from her man.'[77] Thus Adam [was] a man before the union of marriage, just as [1218] Eve too [was] a woman. In both cases the apostle has mentioned enough about the universal species of each sex by so well-constructed a definition that is both concise and [yet] thorough when he says, 'every woman'.[78] What is 'every' if not of every genus, of every class, of every situation, of every rank, of every age, since 'every' is whole and complete and in no part defective? Moreover, 'virgin' is part of [the designation] 'woman'. Equally he says 'every' about not veiling a man.[79] **8.3** Consider the two different names: man and woman. Both [mean] 'every'. The two laws [are] mutually exclusive: one of veiling, the other of leaving bare. Therefore, if by the fact that it said 'every man', the name 'man' is common to a man as yet not a man, to a beardless male[80] – moreover, since the name is common according to nature, the law also is common of not veiling him who is a virgin among men,[81] according to [ecclesiastical] teaching – why, in a similar way also, might it not have been decided previously that every female virgin is included by association with the name 'woman,' so that she may be included in the sharing of the law? If a virgin is not a woman, neither is a beardless youth a man. If a virgin is not hidden [under a veil] since [you consider that] she is not a woman, let the beardless youth be hidden [under a veil] since [you would have to concede that] he is not a man! The same forbearance should be afforded to both types of virginity. Just as virgins are not compelled [by you] to be veiled, so [it must follow that] boys may not be bidden to be unveiled! **8.4** Why on the one hand do we recognize the definition of the apostle as applying completely to every man and decline to accept the reason why he still has not mentioned a boy, but on the other hand we evade the issue when equally it is completely applicable to every woman?[82] He says, 'If anyone is quarrelsome, [remember that] we do not have such a custom, nor [does] the church of God.'[83] He shows that there was some debate about that view. In order to counter it he employed complete brevity: not naming the virgin, in order that he might show that there was no doubt about veiling, and naming every woman, although he had <not> mentioned the virgin.[84] The Corinthians themselves have understood [this] in this way. Indeed, the Corinthians today veil their virgins. They who have learnt what the apostles taught, approve [it].

9.1 Now let us see whether, just as we have pointed out that the arguments from nature and from reason are suitable for a virgin, even the precepts of ecclesiastical teaching about women apply in this way to virgins.

'It is not allowed for a woman to speak in church',[85] but also neither to teach,[86] nor to baptize, nor to offer [sacrifice at the altar], nor to claim a share of any male function, much less {1219} of priestly office, for herself. Let us ask if any of these is permitted to a virgin. If it is not permitted to a virgin, but she is subjected to the same situation in everything, and the necessity of humility is adjudged the same as for a woman, why will this one [function] be permitted to her which is not permitted to every female?[87] What privilege is earned contrary to her situation, if she who is a virgin also has decided to sanctify her flesh? Is the reason for [your] indulgence concerning the veil made for her so that she may enter the [gathered] church notable and distinguished? In order that she may show the honour of sanctity in the freedom of her head? It was possible to be honoured more deservingly by some male privilege of either rank or office!

9.2 In addition, I know of a virgin somewhere who was placed among the order of widows before she was twenty. If the bishop had owed something by way of assistance to her, he could have fulfilled [it] in some other way, especially with a healthy respect for [church] teaching, so that she would not now be branded such an oddity in the church, not to say a monstrosity – a virgin widow. This indeed [is] the more unusual because as a widow she has not covered her head, denying herself both ways – both as a virgin who is considered a widow and as a widow who is called a virgin. 9.3 But by that authority she sits there indeed as an uncovered virgin. To that [reserved] seat [in the church], not only those women who have had one husband[88] – that is married women – and who are over sixty, but even mothers and nurturers of children too are selected. No doubt [the widows sit there], having been prepared by the experiences of all moods, that they might know [how] to help others more easily both with counsel and solace, and notwithstanding [that this virgin and others sit with the widows, they sit there] in order that they might undergo those things by which a female may be approved.[89] To such an extent no honour is allowed to a virgin with regard to the position [which widows hold].

10.1 Also, [it is] not [permitted] on the grounds of any distinctions. Otherwise it is extremely rude enough if females, having been placed under men in everything, should display an honourable[90] mark of their virginity by which they should be respected, be looked round at, and be esteemed by the brothers, while so many men [who are] virgins, so many voluntary eunuchs, go around with their goodness hidden, carrying nothing which would make them noticeable too. 10.2 They would be bound to defend some distinctions for themselves, either the feathers of the Garamanantes,[91] or the ribbons of the foreigners, or the cicadas of the Athenians, or the tufts of hair of the Germans,[92] or the brands of the Britons. Or let it happen in the opposite way: let them be kept out of sight in the church with a veiled head.

We are sure that the Holy Spirit was more able to attach something of this kind to males {1220} if [the Spirit] attached [it] to females, since it was appropriate that males were more honoured, even by reason of their self-control in addition to the authority of their gender. 10.3 The more their gender grows eager and hot for females, the more the self-control of the greater inflamed passion grows difficult, and for that reason the more deserving of all display, if the display of virginity is a dignified thing. In fact, is not self-control superior to virginity, whether of widows or those who by agreement have already protested against the common hardship?[93] For virginity endures by favour, self-control by true virtue. 10.4 The struggle of not desiring is great [for the one] for whom desiring has taken root. However, [if] you have not known the enjoyment of this desiring, it will be easy for you not to desire, because you do not have as an opponent the desire for enjoyment. Therefore, how would God not have approved something like this even more for the honour of men: namely, either naturally, because they belong more to the image [of God],[94] or because of their greater effort?[95] If however nothing [is approved] for a male, to a greater extent [is nothing approved] for a female.

11.1 But now let us settle by means of a response what we interrupted above for the sake of the subsequent debate, in order not to break up its coherence. For whereas we stood our ground about the unconditional definition of the apostle, which ought to be understood [as applying to] every woman, of every age as well,[96] – the other side was able to respond that therefore from birth and from the first sign of her [coming of] age, a virgin should be hidden [under a veil]. However, this is not the case. But [it is the case] from when she has begun to understand herself, and to feel a sense of her nature, and to pass from [the state] of a virgin, and to undergo that which is new of her higher age. 11.2 For the first of the race, Adam and Eve, as long as they were without understanding, lived naked.[97] But when they tasted [the fruit] from the tree of knowledge, at first they sensed nothing other than shame.[98] Thus each marked their understanding of their own sex with a covering. But even if she ought to be veiled on account of the angels,[99] without a doubt the law of veiling will be in operation from that age from which the daughters of men were able to draw desire to themselves and experience marriage. For a virgin ceases [to be a virgin] from the time when she is able not to be [one]. And for that reason it is illegal within Israel to hand [a virgin] over to a man except after the attestation of her maturity by the blood [of menstruation]. Thus, before this indication her condition is immature. Therefore, if she is a virgin for as long as she is immature, she ceases [to be] a virgin when she is recognized as mature and, as not a virgin, is now subject to the law, just as also to marriage.[100]

11.3 The engaged have the example of Rebekah who, unknown up to the time when she was brought to her unknown husband, at once recognized that he was the one whom she had seen from a long way off. She did not undergo the embrace of the hand, nor the meeting {1221} of the eyes, nor the exchange of greeting but, having acknowledged what she had felt, that is [that she was] a married woman in spirit, denied [that she was] a virgin by having veiled [herself] on the spot.[101] O woman already [obedient] to the teaching of Christ! In fact, she showed that even marriage is realized by appearance and attitude, just as defilement [is realized],[102] except that, even now certain ones still veil Rebekah.[103]

11.4 About the rest, that is those who are not engaged, let the delay of their parents, who give in out of poverty[104] or anxiety, consider [the example of Rebekah]. Also let [their delay] consider the vow of self-control itself. [The delay] has nothing to do with age that runs through its own stages and pays its own debts to maturity. Another hidden mother, nature, and another concealed father, time, have given their own daughter in marriage according to their own laws. Look upon that virgin of yours as already married – both her mind by expectation and her flesh by transformation – for whom you prepare a second husband. And now her voice has changed, and her limbs have finished growing, and the shameful {part of her body} is clothed completely, and the months pay their tributes.[105] And do you deny [she is] a woman whom you say is experiencing womanhood?[106] If the union of man makes a woman [which it does not],[107] let them not be covered except after the experience of marriage itself! At any rate, even among the pagans,[108] they are led veiled to a man.[109] 11.5 However, if they are veiled at the engagement because both in body and in spirit they have associated with a male by a kiss and [the joining of] their right hands,[110] through which they surrendered in spirit their original shame, through the common pledge of awareness by which they have fixed the entire union, by how much more will time, without which they are not able to be promised in marriage[111] and by whose insistence they cease being virgins without engagements,[112] veil them? 11.6 Even the pagans respect time, such that, from the law of nature, they accord to the different ages their own rights. For they send females at twelve years, a male at two years more, to the occupation [of marriage], determining puberty by years, not by engagements or marriages. She is called 'mother of the family', although a virgin, and [he is called] 'father of the family', although a beardless youth. What is natural is not respected by us, as if there be a God of nature other than ours. 12.1 Recognize the woman also – recognize the married woman – also from the testimonies both of body and of spirit that she experiences both in awareness and in the flesh. These are the earlier writing tablets of natural engagements and weddings. Place a veil outwardly for those having a covering inwardly. Let her upper parts be covered whose lower parts {1222} are not naked. Would you like to understand what the importance of age is? Consider both [females]: [one] immaturely having been squeezed into the dress of a woman, and [the other] who, of a mature age, still maintains a virgin's mode of dress. The former will more easily be denied [to be] a woman than the latter will be believed [to be] a virgin. So great is the reliability of age that it cannot be impeded by dress. 12.2 What [can be said about the fact] that these [virgins] of ours[113] confess a change of age by [the rest of their] dress and at the same time understand themselves [to be] women, they are moving away from [being] virgins? Indeed, from the head they lay aside what they were; they change their hair and implant their coiffure with an outlandish hairpin, asserting open womanhood by parting their locks of hair from the front. And then they seek beauty advice from the mirror and they torment their more fastidious face with washing, perhaps they even falsify it with some rouge, fling a mantle[114] around themselves, cram [their foot into] an oddly-shaped shoe, bring more implements to the baths. Why should I go into detail? However, the obvious preparations alone proclaim complete womanhood, but they want to act like a virgin with only the head naked, denying by one [item of] dress what they acknowledge by their total demeanour.[115]

13.1 If on account of men they misuse their appearance, let them complete that [appearance] in this [situation I describe] as well, and as they veil their head in the presence of pagans, surely in the church let them conceal their virginity, which they keep secret outside the church. Let them fear strangers and let them respect the community,[116] or let them have the courage to be seen in the streets as virgins as well, just as they dare [to be seen] in the church. I shall praise their effort if they shall have marketed something of virginity even among pagans. Her nature [is] the same outdoors as well as indoors. The same practice in the presence of men and the Lord is consistent with the same freedom [before both]. 13.2 Why then do they hide their goodness outdoors when they parade [it] in the church? I demand a reason. Is it in order to please their community or God?[117]

If in order actually [to please] God, [God] is just as capable of perceiving whatever is done in secret as [God] is fair in rewarding those things done for [God] alone.[118] Finally, [God] instructs us not to trumpet anything that shall be used to obtain a reward in the presence [of God], nor let us receive compensation for it from people. Since if we are prohibited from the left hand knowing of [the giving of] one victory coin or whatever act of almsgiving [we perform], how much should we surround ourselves with darkness when we are offering so great a gift to God as our body itself and our spirit itself, when we are consecrating our nature itself to [God]?

[1223] Therefore, because it cannot be seen to be done on account of God – as God does not want it to be done thus – it follows that it is done for the favour of men, which, in the first place, is as illicit as the lust for the spotlight.[119] In fact, the spotlight is an illicit thing for those whose trial consists of every humility. 13.3 And if the virtue of self-control is conferred by God, 'why are you boasting as if you have not received [it]?'[120] But if you have not received [it], what do you have which has not been given to you? For this reason, therefore, that you attribute it not to God alone, it is clear that it was not given to you by [God]. Therefore, let us see whether what is human may be lasting and true.[121] 14.1 Sometimes they refer to the saying of a certain person when that question – 'And how shall we rouse others to action of this kind?' – was first addressed. Of course, if they will grow in number, they – and not the favour of God or the merits of each – shall make us happy![122] Do virgins adorn or commend the church to God or does the church adorn or commend virgins? Therefore it is acknowledged that the spotlight is the motive. Further, where [there is} the spotlight, there [is] anxiety. Where [there is] anxiety, there [is] pressure. Where [there is] pressure, there [is] compulsion. Where [there is] compulsion, there [is] weakness.[123]

14.2 And thus, while they do not cover their head, in order that they may be seduced for the sake of the spotlight, it is appropriate that they are forced to cover their stomachs because of the catastrophe of their weakness. For envy not piety led them.[124] Sometimes too their god is their stomach itself[125] because the brotherhood readily supports the virgins. It is not so much [that] they go to ruin but also [that] they draw a long string of offences.[126] For, having been brought forth into the public eye and elated by their goodness having been made public and having been overloaded with every honour and esteem and charity by the community – as long as they do not live concealed [under a veil] – when some [other offence] has been committed the [community] considers it as great a disgrace as [before] they held it an honour.[127] 14.3 If an uncovered head is ascribed to virginity, if any virgin has fallen at all from the grace of virginity, she continues with an uncovered head lest she be found out, and then she walks about with the dress that now belongs to someone else (that is, which virginity claims for itself. She continues nevertheless in the dress reserved for someone else, lest of course she be found out by the change). Conscious of a now undoubted womanhood, they dare to approach God with a naked head. But a jealous God and Lord,[128] who said, [1224] '[There is] nothing that has been hidden which will not be revealed,'[129] brings most of them even into [public] view. For they will not confess unless they have been betrayed by the cries of their infants themselves. 14.4 But the more there are of these [false virgins] the more you will have to suspect them of further offences. Let me say, though I would prefer not, that it is difficult to become a woman the first time for one who fears it, and she who has already become [pregnant] is able to pretend that she is a virgin under God. How much will she dare [to pretend] likewise about her womb lest she be detected as a mother too? God knows how many infants now [God] has allowed to be brought to term and be delivered to birth intact, after the battle from their mothers [to hide their existence] has been over for some time. Virgins of this kind always conceive most easily and give birth most happily and [to offspring] in fact most similar to their fathers. 14.5 A pressured and unwilling virginity allows these shameful actions [to occur]. The very desire of not keeping out of sight is not a modest [one]. She experiences something that is not proper to a virgin – the enthusiasm for pleasing, and men especially. However much you may wish she endeavour with her good intention, it is unavoidable that she be in danger by the exposure[130] of herself, while she is transfixed by many untrustworthy eyes, while she is tickled by the fingers of those who point, while she is greatly delighted in [by others], while she glows during the ever-present embraces and kisses. Thus the brow is hardened, thus decency is eroded and loosened, thus she now learns to desire to please in a different way.[131]

15.1 For true, complete and pure virginity certainly fears nothing more than itself. It does not even want to experience the eyes of females. It itself has other eyes. It seeks refuge in the veil of the head as in a helmet, as in a shield, in order to cover its own goodness against the blows of temptations, against the barbs of scandals, against suspicions and mutterings and jealousy, as well as envy itself. For there is something to be feared even among the pagans, which they call witchcraft, the unhappy consequence of excessive praise and celebrity. 15.2 Sometimes we understand this [to be] from the devil, for hatred of good belongs to [the devil]. Sometimes we consider [this to be] from God, for the power of judging arrogance is [God's], 'of exalting the lowly and of bringing down to earth the conceited.'[132] And so the more holy virgin will fear, especially in the name of witchcraft, the devil, on the one hand, and God, on the other. [She will fear] the malicious character of the former and the severe light of the latter. And she will be glad when she is known to herself alone and to God. 15.3 But even if she becomes known to someone, she is sensible if she blocks the path for temptations. For who will dare to pursue an enclosed face with his eyes, an expressionless face, a melancholy face, might I say? Any evil thought whatever will be shattered by the very severity itself. Now she who keeps secret [that she is] a virgin even denies [that she is] a woman.

[1225] 16.1 The defence of our opinion consists of these [arguments] in accordance with Scripture, nature and [ecclesiastical] teaching. Scripture establishes the law, nature is called to witness [to it], [ecclesiastical] teaching carries [it] out. To which of these is the custom that comes from opinion beneficial, or what is the complexion of the opposite way of thinking? Scripture is of God. Nature is of God. [Ecclesiastical] teaching is of God. Whatever is contrary to these is not of God. 16.2 If Scripture is uncertain, nature is clear, and about its testimony Scripture cannot be uncertain. If there is doubt about nature, [ecclesiastical] teaching shows what has been more approved by God. Nothing is more precious to [God than] humility, nothing more acceptable [than] propriety, nothing more troublesome than celebrity and the eagerness to be pleasing to men. And so may Scripture, nature and [ecclesiastical] teaching be that for you which you have discovered to be acceptable to God; just as you have been ordered 'to examine everything and to follow whatever is better.'[133]

16.3 It still remains that we turn to [the women] themselves, so that they may uphold those [three] things more willingly. I beg you, whether mother, sister, or virgin daughter according to the proper description of age which I have named, veil your head! If a mother, [do so] on account of your sons. If a sister, [do so] on account of your brothers. If a daughter, [do so] on account of your fathers. You are a danger for every age group.

16.4 Put on the armour of decency, draw a stockade of reserve around, build a wall for your sex, [of the sort] that neither may reveal your eyes nor give access to [the eyes of] others.[134] Complete the dress of a woman so that you may retain the condition of a virgin. Dissemble to some extent about the things that are within in order that you may display the truth to God alone. Nevertheless, do not pretend to be a married woman. For you are promised in marriage to Christ to whom you have surrendered your flesh, to him you have pledged your maturity. Walk according to the will of your groom. Christ it is who commands both the brides of others and wedded women to be veiled, [and] certainly [he commands] his own much more.[135]

17.1 But we warn you as well, women of the other modesty[136] who have rushed into marriage, lest you so fade away from the teaching of the veil, even for a second, that, because you are not able to cast that [veil] aside, you destroy [it] by another means, walking neither covered nor bare-headed. For certain women, with turbans and wool, do not veil the head, but they bind [it], covering [it] over indeed in the front, yet it is bare as far as the head properly [speaking is concerned]. Others are covered on top of the head to a limited extent by strips of linen – lest they constrict the head, I believe – not hanging down as far as the ears. 17.2 I feel sorry if they have such infirm hearing that they are not able to hear through a covering. Let them know that the whole head is the woman. The limits and [1226] boundaries of it extend as far as from where clothing begins. The veil needs to be as long as the hair is when it is let down, in order that the neck too may be wrapped. For [married women] are the ones who must be subjected, [they are the ones] on account of whom 'power over the head'[137] ought to be had [by men]. The veil is their yoke.

The pagan females of Arabia, who do not cover the head but the total face as well in this fashion, such that they may be content with one eye free to enjoy half the light, rather than to prostitute the whole face, will judge you. 17.3 A female [there] wishes to see rather than be seen. Therefore, a certain Roman queen[138] says that they are most unhappy since they can love deeply more than be loved deeply, although they are happy because of their immunity from the other even more frequent unhappiness, since females [if they did not have their veils] could more easily be loved deeply than love deeply. And yet the restraint of pagan teaching is actually purer and thus, as I have said, more barbaric [than ours].

The Lord has even measured off for us the dimensions of the veil through revelations. For to a certain sister of ours the angel in a dream, beating her neck as if applauding, said, '[This is an] elegant neck and rightly bared! It is good you are uncovered completely from head to loins, lest that freedom of the neck not be beneficial to you!'[139] And certainly what you have said to one, you have said to all.

17.4 However, will they deserve as much castigation as those who during the psalms, or at any mention of God, continue uncovered, who even when they are about to spend time in prayer, most readily place a fringe or a piece of cloth or whatever thread they like over the top of their head and consider themselves covered? They say falsely that their head [is only] that size. Others, whose palm of their hand is clearly greater than every fringe and thread, do not abuse their head any less, just like a certain [animal], which is more beast than bird, even though it is feathered, and has a small head, long neck [and] in other respects walks upright. This [bird],[140] they say, when it has to hide itself, conceals only its head – indeed, the whole [of its head] – into [something] very dense [and] leaves behind the rest of itself out in the open. Thus, while there is safety for its head, the revealed part of it – which is the majority [of it] – is seized together with its head.[141] In fact, this will be the case as well for those who have covered less than is useful. 17.5 Therefore, it is proper at all times and in every place to proceed mindful of the law, prepared and provided for every mention of God, who if present in the heart, will be understood also in the head of females.

To those who will read these things at their leisure, to those who prefer truth to custom, may the grace and peace of our lord, Jesus, abound, and with Septimius Tertullianus, whose little work this is.

NOTES

PART I INTRODUCTION

1 LIFE AND WORKS OF TERTULLIAN

1 On the rhetorical structure of this text see Dunn (2002a): 47–55.
2 Barnes 1985: 58 suggests *c.* 170 as his date of birth. On his name see *On the Veiling of Virgins* 17.5. A full name of Quintus Septimius Florens Tertullianus is attested in some manuscript headings.
3 On Roman education see Bonner 1977.
4 Dekkers (1995: 9) lists *Against the Jews* as a doubtful work. There is debate about Tertullian's involvement in writing or editing *Passion of Sts Perpetua and Felicity*.
5 According to Jerome, Tertullian also wrote six books *On Ecstasy* to which was attached a seventh *Against Apollonius* (*On Illustrious Men* 24.3; 40.4; 53.5). This work was a defence of Montanism. Jerome also mentioned *On the Hope of the Faithful* (*On Illustrious Men* 18.4); *To a Philosophic Friend* (*Letter* 22.22; *Against Jovinianus* 1.13), which is described as an early work; *On Circumcision* and *On Clean and Unclean Animals* (*Letters* 36.1); and *On Aaron's Vestments* (*Letter* 64.23). Tertullian himself referred to *On Paradise* (*Against Marcion* 5.12.8; *On the Soul* 55.5); *Against Apelles* (*On the Flesh of Christ* 8.3); *On Fate* (*On the Soul* 20.5); and *The Origin of the Soul* (*On the Soul* 1.1). Three other works (*On Flesh and Soul*; *On the Submission of the Soul*; and *On the Superstition of the Age*) are known only by titles in the index of the Codex Agobardinus.

2 NORTH AFRICAN CHRISTIANITY

1 Frend (1965: 313) dated the martyrdom of Namphamo and companions to a fortnight before the Scillitan martyrs (cf. Barnes 1985: 261–2). In later works Frend made no reference to Namphamo (Frend 1977: 21).
2 Quispel (1982: 258) states that the Bible read in the Jewish synagogues was the Septuagint, which was translated spontaneously into Latin. Then on 262 he writes that the synagogue lector could have been reading and translating from a Hebrew text. On 265 he suggests further that the lectors read and translated the Greek in the light of their knowledge of Hebrew.
3 On this proconsul see Birley 1992: 37–40.

4 Frend (1977: 23) thinks that they were separate basilicas. Ennabli (1997: 32–4) thinks them to have been the same.

3 SCRIPTURE AND TERTULLIAN

1 In *Against Praxeas* 20.2 he referred to 'both testaments', whereas a few sentences earlier he mentioned Is 45.5 as being 'in the old'. In *Against Marcion* 4.1.1 he referred to two 'instruments' usually known as 'testaments'. In *On the Prescriptions of Heretics* 36.5 he referred to the law and the prophets being united in one volume with the gospels and the letters of the apostles.
2 At *On Flight in Time of Persecution* 11.2, for example, Tertullian's Latin of Lk 8.18 (. . . *ab eo autem, qui non habet, etiam quod uidetur habere auferetur*) is judged to be better than the Old Latin versions that stick more rigidly to the Greek word order (Aalders 1937: 263).
3 As one example, at *Against Marcion* 4.14.14 and 4.26.10 Tertullian borrowed *eicere* from Marcion's version of Lk 6.22 and 11.19, but, in introducing the latter text he had used his own word *expellere* (*Against Marcion* 4.26.10) (Higgins 1951: 17).

4 RHETORIC AND TERTULLIAN

1 On Lactantius as rhetorician see his own *Divinae Institutiones* 5.2.2 and Jerome, *On Illustrious Men* 80.1.

5 PHILOSOPHY AND TERTULLIAN

1 I cannot agree with the idea that *On the Pallium* is an epideictic oration. Tertullian is advocating change (indeed, chapters 2–4 – about one-half of the work – are devoted to the nature of change), which is what one would expect in deliberative oratory. Sider (1971: 120) sees elements of both, with a strongly deliberative focus.
2 González (1974: 21) states: 'What he is saying is simply that these things, which seem impossible, are not really such, because God willed them to happen. In other words, he *is not* saying that the criterion for truth is impossibility. He *is* saying that the criterion of natural reason, usually valid, is not always ultimately valid, for that reason itself shows that God, who is the ultimate deciding factor, does not have to subject himself to it. He *is* also saying that in such cases the criterion of truth is not some inner logic which one can discover purely by rational investigation, but rather whether God did or did not will the event in question – in this case the incarnation and its sequel – to happen.'

7 TERTULLIAN AND PAGANS

1 For an evaluation of the debate about the rhetorical genre of *Apology* see Dunn (2002a: 48–51). For an analysis of its structure see Sider (1973: 405–23).
2 Osborn (1997b: 241–7), in his assessment of Tertullian's Romanness has not taken this point into account, which lessens the value of his statement on 244 that: 'Careful study, therefore, indicates that Tertullian, for all his intransigence and rigour, maintained a positive attitude towards the Roman state.'

3 Barnes (1985: 55) dates it to summer/autumn of 197. On 32 he points out the *terminus post quem* of February 197 because of the historical allusion to the defeat of the imperial usurper Clodius Albinus in February of that year.

4 Barnes (1969: 118) thinks that this reference to rabbits may indicate that Christians are fleeing from persecution. Given the whole tenor of the treatise, though, it would seem a little inconsistent for Tertullian to argue, on the one hand, that God presented the opportunity for martyrdom for the Christian to do battle with the enemy, and, on the other, that avoiding capture was acceptable.

5 In his revision, Barnes (1985: 328) moves back to 211 as the date of composition, although any appropriate date between 208, when Tertullian turned to Montanism, and 211 would be a possibility.

6 Gero's argument only stands because he dates *On Idolatry* to late in Tertullian's literary career. If it is dated earlier it creates problems for his argument of Tertullian's ideas changing over time. The great weakness in his case is *To Scapula*, which is correctly dated late. Its tone contrasts with *On the Military Crown* and *On the Pallium*, as Gero (1970: 293–4) correctly observes, and so contradicts the idea of Tertullian simply changing his mind over the years.

7 On whether this was P. Julius Scapula Tertullus Priscus, the consul of 195, or his cousin C. Julius (Scapula) Lepidus Tertullus, consul between 195 and 197, see Barnes (1986: 202, n. 8); Birley (1991: 81, n. 1); Birley (1992: 53).

8 See Dunn (2002a: 47–55).

8 TERTULLIAN AND JEWS

1 Frend (1977: 27; 1978: 189–90) states that at the site of the largest Christian church, which is just north of the city walls, Damous el Karita, is a large burial ground that contains Jewish and pagan as well as Christian burials.

2 I use this term rather than 'anti-Jewish' to indicate that Tertullian's debate was religious not ethnic, although this may be a distinction that is of importance only in a more modern context.

3 Taylor (1995: 141): 'To the extent that the Judaism portrayed by the church fathers is recognized as a figurative entity which emerges out of Christian theorizing about Christianity, it cannot simultaneously be interpreted as referring to a living Judaism from which useful information can be gleaned about Jewish–Christian interaction.'

PART II TEXTS

11 AGAINST THE JEWS

1 Although in the 1985 revision of his biography on 330 Barnes moderated this view, he did so only to the extent that he admitted that Tertullian knew contemporary Jews in Carthage but still did not engage them in conversation.

2 Here I am revising my opinion (Dunn 1998: 120, 143; 1999b: 317–18; 2000: 3–4) that there was a *narratio* (1.3b–7) and a *partitio* (1.8–2.1a). Tertullian offers more argumentation than would be typically expected in a *narratio*. He seems instead to be moving between the question as it was defined in the debate and the question as he wished to redefine it for his treatise, which would be more appropriate for a *partitio*.

3 Literally 'on account of the blending sound of the debate'.

4   *Ex gentibus*. On Tertullian's use of *gens* see Balfour (1982:785–9). As a rule, I
    translate *populus* as 'people', *natio* as 'tribe' and *gens* as 'clan' (when unspecified)
    or 'Gentile' or 'foreigner' (when the contrast is with Jews). In general, I have
    avoided the words 'nation' and 'race' as they are more modern constructs not
    applicable, as the sociologists tell us, to the ancient world. MacMullen (1975:
    409) states: 'Through common usage, the perception of what we would call
    nationality is thus exposed for what it was at the height of the empire, a perfect
    chaos of ideas and images.' Buell (2002: 432) writes that race, ethnicity and
    cultural identity overlap in ancient Christian writers. In other words, one could
    change race by changing identity; it was not a genetically inherited feature.
    While she believes that race is an elastic term, I think it is swimming against
    the tide to redefine a popularly understood term and hence I avoid it.
5   Is 40:15.
6   Gen 22:18; 26:4; 28:14; 25:23.
7   On Tertullian's interpretation of this passage in relation to other early Christian
    interpretations see Dunn (1998: 119–45).
8   *In partus editione*.
9   Gen 25:23.
10 Ex 32:1, 23; Acts 7:40.
11 Ex 32:4, 8.
12 On the structure and arguments in chapters 2 to 6 see Dunn (1999b:
    315–41).
13 Rather than translate Tertullian's personal pronouns about God in a gender-
    specific way in English, I have simply used the appropriate term in brackets.
14 Gen 3:3.
15 Dt 6:5; 10:12; 11:13; Mt 22:37; Mk 12:30; Lk 10:27.
16 Lev 19:18; Mt 19:19; 22:39; Mk 12:31; Lk 10:27; Rom 13:9; Gal 5:14; Jas 2:
    8.
17 Ex 20:13–16, 12; Dt 5:17–20, 16, 21; Lev 19:11, 3; Mt 19:18–19; Lk 18:20;
    Rom 13:9.
18 Ex 20:17; Dt 5:21; Rom 13:9.
19 Gen 3:6, 8, 5; 2:7.
20 Ex 32:15–16.
21 Gen 7:1.
22 Is 41:8.
23 Gen 14:18.
24 Ex 12:40; Gal 3:17. Cf. Acts 7:6.
25 Gen 17:14.
26 Gen 4:3–5.
27 Gen 7:23.
28 Gen 5:24.
29 Gen 14:18.
30 Gen 19:12–16.
31 Gen 17:24.
32 Gen 14:17–18. In fact, Abraham was not circumcised until some time after
    (Gen 15:1) the encounter with Melchizedek.
33 Ex 4:24–26.
34 Tertullian ignored the fact that in the Pentateuch the law of circumcision was
    not derived from this incident. The general law that existed already was simply
    being applied in this instance.

35 Tertullian overlooked the fact that the command of circumcision was not given through Moses but through Abraham (Gen 17:14).

36 After the Bar Kokhba revolt of 132–5, the emperor Hadrian had forbidden Jews to enter Jerusalem. For the details see Smallwood (1981: 460). Tertullian's reference to this event is mentioned again in this text at 13.4. Tertullian's point that circumcision became the way in which the Romans could check on those trying to enter Jerusalem does not take into account that under Hadrian the practice of circumcision was universally banned. Only under Antoninus Pius was an exemption made for the Jews to resume this practice. This is one of Tertullian's few references to near contemporary events and it is likely that Justin Martyr's *Dialogue With Trypho* was his source.

37 Is 1:7–8.

38 Is 1:2.

39 Is 1:15.

40 Is 1:4.

41 Jer 4:3–4.

42 Jer 31:31–32.

43 Is 2:2.

44 Is 2:2–3.

45 Dan 2:34, 45.

46 Is 2:3–4.

47 Ex 21:24; Lev 24:20; Dt 19:21.

48 Ps 17 (18):43–44.

49 Ps 77 (78):12–13, 24, 11; Ex 16:4, 35; Wis 16:20; Dt 8:16.

50 Ex 32:1.

51 Gen 2:2–3; Ex 20:11.

52 Ex 20:8, 10; 12:16.

53 Is 1:13. The arguments in this and the following chapter about sabbaths and sacrifices appear also in *On Idolatry* 14.6 in a much briefer fashion, which may suggest that *Against the Jews* was written earlier.

54 Ezek 22:8.

55 Is 66:23.

56 Is 54:15?

57 Jos 6:3–5.

58 Jos 6:15–20.

59 Jos 6:16, 21.

60 The Hebrew has 'the one crouching', i.e. the devil. The Latin text is difficult to determine here, possibly because Tertullian has misunderstood the scriptural text or had a poor text from which to work.

61 Gen 4:3–11, 14.

62 Mal 1:10–11.

63 *Gentium*. Ps 95 (96):7.

64 Ps 95 (96):7–8.

65 Ps 50 (51):19.

66 Ps 49 (50):14.

67 Is 1:11.

68 Is 1:13.

69 Is 1:11–12.

70 Mal 1:10–11.

71 Mal 1:11.

72 Is 9:1.
73 I have attempted to use the definite article when Tertullian referred to the messiah. I have omitted it when it is obvious that he used it as an alternative name for Jesus. It is not always an easy distinction to make.
74 Is 45:1.
75 Ps 18 (19):5.
76 Acts 2:9–10, 5. On Tertullian's change to Acts see Dunn (2000: 10–11).
77 Is 45:1–2.
78 Ps 9 (10):16; Jer 10:10.
79 1 Kgs 4:25 (5:5).
80 Dan 9:26. On Tertullian's interpretation of this passage of Daniel in this chapter see Dunn (2002b: 330–44; 2003b: 140–55). In particular it should be noted that Tertullian, dependent upon Theodotion, has inverted the order of the first two blocks of weeks as found in Daniel (and expanded them to eliminate the third block) from 7 and 62 to 62.5 and 70.5.
81 On the importance of these sentences for the structure of the treatise see Dunn (2000: 5–6).
82 Dan 9:1–2.
83 On whether or not to include *septem et dimidia et ebdomades* in the text see Dunn (2002b: 339–40). The problem appears to be that the Greek translation by Theodotion with which Tertullian seems to have been familiar has misunderstood Daniel. While Daniel saw 7 and 62 weeks as quite separate, Theodotion joined them. I do not believe this phrase ought to be included in Tertullian's text.
84 Dan 9:21–27. Given that Tertullian was dependent upon Theodotion's flawed Greek version of Daniel in the LXX (either by translating the Greek to Latin himself or working from someone else's Latin translation of Theodotion), it is not surprising that, in a number of instances, there have been changes to what was originally in Daniel, making Tertullian's version in those places rather unintelligible.
85 Dan 9:25. I have suggested that Tertullian seems here to be referring to the possibility of a third temple, not to the second temple. See Dunn (2002b: 338).
86 Dan 9:26. Note the mixture here of the two different versions of Dan 9:26 previously used by Tertullian in this treatise (8.1 and 8.6).
87 I have turned this question into a statement.
88 Dan 9:23b, 25.
89 On the accuracy of Tertullian's names and figures throughout this chapter see Dunn (2003b: 145–51).
90 It is necessary to omit repetitive and superfluous text and to punctuate it this way in order for this passage to make sense.
91 See Dan 9:24.
92 Mt 11:13.
93 Following *TPNFR Ven – Tiberius Claudius annis XIII, mensibus VII, diebus XX*. On whether to include mention of Claudius in Tertullian's text see Dunn (2003b: 151).
94 Ps 21 (22):17.
95 Ex 12:5–6.
96 Mt 27:25; Jn 19:12; Mt 26:56.
97 *Against the Jews* 9.1–3 = *Against Marcion* 3.12.1–3.
98 Is 7:13–15; 8:4.

99 *Against the Jews* 9.4–18 = *Against Marcion* 3.13.1–3.14.3.
100 Is 8:4.
101 Or diapers, as the Americans say.
102 Is 7:14.
103 Zech 14:14.
104 Ps 71 (72):15, 10.
105 This is the earliest evidence of what would become the popular Christian opinion that the magi were kings. Powell (2000: 474–5), in examining the development of this tradition, does not consider Tertullian's *Against the Jews*, only *Against Marcion*. His argument is that Tertullian was not interested in the status of the magi as much as he was making an argument against an anti-pacifist interpretation of Psalm 72. On 474 he writes that 'they [the magi] are symbols of hostile kings from the past who were conquered by Christ rather than images of pious or present kings who worship him.' Powell goes further and translates the Latin *fere* (which I here translate as 'generally' and Evans translated as 'for the most part') as 'almost' and argues on 475 that '. . . the magi must remain "almost" kings, symbols at best of hostile kings who in a bygone era were conquered by Christ "without fighting or armament". . .' and that '. . . the story must be explicitly identified as a figurative story illustrating the manner of Christ rather than describing an actual conversion of earthly rulers, which neither Tertullian nor Matthew could envision.' I cannot agree with Powell when, on 477, he writes that 'he [Tertullian] does not identify the magi as kings'. If we look at the end of *Against the* Jews 9.12 (and *Against Marcion* 3.13.8), we find Tertullian commending the magi for worshipping Jesus. Powell's argument that Tertullian's focus was on pacifism cannot be correct either; the focus is on the age of one who does not need arms. If one alters Powell's translation then what Tertullian has to say about the magi is more in line with the way Powell interprets Augustine on the magi – they are models for earthly rulers.
106 Justin, *Dialogue with Trypho* 78.10, reports this transfer of Damascus from Arabia to Syrophoenicia, but without indicating that it happened when Syria was split into two. Herodian 2.7.4 reports that Pescennius Niger was governor of the whole province in 193. It was soon after this that Septimius Severus divided Syria into Syria Coele and Syria Phoenicia. See Birley (1988: 114). If this is correct then the comment in Justin must be a later gloss or an indication that even before the split Syria had acquired the name Syria Phoenicia.
107 Mt 2:9–11.
108 1 Kgs 13:33–34.
109 Is 1:10.
110 Ez 16:3.
111 Is 1:2.
112 Is 19:1–24.
113 Rev 17:5.
114 Ps 44 (45):3.
115 Ps 44 (45):2.
116 Ps 44 (45):5.
117 Rev 2:12; Heb 4:12; Mt 16:27.
118 *Against the Jews* 9.19–20a = *Against Marcion* 3.14.5–7.
119 Ps 44 (45):5–6; Heb 4:12.
120 *Against the Jews* 9.21–23a = *Against Marcion* 3.16.3–5.
121 Num 13:16.

122 Jos 5:2–3.
123 Num 12:5–8.
124 Ex 23:20–21.
125 Mal 3:1; Mt 11:10.
126 Ps 131 (132):17.
127 Jn 5:35; 1:29.
128 *Against the Jews* 9.25 = *Against Marcion* 3.16.5–6.
129 Is 11:1–3. *Against the Jews* 9.26b–29 = *Against Marcion* 3.17.3–5.
130 On Mary being a descendant of David see Dunn (2001b: 349–55).
131 Is 53:3, 7.
132 Is 42:2–3.
133 Is 60:1–2.
134 For the next few sentences, Tertullian deviated from the arrangement of topics he had set for himself to consider this twofold pattern.
135 Is 58:1–2.
136 Is 35:4–6.
137 Jn 5:16.
138 *Against the Jews* 10.1 = *Against Marcion* 3.18.1.
139 Gal 3:13 (Dt 21:23). Both Tertullian and Justin, *Dialogue with Trypho* 96.1, like Paul, cite this from the LXX, which has the addition of 'on a tree', and omit from the LXX 'by God'.
140 Dt 21:22–23. Here Tertullian included 'by God' and went on to explain this in a positive way.
141 Is 53:9; Mt 5:39; 1 Pt 2:22.
142 Ps 34 (35):12.
143 Ps 68 (69):5.
144 Ps 21 (22):17.
145 Ps 68 (69):22.
146 Ps 21 (22):19.
147 *Against the Jews* 10.5b–16 = *Against Marcion* 3.18.2–3.19.9.
148 Gen 22:6; Rom 8:32; Jn 19:17.
149 Gen 37:27.
150 Dt 33:17. See Justin, *Dialogue with Trypho* 91.1–2.
151 Gen 49:5–6.
152 The sense of this sentence is not easy to determine.
153 Ex 17:10–11. See Justin, *Dialogue with Trypho* 90.
154 Ex 20:4; Num 21:8–9. See Justin, *Dialogue with Trypho* 91.4.
155 Ps 95 (96):10, although without reference to the tree.
156 Is 9:6.
157 Is 9:6.
158 Jer 11:19.
159 Mk 14:22; Mt 26:26; Lk 22:19; 1 Cor 11:24.
160 This is confirmation that Tertullian was using the LXX.
161 Ps 21 (22):17.
162 Ps 21 (22):22.
163 Is 53:8–10.
164 Is 57:2.
165 Is 53:12.
166 Amos 8:9–10.
167 Ex 12:2–10; Num 9:10; 28:16; Dt 16:1–8; Jn 19:14.

168 Ez 8:12–9:6.
169 Dt 28:63–66.
170 See 8.12.
171 11.10b–11a is a repeat of 8.15.
172 *Against the Jews* 11.11b–12.2 = *Against Marcion* 3.20.1–5.
173 Ps 2:7–8.
174 Here I reject Kroymann's text (*Nec poterit alium deum dei filium uindicare quam Christum*) and Tränkle's text (*Nec poteris alium dei filium dicere quam Christum*) and offer *Nec poteris alium Dauid filium uindicare quam Christum.* (I have changed the opinion I expressed in Dunn (2000:17–18), yet I continue to read *Dauid* as accusative rather than genitive.)
175 *Generis.*
176 Is 42:607.
177 Mic 5:1.
178 Is 1:7.
179 Is 33:17.
180 Is 33:18.
181 Dan 9:26.
182 See *Against the Jews* 8.3.
183 Dan 9:26. See *Against the Jews* 8.1, 6, 8.
184 Is 65:2–3.
185 Ps 21 (22):17–18.
186 Ps 68 (69):22.
187 Ps 66 (67):7.
188 Jl 2:22; Ps 1:3.
189 Ex 15:25.
190 Jer 2:10–12.
191 Jer 2:13.
192 Amos 8:9; Mk 15:33, 38; Mt 27:51–52; Lk 23:44–45.
193 Jer 2:13.
194 Is 65:13a, 14b–16.
195 2 Kgs 6:4–7.
196 Gen 22:1–14.
197 Is 53:7.
198 Is 53:8.
199 Is 53:8.
200 Hos 5:15–6:2.
201 *Against the Jews* 13.24–29 = *Against Marcion* 3.23.1–7.
202 Is 3:1–2.
203 Is 5:6.
204 Mt 11:13.
205 Jn 5:1–4.
206 Is 52:5.
207 Scholer (1982: 825) argues that the text is corrupt here and that we should be guided in our interpretation by what we find in *Against Marcion* 3.23.3: 'for from them began that infamy – and they failed to understand that the time that intervened between Tiberius and Vespasian was [a time for] repentance . . .'. On the basis of this revised reading, Scholer finds no evidence in *Against the Jews* for Tertullian charging contemporary Jews with the persecution of Christians.
208 Jer 46:21. These two sentences are difficult to punctuate.

209 Is 1:7–8.
210 Is 1:3–4.
211 Is 1:20.
212 Ps 58 (59):12.
213 Is 50:11.
214 *Against the Jews* 14.1–7 = *Against Marcion* 3.7.1–6.
215 Is 53:7. This is the third time in this treatise that Tertullian has used this passage, although once would have been enough.
216 Is 53:2–3.
217 Is 8:14.
218 Ps 8:8.
219 Ps 21 (22):7.
220 Dan 2:34–35.
221 Dan 7:13–14.
222 Ps 44 (45):3–4.
223 Ps 8:6.
224 Jer 17:9.
225 Is 53:8.
226 Zech 3:1–5.
227 Jn 13:27.
228 *Against the Jews* 14.9–10 = *Against Marcion* 3.7.7–8.
229 Lev 16:5–29. On Tertullian's interpretation and for a comparison with other early Christian interpretations see Dunn (1999c: 245–64).
230 On the relationship between 14.11–12a and 11.11b–12.2a see Dunn (2000: 15–18). I have argued that these last sentences of the treatise are the only ways that were obviously not written by Tertullian himself on the basis of the misinterpretation of Tertullian's earlier interpretation of Ps 2.
231 Ps 2:7–8.
232 These last two sentences seem very awkward.

12 ANTIDOTE FOR THE SCORPION'S STING

1 Barnes (1985: 178) considers that Tertullian kept his promise in *On Flight in Time of Persecution*.
2 This is the juridical or qualitative issue as found in *To Herennius* 1.14.24; Cicero, *On Invention* 2.21.62–2.39.115; and Quintilian, *Oratorical Instruction* 3.6.
3 The elder Pliny, *Natural History* 28.24, could not mention the scorpion without thinking of Africa.
4 As one would expect from a competent orator, Tertullian has put some effort into his opening comments, here employing rhyming pairs, something of which I have tried to capture in English.
5 Nicander of Colophon flourished *c.* 130 BC and wrote, among other things, the poem *Theriaca* about scorpions (769–804), snakes, spiders and other such creatures.
6 See Pliny the elder, *Natural History* 11.86–91, 100.
7 The Roman military catapult for hurling arrows or stones was known as a scorpion. It derived its firepower from a bow, the tension for which came from twisting springs of sinew or hair. See Vitruvius, *On Architecture* 10.10.
8 The elder Pliny, *Natural History* 11.88, reports Apollodorus as having stated that some scorpions use the south wind to fly.

9 Pliny the elder, *Natural History* 27.5, describes aconite (wolfsbane) as being a remedy for scorpion's stings, but not as a preventative. Taken by a healthy person, it is a poison that kills. In 27.6 Pliny suggested that aconite numbs scorpions when applied to them, against which they use white hellebore to reverse the numbness.

10 Azzali Bernardelli (1990b: 178) suggests that Tertullian was arguing either that making the sign of the cross, praying or anointing (and I follow her reading of the manuscripts here) was an indication of the lack of a Christian's faith or that faith was undermined by the incorrect performance of these actions. I am not inclined to the second position. Tertullian was saying that the Christian needed no superstitious practices; the promise of God was sufficient.

11 The use of *ethnicus* is usually an indication of the late date of composition. See Balfour (1982: 786).

12 Acts 28:3–5. See also Mk 16:18.

13 Ex 3:2.

14 Heb 7:27; 9:28; 10:12, 14; Rom 6:9–10; 1Pt 3:18.

15 Is 1:11; Ps 49 (50): 13; Heb 7:27.

16 Ez 18:23; 33:11; 1 Tim 2:4; 2 Pt 3:9.

17 *Canicula* is the lesser dog star, Canis Minor, in the mouth of the canine constellation. This star would become visible on the horizon, after having been obscured for some period of time by the sun, at the hottest time of the year. Hence, it was another way of referring to the height of summer. The word was also used to refer to the worst dice throw. Tertullian, *Against Marcion*, 1.1.5, described Diogenes, the Cynic philosopher, as *canicola* (dog-like) because of his shamelessness.

18 In *Apology* 6.8, Tertullian's reference to the dog-headed one is certainly to an Egyptian god, either Anubis, the jackal-headed god of the underworld or Thoth, the dog-headed baboon god of the moon, wisdom, speech and time (who was also sometimes depicted as an ibis). Barnes (1969: 123) takes this not as a reference to Caracalla or any governor but to the devil.

19 *Venationes* could describe the amphitheatre entertainment that involved not gladiatorial combat but mock animal hunts. I would emend *uenatio* to *uenatione*.

20 Barnes (1986: 118; 1985: 176) takes this an indication that this work must be early, when Tertullian accepted the legitimacy of flight from persecution. Azzali Bernardelli (1990a: 60–1) rejects this. Here I would agree with her because the verb *obsido* does not have any sense of Christians in flight.

21 Ps 18 (19): 10; 118 (119): 103.

22 Ex 3:8, 17.

23 Is 5:20.

24 Ex 20:2–5.

25 Ex 20:22–3.

26 Dt 6:4–5.

27 *Nationum*, i.e. the Gentiles. As Balfour (1982: 788) points out, when Tertullian was contrasting Jews with others (as one would find in the pages of the Hebrew Scriptures), *natio* was Tertullian's regular word choice.

28 Dt 6:12–15.

29 Dt 11:26–8.

30 Dt 12:2–3.

31 Dt 12:29–30.

32 Dt 13:2–6.
33 Literally 'who is in your bosom'.
34 Dt 13:7–11.
35 Dt 12:13–17.
36 Dt 13:17–18.
37 Dt 27:15.
38 Lev 19:4.
39 Lev 25:55–26:1.
40 Ps 113 (115): 4–8; 134 (135): 15–18.
41 Ex 32:1–6, 20.
42 Ex 32:2.
43 Mt 6:21. On the phrase 'fire of wisdom' see Minucius Felix, *Octavius*, 35.
44 In Egyptian mythology the goddess Hathor is often depicted as a woman with a cow's head. The goddess Isis is often depicted with a cow-horned head-dress. The god Ptah is sometimes in Memphis depicted as the bull Apis, while Osiris could be depicted in Helopolis as the bull Mneus. There was a cult of Buchis at Hermothis near Thebes. The white bull was sacred to Min, a harvest and fertility god.
45 Ex 32:27–9.
46 Num 25:1–3.
47 Num 25:5, 8–9. The number is given as 24,000.
48 Jud 2:8, 12–14.
49 The censor traditionally was the highest Roman magistracy. It used to be held by two ex-consuls every five years for an eighteen-month period. Their responsibility was to update the census of the citizen body and the Senate, which led to them being involved in safeguarding public morality. Under the empire this office was often held by the emperor as part of the basis of his authority.
50 Jud 2:20–1.
51 Barnes (1985: 40) takes this as a reference to *On the Prescriptions of Heretics* and possibly the first edition of *Against Marcion*.
52 Ex 23:13.
53 Ex 20:4–5.
54 Barnes (1969: 107) does not find this helpful in dating this treatise because *Against Marcion* underwent three editions over a number of years.
55 See the elder Pliny, *Natural History*, 20.22.
56 Gen 2:16–17.
57 The *pythicus agon* was a musical contest with singing and dancing. Barnes (1969: 125–8) dates the awarding of these games to Carthage with the visit of Septimius Severus, which he places in the middle of 203, which would have been the occasion for the construction of the odeon, which backs onto the theatre, on the hill of Juno. Birley (1988: 146) is more inclined to date the visit to Carthage in mid-202, before the visit to Lepcis. The stadium was the venue for foot races and it has not been located in Carthage.
58 This reference here is to more than foot races or the Pythian games, including as it does mention of wrestling, boxing and horse racing.
59 Jn 14:2.
60 1 Cor 15:41.
61 Gen 2:7.
62 The reference would seem to be to Mt 22:11.
63 Mt 25:3.

64 Lk 15:4–5.
65 Ps 31 (32):1–2.
66 Prov 10:12; 1 Pt 4:8.
67 Sophia is the youngest of the aeons in the Valentinian cosmology, the one who splits from the others by acting without her pair, Teletus (or Theletus), who becomes the mother of the demiurge (the God of the Old Testament). In contrast to the Valentinians, Tertullian presents Christ as the only-begotten son of Sophia, not as a separate aeon. See Stead (1969: 75–104).
68 Prov 9:2.
69 Prov 1:20–1.
70 Is 44:5.
71 Zech 13:9.
72 Rom 8:32.
73 Rom 4:25.
74 Is 40:13–14; Wis 9:13; Rom 11:34.
75 On human sacrifice in Carthage see Stager (1980: 1–11).
76 Rome itself.
77 Ps 115:5 (Ps 116:15).
78 Is 57:1–2.
79 Gen 4:5–8.
80 1 Sam 19:1–2.
81 1 Kgs 19:3.
82 Heb 11:37 speaks of prophets sawn in two. This is found with reference to Isaiah in the apocryphal *Ascension of Isaiah* 5.9, 14, which is in the first section known as *The Martyrdom of Isaiah*, which was a Jewish Midrash of 2 Kgs 21: 16, probably written in the first century AD. Tertullian, *On Patience* 14.11, mentioned the same incident. Tertullian probably derived his information from Justin's *Dialogue with Trypho* 120.5.
83 2 Chr 24:21; Mt 23:35; Lk 11:51.
84 Lk 16:16.
85 Mk 1:2; Mt 3:3; Lk 3:4; 7:27.
86 Mt 14:6–11; Mk 6:22–8.
87 Dan 3:1–15.
88 Bar 6:3.
89 Dan 3:16–18.
90 Tertullian's aim is to show that both Old and New Testaments teach the same thing with regard to the need for martyrdom and that the argument of his opponents – that there is no teaching that Sophia cuts the throats of her children – is proven wrong from both.
91 Mt 5:10. Tertullian has presented the Valentinian position and, in the extract from the Beatitudes, a quick indication that their position was absurd (unless it was interpreted figuratively, something that he would not here accept).
92 Mt 5:11–12.
93 Barnes (1969: 115–16) argues that Tertullian would not have made this kind of statement during his Montanist years. Azzali Barnardelli (1990a: 57–8) thinks this is really only an argument from silence on Barnes' part.
94 Mt 10:16; Lk 10:3.
95 Mt 10:17–18.
96 Mt 10:21; Mk 13:12.
97 Mt 10:22.

98 Mt 10:22.
99 Mt 10:24.
100 Mt 10:28.
101 Mt 10:29.
102 Mt 10:30.
103 Mt 10:31.
104 I have not wanted to use the English 'confess' to translate *confiteor* because of its additional modern penitential meaning. At the same time I need to find a term in English that can be both transitive and intransitive, as will become clear in Tertullian's argument in 9.11.
105 To avoid gender-specific problems in English, I have translated the Latin singular into the English plural. That Tertullian was not being gender-specific is clear from his use of *omnis*. I shall continue to do this unless it is clear that the reference is specifically to one gender alone.
106 Mt 10:32–3.
107 Note that this is the transitive form, unlike the intransitive in 9.8.
108 This would make more sense if it simply said 'have denied Christ'.
109 The Latin is corrupt. Azzali Barnardelli reconstructs it as *pro <bro> auspice* and I have followed that here.
110 Mk 8:38; Lk 9:26.
111 Here Tertullian referred cynically to Valentinian cosmology. Acinetus, which means motionless or unmoveable one, was one of the thirty aeons in the Valentinian Pleroma according to Hippolytus, *Refutation of All Heresies* 6.25. In Tertullian's *Against the Valentinians* 8.2, 4, Acinetus is mentioned while Theletus (note the variant spelling), which means perfect and who was paired with Sophia, is mentioned is 8.2, 4; 9.2; 12.1; 30.1; 32.5. Abascantus, which means resistant to the spiteful, is not mentioned.
112 Is 40:5.
113 See Is 40:22.
114 Ps 48 (49): 13, 21.
115 Mk 8:27; Mt 16:13; cf. Lk 9:18.
116 Mt 7:12; Lk 6:31.
117 Aratus was a Valentinian. The other four are mythological characters after whom celestial constellations are named. Erigona is the constellation Virgo. Although some of these were also named in Tertullian's *To the Heathens* 2.15.1, the point here is that the only thing to be found in the heavens are the stars and not the Valentinian superior 'spiritual' or 'heavenly' Christians.
118 Cf. Mt 10:32. That the Lord did not say 'heavenly' tells against the Valentinians according to Tertullian.
119 Following Azzali Bernardelli in reading *Carnam*. As Barnes (1969: 120) points out, Tertullian referred to Carna (corrupted in the manuscripts to Cardea) in three other treatises: *To the Heathens* 2.15.5; *On Idolatry* 15.5 and *On the Military Crown* 13.9. These were primitive Roman household deities of hinges, doors and thresholds. See also Ovid, *Fasti* 6.101; Augustine, *On the City of God* 4.8; 6.7; Arnobius of Sicca, *Against the Nations* 1.28; 4.9.
120 Ps 23 (24): 7, 9.
121 Amos 9:6.
122 On the significance of this for Tertullian's thoughts about the Roman church, see Dunn (2003a: 14). Even this passage makes it clear that the power of the keys was inherited by every Christian.

123 Cf. Mt 10:28. Tertullian's accusation against the Valentinians is that they have misinterpreted this passage, by turning a negative command into a positive one.

124 One should note Tertullian's sarcasm here.

125 Tertullian again sarcastically stated his opponents' view.

126 Ps 109 (110):1; Mt 22:44; Heb 1:13; 10:12.

127 This statement has been the source of its own controversy about how to interpret Tertullian. Barnes (1969: 132) states that context – the reference to the fate of the apostles – would indicate that Tertullian was referring to Christianity at its origins, while the reference to the pagans was a more contemporary one. Frend (1965: 334; 1968: 8–9 and 1970b: 92–6) argues that the references both to the Jews and the pagans referred to contemporary events. Like Frend, I believe that Tertullian often had contemporary relationships between Christians and Jews in mind when he wrote, but I do not believe, in this instance, that he was saying that the Jews were persecuting Christians. It would seem to me more of a statement that he was blaming the Jews for starting the persecutions, which now were being continued much more forcefully by the pagan authorities. I take this statement as evidence of ongoing feelings but not ongoing persecutions. I would think it to be the same thing at 15.2 where there is a mixture of scriptural and more contemporary references.

128 i.e., the Gentiles.

129 I have resisted translating *genus* as 'race' here because the distinction is one of religious affiliation not race or ethnicity (however we define those terms), just as his reference to a third *genus* (the existence of which he rejected) in *On the Veiling of Virgins* 7.1 was on the basis of sexual distinction. As we find in Clement, *Miscellanies* 6.42.2, what Tertullian said here is that only the third *genus*, the Christians, will reach heaven, while the other two (Jews and pagans) will not.

130 Lk 21:16.

131 Once again, Tertullian is being sarcastic.

132 A reference to the two constellations Ursa Major and Ursa Minor.

133 A reference to the constellations Taurus and Leo.

134 Mt 10:34–6.

135 Mt 10:21; Mk 13:12.

136 Mt 10:22.

137 Mt 10:37; Lk 14:26.

138 Mt 16:25; Lk 17:33; Jn 12:25.

139 I have added this to give the sense of Tertullian's sarcasm and to balance with the point he makes in the next sentence.

140 Mt 10:19.

141 Mt 10:20.

142 Mt 25:36.

143 Lk 18:7.

144 Mt 13:5–6, 20–1.

145 Tertullian's logic is difficult to follow here. In this instance, because it suited his argument, he was arguing for a rather literal interpretation of Scripture against the Valentinians who were advocating other events than the ones that were most obvious as the fulfilment of scriptural prophecy. Tertullian wanted to argue here (and it must be remembered that he could argue for a more allegorical interpretation of Scripture when it suited him) that any event could be seen as the fulfilment of a prophecy if one were not to take the words at face value.

Those events, like persecution, that seemed to match the literal fulfilment of the words of Jesus must therefore be taken to be those to which Jesus referred. I have the impression that one is not meant to understand Tertullian's logic here with great clarity; its very complexity and obscurity could well have been meant to overwhelm a reader into accepting his point.

146 Mt 17:1; Mk 9:2; Lk 9:28; 1 Cor 15:8.
147 2 Cor 1:4.
148 Again, Tertullian is being sarcastic.
149 1 Pt 2:20–1.
150 1 Pt 4:12–16.
151 1 Jn 3:16.
152 1 Jn 4:18.
153 Mt 10:28.
154 Rev 2:10.
155 Rev 2:13.
156 Rev 3:7–8.
157 Rev 2:7.
158 Rev 2:17.
159 Rev 2:27–8.
160 Rev 3:5, 12.
161 Rev 3:21.
162 Mt 20:21; Mk 10:40.
163 Rev 6:9–11.
164 Rev 7:9.
165 Rev 7:14.
166 Is 1:18.
167 Rev 17:5–6.
168 Rev 21:8.
169 1Jn 4:18. See *Antidote for the Scorpion's Sting* 12.4.
170 Is 2:4.
171 Gen 49:27. On Paul's Benjaminite membership see Rom 11:1; Phil 3:5. In *Against Marcion* 5.1.5 Tertullian also made the connection between Paul and the imagery of his tribe as a ravenous wolf.
172 Gen 25:34; 27:25.
173 2 Thess 1:4–5.
174 Rom 5:3–5.
175 Rom 8:17–18.
176 Rom 8:35–9.
177 2 Cor 11:23–5.
178 2 Cor 12:10.
179 2 Cor 4:8–10.
180 2 Cor 4:16–18.
181 This is not from either letter to the Thessalonians but from Phil 1:30. Is this an indication that Tertullian was trying to cite from memory?
182 Phil 2:17–18.
183 2 Tim 4:6–8.
184 2 Tim 2:11–13.
185 2 Tim 1:8.
186 2 Tim 1:7.
187 Rom 13:1.

188 Rom 13:4.
189 Rom 13:3–4.
190 Rom 13:7.
191 Mt 22:21.
192 1 Pt 2:13.
193 Acts 5:40.
194 Acts 7:59.
195 Acts 12:2.
196 Acts 14:19.
197 Lk 19:40.
198 See Tacitus, *Annals* 15.44. Cf. Suetonius, *Nero* 16.
199 Jn 21:18.
200 As I point out in Dunn (2001a: 410–11), while in *On the Prescriptions of Heretics* 36.3, Tertullian also referred to the manner of the two apostles' deaths and the location, only here was it linked specifically with Nero.
201 Acts 21:10–12.
202 Acts 21:13.
203 Acts 21:14.
204 Mt 4:10; Dt 6:13. Cf. Mt 16:23; Mk 8:31.

13 ON THE VEILING OF VIRGINS

1 Literally 'from the time when they shall have completed the changing of their age'. That Tertullian felt the need for a Latin edition of his Greek original should be an indication that he wanted it to be read more widely. We may speculate that the Greek original had been addressed to the virgins themselves. If so, this could suggest either that these girls came from better-off local families where they could afford to have learnt several languages or that they came from Greek-speaking migrant families where such a non-veiling had been the custom and which they wished to maintain (and extend) in Carthage. This latter idea would make sense of why, in 2.1, Tertullian mentioned other communities in the Greek world that did veil their virgins. Stücklin (1974: 108) thinks it not out of the question that Tertullian's reference to an earlier work was to *On Prayer*, but I am not inclined to agree.
2 One should contrast these early chapters here, where Tertullian argued against custom when it was contrary to the truth, with what he wrote in *On the Military Crown* 3 where he described much of Christian liturgical life as being derived from custom and not from Scripture. Like a good orator, he was able to speak either for or against a position depending upon the particular circumstances.
3 Jn 14:6.
4 Col 1:17.
5 *Resuscitatum.* The same verb is used in *Against Praxeas* 2.1 but not in *On the Prescriptions of Heretics* 13.4, which uses *resurgo*. While *resuscito* does mean 'raise up again', I am wanting to emphasize the difference between the two verbs, perhaps suggesting that *resuscito* is a more primitive, less theologically precise word than the later *resurgo*.
6 See Countryman (1982: 208–27). It is surprising, in a supposedly Montanist work, that the rule of faith contains no reference to the Spirit.
7 Reference to the Holy Spirit as Paraclete is taken by Barnes (1985: 44) as one of

the indicators of a work being written later in Tertullian's career, when he was most under the influence of Montanism.

8   Jn 16:12–13. Gramaglia (1984: 22612) points out that Tertullian was translating this passage from the Greek and not the Old Latin version.

9   Jn 14:26.

10 One should note how this sentence gives structure to the rest of the treatise, in a very similar way to which the threefold pattern of faith, teaching and truth gives shape to *On the Shows* (Sider 1978: 339–65). Throughout this treatise I have translated *disciplina* as 'teaching'. Tertullian used the word to refer to teaching about how one should live one's life rather than teaching about matters of what to believe intellectually, so perhaps it could even be rendered as 'practical teaching'. The emphasis throughout is on the theory of how a Christian should live rather than on how Christians actually did live, hence my preference for 'teaching' over 'conduct' or 'discipline'. In *On the Shows*, discussion about practical teaching comes in the section on truth, while the heading *disciplina* is used to refer to Scripture, in contrast with *On the Veiling of Virgins*.

11 Ecc 3:17.

12 A reference to Tertullian's opposition to Marcion, who had argued that the god revealed in the Old Testament (the creator) was an inferior god to the one revealed in the New Testament (the God of justice).

13 Rather than gender-specific language about God (in this instance the Paraclete), I prefer to use the substantive, putting it in brackets to indicate where Tertullian simply used a personal pronoun.

14 Mt 23:8.

15 Jn 14:26; 16:13b. Tertullian had not included this part of verse 13 in his earlier extract from chapter 16.

16 It is only in this text that Tertullian used *antecessor* in its sense of 'law professor' (with it parallels with the usual Latin translation of παράκλητος as *advocatus* – see Tertullian, *Against Praxeas* 9.3 – rather than *intercessor*) rather than its usual sense of 'predecessor'.

17 Balfour (1982: 786) points out that *gentiles* never appears in any of Tertullian's works after *Against Marcion*. The fact that the related noun (*gentilitas*) appears here is either an exception, or an indication that the work ought to be dated earlier. Here the word does not mean Gentile (as opposed to Jew) but pagan (as opposed to Christian).

18 Tertullian's final comment (*et puto ante quosdam*) is ambiguous in that it depends upon something else. If that verb is *proposui* ('I have proposed') then Tertullian was saying that he believed that he had proposed apostolic churches as setting a precedent before anyone else had proposed this. I have taken the reference to be to the apostles and their associates. Gramaglia (1984: 23324) finds a reference to the bishop of Carthage as the 'certain others'. I think it more likely to be a reference simply to the other churches to which the unveiled virgins turned for their precedent.

19 What Tertullian argues is that not only do a great number of churches veil their virgins but the apostolic churches in particular, which set precedent, veil them. The later churches, as he refers to them, i.e., those of more recent, non-apostolic origin, are those that do not veil them. As Rankin (1995: 99) points out in another context, it is a church's conformity to apostolic teaching that is of most importance, more so even than its ability to trace some apostolic succession.

20 Tertullian's argument is that, just because the practice of veiling virgins is found

in Greek and foreign churches, this is no reason for it to be rejected in Africa. He offers three reasons: the practice is also found in Africa, some of those other (Greek) churches are apostolic churches (which ought to be imitated by others), and they are not foreign churches but form part of the one body.

21 Eph 4:4–6.

22 1 Cor 12:25. Rankin (1995: 104) takes this passage as indicating that, even as a Montanist, Tertullian remained a member of the church and was not schismatic.

23 *Includit*. The word is used here to mean 'encloses them in a veil'. Yet the verb also means to 'shut in' and even 'control', and there is a sense that this is Tertullian's motive in wanting virgins veiled.

24 Jn 5:44; 12:43.

25 What Tertullian said was that praising virgins would cause them to blush and, not being veiled, the visible sign of the offence of being singled out for praise (their blushing), would last long after the words were spoken.

26 Schulz-Flügel (1997: 207) suggests that Tertullian is being pointed here in his reference to his opponents.

27 *Prostitui*. This verb more commonly meant 'to be exposed to prostitution' or simply 'to prostitute oneself'. Tertullian's choice of words is very revealing.

28 1 Cor 7:25–39.

29 1 Cor 7:22, 34.

30 Stücklin (1974: 122–3) finds a reference to Seneca's *Letter* 94 here.

31 The adjective *nundinaticius, -a, -um* is connected with a word for market and is used to imply that those virgins who went about unveiled were offering themselves for sale. Again, the overtones of prostitution are present behind Tertullian's choice of words.

32 *Publicatio* could also have the sense of public exposure (Schulz-Flügel 1997: 210). I am more inclined to use it in the more traditional sense of confiscation, especially because of the reference to the veil having been taken (*sublato*) in the next sentence.

33 Tertullian seems to suggest here that the loss of physical virginity is less of a degradation than the loss of spiritual virginity because, while sexual intimacy is at least natural, ripping of a woman's veil is unnatural. I do not think Tertullian meant rape when he referred to physical violence, but the violence done to virginity through any kind of sexual intimacy (even consensual) involving a dedicated virgin.

34 *Habitus* can refer both to what one wears as well as to one's character or nature or deportment. If Tertullian's statement applies to an item of clothing, then he provides us with information about its blessing. If the statement applies more to one's appearance, then he seems to suggest that the virgins make a commitment to God to appear a certain way (that is to say veiled). The veil becomes the sign of that commitment.

35 Ps 73 (74):22.

36 Tertullian is saying that the custom of letting virgins themselves choose whether to be veiled or not was destroyed by those virgins who wanted to force their still-veiled sisters to be liberated.

37 1 Cor 11:5–16.

38 1 Cor 7:34.

39 Most of this section of 4.1 (with the exception of the reference to 1 Cor 7:34) parallels *On Prayer* 21.2–4.

40 1 Cor 7:34.

41 This section of 4.2 parallels *On Prayer* 22.2.

42 1 Cor 7:34.

43 As one can tell from the number of additions a translator has to add to this treatise in order to make it make sense, in this work Tertullian himself is giving us an example of this maxim in action. Indeed, this could be his own motto for his mature style as an author.

44 Here we have an appeal to simple Aristotelian biology. The general, antecedent, universal genus is 'woman' to which belongs any number of particular, subsequent, partial species, including 'virgin', 'widow' and 'married woman'. In 1 Corinthians 7, Paul had used the term 'woman' as equivalent to 'married woman' – this is Tertullian's interpretation – while in 1 Corinthians 11 he used the term 'woman' in its more general sense.

45 Gen 2:18.

46 Gen 2:23.

47 This section parallels *On Prayer* 22.1.

48 Gen 2:24.

49 Gen 2:19–20.

50 Gen 2:25.

51 Gen 2:23.

52 This sentence parallels roughly with *On Prayer* 22.3.

53 Gen 2:24.

54 Gen 2:23.

55 Gen 3:20.

56 Tertullian's rather long-winded statement appears to be that it is not the term 'woman' that indicates Adam's helpmate as his future wife, but the very name Eve itself that indicates her future status as mother (and wife too).

57 Gal 4:4.

58 Ebion is reputed by Tertullian and Hippolytus to have been the founder of the Ebionites, a group of Christians who observed many Jewish ritual practices and who were branded as heretics because of their belief that Jesus was born of normal human sexual intercourse and was invested by God with extraordinary powers and yet was not divine. Scholars today debate whether the Ebionites were a particular sect or whether the term applied to Christian Jews in general.

59 Lk 1:26–8.

60 The use of the substantive derived from the verb *desponso*, which we find a number of times in this chapter and in chapter 11, suggests an agreement to marry, probably still negotiated between families rather than between the marrying couple, that was less formal than the arrangement that involved the use of the verb *spondeo* or *sponso*. See Treggiari (1991: 141–2).

61 1 Cor 11:3. It is to be noted that in this section of the treatise, where the argument is drawn from reason and nature, that Tertullian still appeals to Scripture.

62 *Nubere* is a verb that means to veil. As the wearing of the *flammeum*, the flame-coloured mantle, was an integral part of the Roman wedding ceremony, the verb came to mean to marry. I want to capture this twofold meaning in my translation.

63 1 Cor 11:6.

64 This sentence parallels *On Prayer* 22.7b.

65 1 Cor 11:7.

66 1 Cor 11:8–9.

67 Gen 2:23.

68 1 Cor 11:10.

69 1 Cor 11:10.

70 Tertullian argued that if even the angels lusted after virgins, it was to be expected that men would do the same, and that as a consequence virgins ought to be veiled to protect themselves. This section of 7.2b parallels *On Prayer* 22.5.

71 Gen 6:1–2.

72 This is an indication that Tertullian was using a Greek text of Genesis.

73 7.2c–3a parallels *On Prayer* 22.6.

74 1 Cor 11:14–15.

75 1 Cor 11:7.

76 1 Cor 11:3.

77 Gen 2:23.

78 1 Cor 11:5.

79 1 Cor 11:4.

80 *Investis* can also refer to an unmarried man.

81 Here we have a clear instance of Tertullian applying the term *uirgo* to males.

82 8.3–4a parallels *On Prayer* 22.4b not 22.8a as Schulz-Flügel (1997: 28) suggests.

83 1 Cor 11:16.

84 Stücklin (1974: 42) omits the negative particle.

85 1 Cor 14:34.

86 1 Tim 2:12.

87 Cardman (1999: 325, 32) says that here 'Tertullian rails against women speaking . . .'. I certainly agree that Tertullian repeats the Pauline instruction but I would not go as far as to say that he rails. Indeed, the Montanist style of Christianity to which Tertullian was attracted was founded upon three prophets, two of whom had been female. In *On the Soul* 9.4 Tertullian mentioned a (Montanist) woman who was inspired by the Paraclete during the liturgy and who delivered her message (to those in the assembly who were of Montanist leanings) when the liturgy was concluded. Here in *On the Veiling of Virgins*, it suits Tertullian's purpose to portray himself as being submissive to Scripture as he wants the unveiled virgins to be equally submissive. Cardman's statement does not take into account what we find in *Against Marcion* 5.8.11 where, using the same piece of Scripture (1 Cor 11:5–6), Tertullian was able to argue that women could utter prophecy as long as they were veiled. The closest parallel to this section in *On Prayer* is 22.4a.

88 1 Tim 5:9.

89 1 Tim 5:10. This is a difficult passage to translate and my result must remain rather conjectural. The German and Italian translations have the two *ut* clauses referring to the widows (which certainly seems to make most sense of the first clause), while the French translation has them referring to the virgin (which makes most sense of the second clause). I am making the first refer to the widows and the second to the virgin (and others like her).

90 The honourable mark is their unveiled condition. It is obvious that Tertullian here is being sarcastic.

91 These were an inland African people. The elder Pliny refers to them in his *Natural History* 5.36, 38, 45.

92 Stücklin (1974: 124) believes that Tertullian's information comes from Tacitus,

Germany 38, where he describes the practice of the male Suebi, who sweep up their hair and tie it in a knot to give them the appearance of greater height. This practice distinguishes them from other Germans.

93 1 Cor 7:5. The common hardship may be taken as a reference to marriage, thus those who have protested against marriage are the virgins.

94 Gen 1:27; 1 Cor 11:7.

95 On the question of whether or not Tertullian accepted that women were, like men, created in the image of God, see Church (1975: 90–1).

96 See 8.2. The opponents have argued that if Tertullian were right, that 'women' referred to females of every age, then he ought to be consistent and argue for the veiling even of prepubescent girls, which he does not. In a wonderful display of rhetoric Tertullian will now go on to argue further about the definition of virgin. Up until this point he has put the case that 'virgins' (a species of the generic term 'woman') meant unmarried adolescent and unmarried adult females, and they should be veiled. Now he is prepared to agree with his opponents that virgins should not be veiled only because, for the sake of argument, he has redefined 'virgins' to be only those who are prepubescent.

97 Gen 2:25.

98 Gen 3:6–7.

99 1 Cor 11:10.

100 11.1–2 parallels *On Prayer* 22.8.

101 Gen 24:63–5.

102 Mt 5:28.

103 In *On the Military Crown* 4.2, Tertullian also turned to Rebekah to argue that if one were only to follow Scripture (and not take custom into account) then she would be the precedent only for virgins coming to marriage to be veiled at the moment they recognized their intended husbands. No other females and virgins at no other times should be veiled. As this was obviously not the case, Tertullian argued that Christians sometimes needed more than Scripture in order to devise rules for life. 11.3 parallels *On Prayer* 22.10c.

104 This is how the German, Italian and French translations render *ex angustiis*, yet the term can also have the sense of narrow-mindedness.

105 This is a reference to the changes of puberty, including the onset of menstruation.

106 Here Tertullian seems to be using the term 'woman' now to indicate a particular species (adult females) rather than the genus.

107 I add this to make clear how Tertullian can seem to have made a statement contrary to his overall position.

108 The use of *ethnicus* is an indication of the late date of composition. See Balfour (1982: 786).

109 For classical references to the *flammeum*, the flame-coloured wedding veil, see Juvenal, *Satires* 6.224–6; Pliny the elder, *Natural History* 21.46; Festus 79.23L; 32.6L.

110 See Lucan, *Pharsalia* 2.370–1. Treggiari (1991: 149–50) makes the point that it is only on the basis of Tertullian's 'tendentious' evidence that we may conclude that the wearing of the veil, the kiss and the joining of the right hands was part of the engagement ceremony. At her engagement '[t]he physical contact with a male body and the mental awareness make her to all intents and purposes a married woman already'. Tertullian's overall point is clear: it is not marriage (or even engagement) that makes a girl a woman but her age.

111 The use of the Latin verb *sponso* indicates the Roman practice of an agreement to marry being reached between two families. I have translated this term here and at 16.4 with the idea of promise to indicate that this first step did not involve those to be married. See Treggiari (1991: 138–46).

112 *Sponsalia* refers to the ratification of the promise to marry that had been made by the families. The ratification needed to be made by the couple themselves. The term also refers to the celebration of the engagement. See Treggiari (1991: 145–8).

113 I would not take Tertullian at face value here, for although he says 'ours' he really meant that in a very loose sense. His comments are about the unveiled virgins who, although in every other respect dress as adults from the time of puberty onwards, continue to dress as children when it comes to the wearing of the veil.

114 The *pallium* was a Greek rectangular mantle unlike the Roman curved *toga*. Women wore a *palla* rather than a *pallium*, so it is interesting to find this term, about which Tertullian wrote so much in *On the Pallium*, associated with women.

115 12.1b–2 parallels *On Prayer* 22.9a.

116 Literally 'the brothers'. I have offered the more inclusive translation to indicate that perhaps Tertullian meant that these virgins ought to show respect to the other females in the community (as well as the males).

117 Cf. Gal 1:10. 13.1–2a parallels *On Prayer* 22.9b.

118 Mt 6:4.

119 *Gloria*. Groh (1971: 11) notes that *gloria* is self-exaltation, the very opposite to Christian humility and that in this part of his work, Tertullian points to its manifestation in clothing and personal appearance.

120 1 Cor 4:7.

121 13.3 parallels *On Prayer* 22.9c.

122 Tertullian was being ironic, even sarcastic, here.

123 This is an excellent example of the rhetorical figure of *gradatio*. See *To Herennius* 4.25.34; Quintilian, *Oratorical Instruction* 9.3.55–7. One may note the parallel with *On the Shows* 15.3–4.

124 *Produco* can have the sense that it is envy that 'leads' them to behave the way they do, that their pregnancies are 'exposed' to common knowledge, and that it is their envy that makes their stomachs 'grow and bear'.

125 Phil 3:19.

126 Prov 5:22; Is 5:18.

127 There seems to be something missing in what Tertullian wrote at this point, which makes interpretation of what he meant difficult.

128 Ex 20:5; Dt 5:9.

129 Mt 10:26; Lk 12:2.

130 Here I take *publicatio* in its secondary sense. Cf. 3.4.

131 14.1–5 parallels *On Prayer* 22.9d.

132 1 Sam 2:7; Ps 74 (75):8; 146 (147):6; Lk 1:52.

133 1 Thess 5:21.

134 Eph 6:11, 13.

135 This section parallels *On Prayer* 22.9e.

136 *Pudicitia*. Tertullian has a treatise entitled *On Modesty*. The word can also mean decency, virtue, good character or chastity. Tertullian's *On Exhortation to Chastity* uses the Latin word *castitas*, which more commonly means purity. Classical

literature praised the woman of good character as suitable for marriage and by that is meant a woman of restraint or modesty in all things, and one part of that would have been sexual modesty, or chastity. See Treggiari (1991: 103–7, 218–19, 236).

137 1 Cor 11:10.

138 Her identity is unclear. Indeed, these couple of sentences seem to make awkward sense. I have taken the 'they' to refer to the pagan females who wear their veil: they are unhappy because they can see what they are loving, whereas men cannot see them to decide whether or not to love them; yet they are happy because they do not have the constant attention of men which they would if they were not veiled.

139 Is the Christian woman in question of Montanist persuasion, for whom prophetic revelations were an important dimension of their religious identity, or not? Such revelations did not seem as important to non-Montanist Christian women. If she were a Montanist, though, one would presume that she would already have been veiled, as demanded by their more rigorous way of Christian life. That the angel can see the certain sister's neck could indicate that she was a non-Montanist Christian woman (who were generally of a more libertine persuasion than their Montanist-inclined sisters). However, as I suggested at the end of the introduction to this text, perhaps it is more likely that some of the Montanist virgins had been seeking liberation from the veil and that this female prophet was indeed a rebellious Montanist woman. The sarcastic tone of the angel's comment would indicate that the prophecy was a warning to be veiled down to the base of the neck. Whether or not the woman responded positively to the warning we cannot tell, though if she had, one would imagine Tertullian would have mentioned her change as it would have been so useful to his position.

140 It would seem that Tertullian was describing the ostrich.

141 Stücklin (1974: 123–4) finds a parallel with the elder Pliny's *Natural History* 10.1 here.

BIBLIOGRAPHY

TEXTS AND TRANSLATIONS OF TERTULLIAN

Aulisa, Immacolata (ed.) (1998) *Tertulliano. Polemica con i Giudei*, Rome: Città Nuova (Collana di Testi Patristici 140).

Azzali Bernardelli, Giovanna (ed.) (1990b) *Tertulliano. Scorpiace*, Florence: Nardini Editore (Biblioteca Patristica).

Dekkers, E., Borleffs, J. G. Ph., Willems, R., Refoulé, R. F., Diercks, G. F. and Kroymann, A. (eds) (1954) *Tertulliani*, pars I: *Opera catholica – Adversus Marcionem*, Turnhout: Brepols (Corpus Christianorum, Series Latina 1).

Evans, Ernest (trans. & ed.) (1972) *Tertullian. Adversus Marcionem*, 2 vols, Oxford: Clarendon Press (Oxford Early Christian Texts).

Gerlo, A., Kroymann, A., Waszink, J. H., Borleffs, J. G. Ph., Reifferscheid, A., Wissowa, G., Dekkers, E., Thierry, J. J., Evans, E., Willems, R. and Harnack, A, eds (1954) *Tertulliani*, pars II: *Opera montanistica*, Turnhout: Brepols (Corpus Christianorum, Series Latina 2).

Gramaglia, Pier Angelo (ed.) (1984) *Tertulliano. De virginibus velandis: La condizione femminile nelle prime comunità cristiane*, Turin: Edizioni Borla (Collana di testi e studi).

Schulz-Flügel, Eva (ed.) (1997) *Tertullien. Le voile des vierges*, trans. Paul Mattei, Paris: Les Éditions du Cerf (Sources Chrétiennes 424).

Stücklin, Christoph (1974) *Tertullian. De virginibus velandis. Übersetzung, Einleitung, Kommentar. Ein Beitrag zur altkirchlichen Frauenfrage*, Bern: Herbert Lang (Europäische Hochschulschriften XXIII, 26).

Tränkle, Hermann (1964) *Q. S. F. Tertulliani. Adversus Iudaeos: Mit Einleitung und kritischem Kommentar*, Wiesbaden: Franz Steiner.

REFERENCE WORKS

Allenbach, J., Benoit, A., Bertrand, D. A., Hanriot-Coustet, A., Maraval, P., Pautler, A. and Prigent, P. (eds) (1975) *Biblia Patristica* t. 1: *Des origines à Clément d'Alexandrie et Tertullien*, Paris: Éditions du Centre National de la Recherche Scientifique.

Braun, R., Chapot F., Deléani, S., Dolbeau, F., Fredouille, J.-C. and Petitmengin, P.
(eds) (1999) *Chronica Tertullianea et Cyprianea 1975–1994*, Paris: Institut d'Études
Augustiniennes (Collection des Études Augustiniennes Série Antiquite 157).

Claesson, Gösta (1974–5) *Index Tertullianeus*, 3 vols, Paris: Études Augustiniennes
(Collection des Études Augustiniennes Série Antiquite 62–4).

Dekkers, Eligius (ed.) (1995) *Clavis Patrum Latinorum, Corpus Christianorum, Series
Latina*, 3rd edn, Steenbrugge: Brepols.

Stevenson, J. (1987) *A New Eusebius: Documents illustrating the history of the Church to
AD 337*, rev. W. H. C. Frend, London: SPCK.

SECONDARY LITERATURE

Aalders, G. J. D. (1937) 'Tertullian's Quotations from St Luke', *Mnemosyne* 5 series
3: 241–82.

Anderson, Graham (1993) *The Second Sophistic: A Cultural Phenomenon in the Roman
Empire*, London and New York: Routledge.

Aziza, Claude (1977) *Tertullien et le judaïsme*, Nice: Faculté des Lettres et des Sciences
Humaines de Nice (Publications de le Faculté des Lettres et des Sciences
Humaines de Nice 16).

Azzali Bernardelli, Giovanna (1990a) *'De Quaestionibus Confessionum Alibi Docebimus'*
(Tertulliano *Cor* 1,5)', in Jean and Michèle Biraud (eds), *Autour de Tertullien.
Hommage à René Braun*, t. 2, Nice: Faculté des Lettres et Sciences Humaines de
Nice: 51–84 (Publication de la Faculté des Lettres et Sciences Humaines de Nice
56).

Balfour, I.L.S. (1982) 'Tertullian's Description of the Heathen', *Studia Patristica* 17/2:
785–9.

Barnes, Timothy David (1969) 'Tertullian's *Scorpiace*', *Journal of Theological Studies* n.s.
20: 105–32.

—— (1976) 'Tertullian the Antiquarian', *Studia Patristica* 14/3: 3–20.

—— (1985) *Tertullian: A Historical and Literary Study*, rev. edn, Oxford: Clarendon
Press.

—— (1986) 'Proconsuls of Asia Under Caracalla', *Phoenix* 40: 202–5.

Birley, A. R. (1988) *The African Emperor: Septimius Severus*, 2nd edn, London:
Batsford.

—— (1991) 'Caecilius Capella: Persecutor of Christians, Defender of Byzantium',
Greek, Roman and Byzantine Studies 32: 81–98.

—— (1992) 'Persecutors and Martyrs in Tertullian's Africa', *Institute of Archaeology
Bulletin* 29: 37–68.

Bonner, Stanley F. (1977) *Education in Ancient Rome: From the elder Cato to the younger
Pliny*, Berkeley and Los Angeles: University of California Press.

Boyarin, Daniel (1999) *Dying for God: Martyrdom and the Making of Christianity and
Judaism*, Stanford: Stanford University Press.

Braun, René (1977) *Deus Christianorum. Recherches sur le vocabulaire doctrinal de
Tertullien*, 2nd edn, Paris: Institut d'Études Augustiniennes (Collection des Études
Augustiniennes Serie Antiquité 70).

Bray, Gerald (1977) 'The Legal Concept of Ratio in Tertullian', *Vigiliae Christianae* 31: 94–116.

Buell, Denise Kimber (2002) 'Race and Universalism in Early Christianity', *Journal of Early Christian Studies* 10: 429–68.

Caplan, Harry (1921) 'The History of the Jews in the Roman Province of Africa: A Collection of the Sources' (PhD diss., Cornell).

Cardman, Francine (1999) 'Women, Ministry, and Church Order in Early Christianity', in Ross Shephard Kraemer and Mary Rose D'Angelo (eds), *Women and Christian Origins*, Oxford & New York: Oxford University Press, 300–29.

Church, F. Forrester (1975) 'Sex and Salvation in Tertullian', *Harvard Theological Review* 68: 83–101.

Countryman, L. Wm. (1982) 'Tertullian and the Regula Fidei', *The Second Century* 2: 208–27.

Croom, A. T. (2000) *Roman Clothing and Fashion*, Stroud: Tempus Publishing.

Daly, Cahal (1993) *Tertullian the Puritan and His Influence*, Dublin: Four Courts Press.

Daniélou, Jean (1977) *A History of Early Christian Doctrine Before the Council of Nicaea*, vol. 3: *The Origins of Latin Christianity*, trans. David Smith and John Austin Baker, London: Darton, Longman and Todd.

Duncan-Jones, R. P. (1963) 'City Population in Roman Africa', *Journal of Roman Studies* 53: 85–90.

Dunn, Geoffrey D. (1998) 'Tertullian and Rebekah: A Re-Reading of an "Anti-Jewish" Argument in Early Christian Literature', *Vigiliae Christianae* 52: 119–45.

—— (1999a) '*A Rhetorical Analysis of Tertullian's* adversus Iudaeos' (PhD diss., Australian Catholic University).

—— (1999b) '*Pro Temporum Condicione*: Jews and Christians as God's People in Tertullian's *Adversus Iudaeos*' in Pauline Allen, Wendy Mayer and Lawrence Cross (eds), *Prayer and Spirituality in the Early Church*, vol. 2, Brisbane: Centre for Early Christian Studies, Australian Catholic University, 315–41.

—— (1999c) 'Two Goats, Two Advents and Tertullian's *adversus Iudaeos*', *Augustinianum* 39: 245–64.

—— (2000) 'The Universal Spread of Christianity as a Rhetorical Argument in Tertullian's *adversus Iudaeos*', *Journal of Early Christian Studies* 8: 1–19.

—— (2001a) 'Peter and Paul in Rome: The Perspective of the North African Church' in *Pietro e Paolo: Il loro rapporto con Roma nelle testimonianze antiche*, Rome: Institutum Patristicum Augustinianum (Studia Ephemeridis Augustinianum 74): 405–13.

—— (2001b) 'The Ancestry of Jesus according to Tertullian: *ex David per Mariam*' *Studia Patristica* 36: 349–55.

—— (2002a) 'Rhetorical Structure in Tertullian's *ad Scapulam*', *Vigiliae Christianae* 55: 47–55.

—— (2002b) 'Tertullian and Daniel 9:24–27: A Patristic Interpretation of a Prophetic Time-Frame', *Zeitschrift für Antikes Christentum* 6: 330–44.

—— (2003a) 'Clement of Rome and the Question of Roman Primacy in the Early African Tradition', *Augustinianum* 43: 1–24.

—— (2003b) '*Probabimus uenisse eum iam* – The Fulfilment of Daniel's Prophetic Time-Frame in Tertullian's *adversus Iudaeos*', *Zeitschrift für Antikes Christentum* 7: 140–55.

Efroymson, David P. (1979) 'The Patristic Connection' in Alan T. Davies (ed.), *Anti-Semitism and the Foundation of Christianity*, New York: Paulist, 98–117.

—— (1980) 'Tertullian's Anti-Jewish Rhetoric: Guilt by Association', *Union Seminary Quarterly Review* 36: 25–37.

Ennabli, Liliane (1982) *Les inscriptions funéraires chrétiennes de Carthage* t. 2: *La basilique de Mcidfa*, Rome: École française de Rome (Collection de l'École française de Rome 62).

—— (1997) *Carthage: Une métropole chrétienne du IVᵉ à la fin du VIIᵉ siècle*, Paris: Éditions du Centre National de la Recherche Scientifique (Études d'Antiquités africaines).

Evans, R. F. (1976) 'On the Problem of Church and Empire in Tertullian's *Apologeticum*', *Studia Patristica* 14: 21–36.

Fredouille, Jean-Claude (1972) *Tertullien et la conversion de la culture antique*, Paris: Institut des Études Augustiniennes (Collection des Études Augustiniennes Série Antiquite 47).

Frend, W. H. C. (1958) 'The Persecutions: some Links between Judaism and the Early Church', *Journal of Ecclesiastical History* 9: 141–58.

—— (1961) 'The *Seniores Laici* and the Origins of the Church in North Africa', *Journal of Theological Studies* n.s. 12: 280–4.

—— (1965) *Martyrdom and Persecution in the Early Church*, Oxford: Blackwell.

—— (1968) 'Tertulliano e gli Ebrei', *Rivista di Storia e Letteratura Religiosa* 4: 3–10.

—— (1970a) 'A Note on Tertullian and the Jews', *Studia Patristica* 10: 291–6.

—— (1970b) 'A Note on the Jews and Christians in Third-Century Africa', *Journal of Theological Studies* n.s. 21: 92–6.

—— (1977) 'The Early Christian Church in Carthage' in J. H. Humphrey (ed.), *Excavations at Carthage 1976 Conducted by the University of Michigan*, vol. 3, Ann Arbor, MI: The University of Michigan, 21–40.

—— (1978) 'Jews and Christians in Third Century Carthage' in *Paganisme, Judaisme, Christianisme. Influences et affrontements dans le monde antique*, Andre Benoit (ed.), Paris: Éditions E. de Boccard, 185–94.

Gager, John (1985) *The Origins of Anti-Semitism: Attitudes toward Judaism in Pagan and Christian Antiquity*, Oxford: Oxford University Press.

Gamble, Harry Y. (1995) *Books and Readers in the Early Church: A History of Early Christian Texts*, New Haven, CT: Yale University Press.

Gaston, Lloyd (1986) 'Retrospect' in Stephen G. Wilson (ed.), *Anti-Judaism in Early Christianity*, vol. 2, *Separation and Polemic*, Waterloo, Ontario: Wilfrid Laurier University Press (Studies in Christianity and Judaism 2), 163–74.

Gero, Stephen (1970) '*Miles Gloriosus*: The Christian and Military Service according to Tertullian', *Church History* 39: 285–98.

González, Justo L. (1974) 'Athens and Jerusalem Revisited: Reason and Authority in Tertullian', *Church History* 43: 17–25.

Groh, Dennis E. (1971) 'Tertullian's Polemic Against Social Co-optation', *Church History* 40: 7–14.

Guerra, Anthony J. (1991) 'Polemical Christianity: Tertullian's Search for Certitude', *The Second Century* 8: 109–23.

Harnack, Adolf (1904) *Geschichte der altchristlichen Literatur bis Eusebius*, teil 2: *Die Chronologie* band 2: *Die Chronologie der Literatur von Irenäus bis Eusebius*, Leipzig: J. C. Hinlichs.

Higgins, A. J. B. (1951) 'The Latin Text of Luke in Marcion and Tertullian', *Vigiliae Christianae* 2: 1–42.

Hoffman, Daniel L. (1995) *The Status of Women and Gnosticism in Irenaeus and Tertullian*, Studies in Women and Religion 36, Lewiston, NY: Edwin Mellen Press.

Horbury, William (1972) 'Tertullian on the Jews in the Light of De Spectaculis XXX.5–6', *Journal of Theological Studies* n.s. 23: 455–9.

Kennedy, George A. (1994) *A New History of Classical Rhetoric*, Princeton, NJ: Princeton University Press.

Le Bohec, Yann (1981) 'Inscriptions juives et judaïsantes de l'Afrique romaine', *Antiquités africaines* 17: 165–207.

Lieu, Judith (1996) *Image and Reality: The Jews in the World of the Christians in the Second Century*, Edinburgh: T & T Clark.

MacLennan, Robert S. (1990) *Early Christian Texts on Jews and Judaism*, Atlanta, GA: Scholars Press (Brown Judaic Studies 194).

MacMullen, Ramsay (1975) 'Tertullian and "National God"', *Journal of Theological Studies* n.s. 26: 405–10.

Moore, George Foot (1921) 'Christian Writers on Judaism', *Harvard Theological Review* 14: 197–254.

Neander, Augustus (1849^2) *Antignostikus, Geist des Tertullianus und Einleitung in dessen Schriften*, Berlin: Dummler.

Noeldechen, E (1888) *Die Abfassungszeit der Schriften Tertullians*, Leipzig: J. C. Hinrichs (Texte und Untersuchungen V.2).

—— (1894) *Tertullian's Gegen die Juden auf Einheit, Echtheit, Entstehung*, Leipzig: J. C. Hinrichs (Texte und Untersuchungen XII.2)

Norman, Naomi J. (1988) 'The Architecture of the Circus in the Light of the 1982 Season', in J. H. Humphrey (ed.), *The Circus and a Byzantine Cemetery at Carthage*, vol. 1, Ann Arbor, MI: The University of Michigan Press, 7–31.

O'Malley, T. P. (1967) *Tertullian and the Bible: Language-Imagery-Exegesis*, Nijmegen: Dekker (Latinitas Christianorum Primaeva 21).

Osborn, Eric (1997a) *Tertullian: First Theologian of the West*, Cambridge: Cambridge University Press.

—— (1997b) 'Tertullian as Philosopher and Roman', in Barbara Aland and Christoph Schäublin (eds), *Die Weltlichkeit des Glaubens in der Alten Kirche. Festschrift für Ulrich Wickert zum siebzigsten Geburtstag*, Berlin and New York: Walter de Gruyter: 231–47 (Beihefte zur Zeitschrift für die neutestamentliche Wissenschaft und die Kunde der älteren Kirche, bd 85).

Powell, Douglas (1975) 'Tertullianists and Cataphrygians', *Vigiliae Christianae* 29: 33–54.

Powell, Mark Allen (2000) 'The Magi as Kings: An Adventure in Reader-Response Criticism', *Catholic Biblical Quarterly* 62: 459–80.

Quasten, Johannes (1953) *Patrology*, vol. 2: *The Ante-Nicene Literature After Irenaeus*, Utrecht: Spectrum.

Quispel, G. (1943) *De Bronnen van Tertullianus' Adversus Marcionem*, Utrecht: Burgersdijk en Niemans.

—— (1982) 'African Christianity Before Minucius Felix and Tertullian', in J. den Boeft and A. H. M. Kessels (eds), *Actus: Studies in Honour of H. L. W. Nelson*, Utrecht, the Netherlands: Instituut voor Klassieke Talen, 257–335.

Rankin, David I. (1986) 'Was Tertullian a Schismatic?', *Prudentia* 18: 73–9.

—— (1995) *Tertullian and the Church*, Cambridge: Cambridge University Press.

—— (1997) 'Was Tertullian a Jurist?', *Studia Patristica* 31: 335–42.

Raven, Susan (1993³) *Rome in Africa*, London: Routledge.

Rives, J. B. (1995) *Religion and Authority in Roman Carthage from Augustus to Constantine*, Oxford: Clarendon Press.

Rokéah, David (1982) *Jews, Pagans and Christians in Conflict*, Leiden: E. J. Brill.

—— (2001) *Justin Martyr and the Jews*, Leiden: E. J. Brill.

Ruether, Rosemary Radford (1974) *Faith and Fratricide: The Theological Roots of Anti-Semitism*, New York: Seabury.

Säflund, Gösta (1955) *De Pallio und die stilistische Entwicklung Tertullians*, Lund: C. W. K. Gleerup.

Scholer, D. M. (1982) 'Tertullian on Jewish Persecution of Christians', *Studia Patristica* 17/2: 821–8.

Setzer, Claudia (1997) 'Jews, Jewish Christians, and Judaizers in North Africa', in Virginia Wiles, Alexandra Brown and Graydon F. Snyder (eds), *Putting Body & Soul Together: Essays in Honor of Robin Scroggs*, Valley Forge, PA: Trinity Press International, 185–200.

Shaw, Brent D. (1982) 'The elders of Christian Africa', in P. Brind'Amour (ed.), *Mélanges offerts à R. P. Etienne Gereau*, Ottawa: Editions de l'Université d'Ottawa, 207–26.

Sider, Robert D. (1971) *Ancient Rhetoric and the Art of Tertullian*, Oxford: Oxford University Press.

—— (1973) 'On Symmetrical Composition in Tertullian', *Journal of Theological Studies* n.s. 24: 405–23.

—— (1978) 'Tertullian *On the Shows*: An Analysis', *Journal of Theological Studies* n.s. 29: 339–65.

—— (1982) 'Approaches to Tertullian: A Study of Recent Scholarship', *The Second Century* 2: 228–60.

Simon, Marcel (1996) *Verus Israel: A Study of the Relations between Christians and Jews in the Roman Empire (AD 135–425)*, trans. H. McKeating, 2nd edn, London: Vallentine Mitchell.

Siniscalco, Paolo (1978) 'Recenti studi su Tertulliano', *Rivista di storia e letteratura religiosa* 14: 396–405.

Smallwood, E. Mary (1981) *The Jews Under Roman Rule: From Pompey to Diocletian*, 2nd edn, Leiden: E. J. Brill.

Stager, Lawrence E. (1980) 'The Rite of Child Sacrifice at Carthage', in John Griffiths Pedley (ed.), *New Light on Ancient Carthage*, Ann Arbor, MI: University of Michigan Press, 1–11.

Stark, Rodney (1996) *The Rise of Christianity: A Sociologist Reconsiders History*, Princeton, NJ: Princeton University Press.

Stead, G. C. (1969) 'The Valentinian Myth of Sophia', *Journal of Theological Studies* n.s. 20: 75–104.

Stroumsa, Guy G. (1996) 'From Anti-Judaism to Antisemitism in Early Christianity?' in Ora Limor and Guy G. Stroumsa (eds), Contra Iudaeos: *Ancient and Medieval Polemics between Christians and Jews*, Tübingen: J. C. B. Mohr (Paul Siebeck), 1–26.

Swift, Louis J. (1968) 'Forensic Rhetoric in Tertullian's *Apologeticum*', *Latomus* 27: 864–77.

Tabbernee, William (1997) *Montanist Inscriptions and Testimonia: Epigraphic Sources Illustrating the History of Montanism*, Macon, GA: Mercer University Press (North American Patristic Society Patristic Monograph Series 16).

Taylor, Miriam S. (1995) *Anti-Judaism and Early Christian Identity: A Critique of the Scholarly Consensus*, Leiden: E. J. Brill.

Telfer, W. (1961) 'The Origins of Christianity in Africa', *Studia Patristica* 4: 512–17.

Treggiari, Susan (1991) *Roman Marriage: Iusti Coniuges From the Time of Cicero to the Time of Ulpian*, Oxford: Clarendon Press.

Trevett, Christine (1996) *Montanism: Gender, Authority and the New Prophecy*, Cambridge: Cambridge University Press.

Waszink, J. H. (1979) 'Tertullian's Principles and Methods of Exegesis' in W. R. Schoedel and R. L. Wilken (eds), *Early Christian Literature and the Classical Intellectual Tradition: In Honorem Robert M. Grant*, Paris: Beauchesne: 17–31.

Williams, A. Lukyn (1935) *Adversus Judaeos: A Bird's-Eye View of Christian* Apologiae *until the Renaissance*, Cambridge: Cambridge University Press.

Wright, David (2000) 'Tertullian' in Philip F. Esler (ed.), *The Early Christian World*, vol. 2, London: Routledge.

INDEX

INDEX OF MODERN AUTHORS